Antique
-10-
TMX
6123
C-48722

Model Soldiers
an Illustrated History

Model Soldiers
an Illustrated History

John G. Garratt

New York Graphic Society Ltd.
Greenwich, Connecticut

Standard Book Number 8212–0487–4
Library of Congress Catalog Card Number 72–80417

First published in Great Britain by
Weidenfeld and Nicolson Ltd., London
Published in the United States of America by
New York Graphic Society Ltd., Greenwich, Connecticut

Designed by Sheila Sherwen for George Weidenfeld and Nicolson Ltd., London
Printed in Germany

Contents

6 Acknowledgments

8 The Background

43 The Makers

51 Austria
53 Denmark
56 France
77 Germany
80 Great Britain
122 Italy
124 Sweden
127 United States of America

140 The Collectors

148 Flats
155 L'Idée Fixe
177 Means to an End
188 New Worlds to Conquer
202 Miscellany
226 The War-gamers
231 The Young Enthusiasts
235 Makers and manufacturers mentioned in the text
240 Places where model soldiers may be seen
241 Bibliography
242 Sources of Illustrations
243 Index

Acknowledgments

This work would not have been possible if it had not been for the co-operation of the makers and collectors discussed in this book.

The author also wishes gratefully to acknowledge the valuable assistance he has received from G. Carol Boeri, Sergeant A. W. Carter, Cornelius Frazer, Derek Frost, Hugh Garrett-Taylor, Guiseppe de Giorgis, Commander Ian Hamilton, RN, Michael V. Hitrovo, I. H. Johansen, Dr Erich Kröner-Grimm, Eugene Lelièpvre, Carlos Maria Naon, Harold R. Pestana, Antonia Costa Ramos, L. W. Richards, Marcel Roubicek, Leonard A. Rowe, Edward Ryan, Samuel Slonim, David Sparkman, J. Tofts White, David and Yvonne Winter, and David C. Young.

The author would also like to thank his wife, who patiently sorted through an at times almost unintelligible manuscript and produced a finished typed copy.

The author and publishers very much regret that since going to press they have learned of the deaths of M. Baldet and F. W. Wilson.

To Michael V. Hitrovo

The Background

One of the most intriguing phenomena of the second half of the present century is the growth of interest in the collection of small objects which, whilst in themselves not perhaps of any great monetary value, afford delight to the possessor.

Our ancestors, if well-to-do, purchased large and bulky pieces of furniture and vast canvases with which to decorate their spacious homes; the present-day collector, in his much more modest house or flat, has to concentrate on smaller treasures. Any dealer in antique furniture will tell you that he cannot get enough small objects of quality, and that the more ponderous ones are at a discount. People in all walks of life take a lively interest in antiques and bygones, and in this they have been greatly assisted by a flood of beautifully illustrated books written by experts on virtually all branches of collecting, by special exhibitions at museums, by television and radio programmes, and generally by a growing awareness that it is both good for the soul and pleasurable to have things to look at which are not the result of mass-production. At the same time it is certain that, whatever ills may be attributable to the 'affluent society', many more people are now able to devote a modest portion of their incomes to the acquisition of small things of beauty.

The virtual impossibility for most people of being able any longer to collect really old pieces has forced the collector to concentrate on products of a more recent date, objects which up to a few years ago would hardly have been considered worthy of preservation. This has resulted in exciting discoveries in many fields. John Betjeman and Nikolaus Pevsner have opened up new vistas in the appreciation of previously ignored or unfashionable styles of architecture, and the same has been done in other directions by Mrs Graham Green, Leslie Daiken, Patrick Murray and Lady Antonia Fraser.

One of the branches of collecting that have taken a great leap forward in recent years is that of the model soldier. A number of authors, including George Augustus Sala and Lloyd Osbourne, had noted them much earlier, but whereas they regarded them as playthings and transitory by their very nature, French collectors saw in them a significance far beyond that of a nursery toy. However, it was not until 1924 that Hampe, in his *Der Zinnsoldat* (1924) and Riff, *Les Étains Strasbourgeois du XVIe au XIXe siècle* (1925) examined these little figures in detail and considered them worthy of collection.

The bibliography of the model soldier since then has been prolific, but much of it is of an ephemeral nature, consisting of newspaper and magazine articles, written with a kind of half-amused tolerance at the idea of presumably responsible and intelligent adults collecting 'toy soldiers'.

During more recent years, however, several books have been published which deal more seriously with the world of the model soldier in all its aspects. It is not our intention to recapitulate all the information that is to be found in these works, but to concentrate on two areas that have not, as yet, been adequately covered. The first of these is a consideration of a selected number of those modern masters of the craft of specialised model making whose creations are worthy of collection, and the second a survey of those who seriously collect both their works and the productions of those commercial manufacturers which were once universally called 'toys'.

To account for the emergence of these complementaries, on one hand the master craftsman, on the other the collector, and to show how the terms 'toy' and 'model' have become virtually synonymous, it is necessary to trace the history of the military figurine from its beginnings in remote antiquity and to give some indication of the various forms it has assumed in different countries, thereby enabling us to appreciate more fully the aims and predilections of the collector.

To begin with it is important to distinguish between the two types of model that figure predominantly in collections. The first is the 'solid' (American: 'full

Previous page Medieval models evoke the romance of Malory and Froissart form'; German: *vollplastische*; French: *ronde-bosse*), the second the 'flat' (American: 'profile'; German: *Zinnfiguren*; French: *plat d'étain*). In simple terms, a solid model is three dimensional, and a flat has the appearance of being cut out of sheet tin. These two are the bases from which all other forms, whether they be hollow-cast, semi-solid, *carton comprimé*, composition, plaster, wood, plastic, semi-flat, or flat-plastic have emerged. The only thing that they have in common is that they depict a military subject.

The making of small figures began far back in antiquity – indeed, as soon as primitive man could handle tools his mind concentrated on reproducing what he could see and embodying what his imagination could invent. On the walls of caves he drew and painted the animals he hunted, and in a variety of materials he made tiny figures of the beings who directed his life. And although the prime object was religious, there is no doubt that at the same time many small figures were made for the pleasure of children. The doll is one of the oldest objects of antiquity – so is the warrior. Diminutive martial models have been unearthed from the soil of Greece, Troy, Crete, Central Europe, Spain, Italy, Mesopotamia and Alexandrian India, and whole regiments have come from the tombs of the Egyptian Pharoahs. Some are of bronze, others of clay or wood, and a number have wheels so that they may be propelled; and there are examples with articulated limbs. An outstanding find was made in

Right Roman terracotta figurine, with articulated legs, first century AD, $7\frac{3}{8}$ inches high

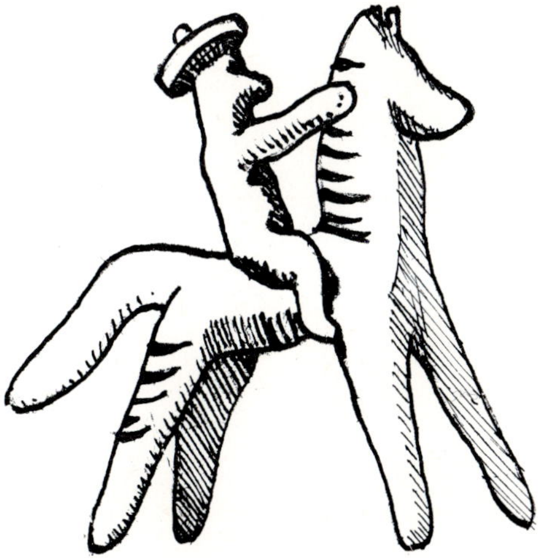

Above left Archaic Greek terracotta rider

Above right Classical Greek terracotta mounted warrior

Right One of the earliest flat lead figures, 6cm high, fourteenth century, probably representing St Denis of France. It is significant that this is not a pilgrim's token, the foot-stands indicating that it was made with a standing position in mind

1942 at Wasit, near Hai in Southern Iraq, comprising some 400 terracotta toys, including a squadron of horse.

The warlike society of the Middle Ages provides a number of examples of military figurines, ranging from the first emergence of the 'flat' as we know it to the bronze and wooden equestrian jousting knights made for the sons of wealthy landowners. Perhaps the most intriguing object, though not itself a warrior, is the miniature (3 by $1\frac{1}{2}$ inches) wooden model found in the Tower of London in 1964. Is it indeed, as one expert thinks, a representation of the Bloody Tower, and was it, perhaps, a plaything used by the prisoner princes;

Above The front and back of a tiny model of the Tower of London, wood, 3 by $1\frac{1}{2}$ inches

Above Front and rear views of a solid lead musketeer, 10cm, made in France in the seventeenth century

and if it was, would there have been, perhaps, even tinier figures to go with it?

The French were the first to make the prototype of the present-day solid, a number of these *petites statues en ronde bosse* dating from the time of Henri IV being preserved in Cluny Museum.

What may be the first mention of tiny military figures being made in England occurs in the third Act of John Webster's *The Duchess of Malfi* (1614):

Delio. He hath read all the late service
As the City-Chronicle relates it:
And keeps two pewterers going, only to express
Battles in model.

The most recent edition of Webster's works has a variant reading: 'painters' instead of 'pewterers'. The editor, the late F. L. Lucas, to whom we are indebted for this information, suggested that in this case 'model' would mean 'plan', as often at that period. If, however, 'pewterers' is allowed to stand, one would still not be sure whether the models were of single figures or of bodies of troops. Lucas also drew our attention to a further reference of the period, in Jonson's *The Devil is an Ass* (Act III. i, 1616), which actually mentions 'leaden men' meant to represent 'Finsbury battles'.

The reign of Louis XIII saw France at its most arrogant, and the Dauphin was surrounded by military playthings, including a collection of three hundred soldiers made of silver, the work of Nicholas Roger, and some in lead, 7cm high, made by himself. Successive Dauphins also possessed armies of pottery, wood, and cardboard to augment the more expensive models (another silver army, made by Merlin in 1650, cost 5,000 écus). *Le Roi Soleil* pressed the great Vauban and the eminent minister Colbert into his service over the arrangements for a magnificent army of foot and mounted soldiery, fitted with automatic devices so that they could carry out manoeuvres. These figures, 7cm high, were made in silver by Jacob Wolrab.

The silver armies have vanished, but a number of

Left Solid lead model of a soldier of the period of Henri IV, French, 8cm

Above Group of Lucotte commercial models, standard size, *c* 1850

museums on the Continent contain collections of cardboard models of the period which give us a good idea of what the Royal armies must have been like, whilst at the Carnavalet Museum in Paris there are a number of 2.15cm-high lead soldiers, said to be the last of a large army owned by the eldest son of Louis XVI. It is not surprising that the theme persisted in France after the Revolution, and there are numerous paintings of the King of Rome playing with model soldiers, some quite large, and presumably of carved wood, given him by the indulgent Emperor. The most notable collection owned by the little prince, however, was the set of 117 pieces made in gold by J. B. Claude Odiot, and intended for drill instruction. A description and illustrations may be found in Henry Harris's *Model Soldiers*, on pages 13–14 and figures 10–11.

Goethe, in his *Dichtung und Wahrheit*, published in 1811, relates a story concerning a boy and girl and some boxes of soldiers, 'round and solid and most finely wrought'. The date is significant, as the most famous early French maker of model soldiers, Lucotte, began work sometime before 1789. None of the models of this period have been traced, and those bearing the characteristic mark of the Imperial bee flanked by the

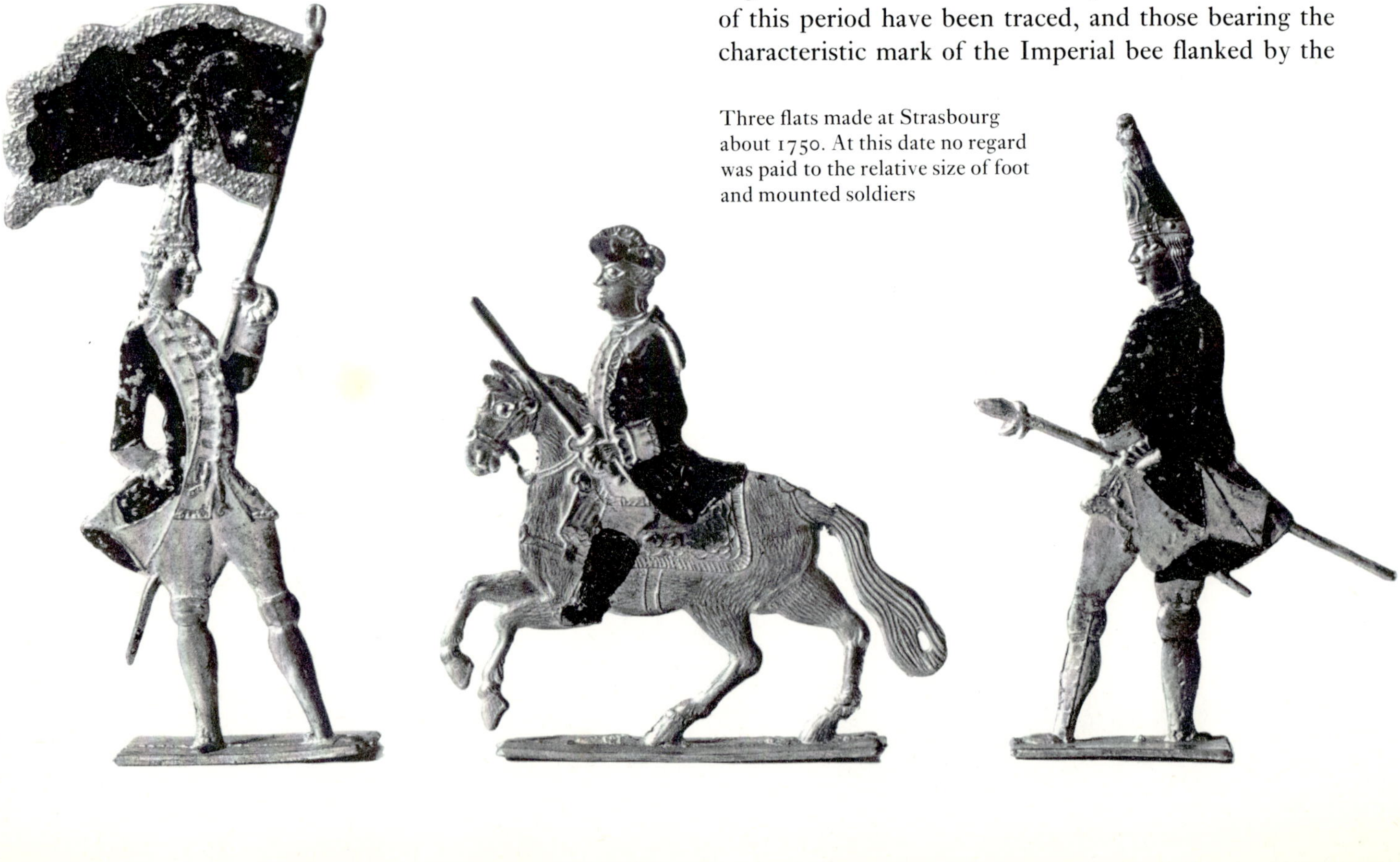

Three flats made at Strasbourg about 1750. At this date no regard was paid to the relative size of foot and mounted soldiers

letters L and C so well known to collectors do not date from much earlier than 1850. (Unforgettable examples of these are on display at Blenheim Palace.) They represent all that is best in solids. Made of a mixture of lead and antimony and heavy in the hand, the foot soldiers – two and a half inches or so in height – are mounted on a thin base, and the accoutrements soldered on. The cavalry are in proportion, the saddlecloths, saddles and men detachable, a small plug in the seat holding them in place. The reins are cast separately. They have an *élan* difficult to match in other commercial makes. Lucotte was absorbed by a group of French toy makers, Cuperley, Blondel and Gerbeau, about 1825 – themselves taken over in 1875 by the firm of Mignot, who adopted the trade initials CBG in 1902. Mignot produced models in much greater numbers than Lucotte, and they are therefore more frequently found in collections. Their range was wide and the standard good, although some evidence of archaism is to be observed – indeed the design of the horses suggests that of a much earlier period – and the cavalrymen are not detachable. Two ranges are available, 45mm and 54mm, the former of inferior quality. The firm still flourishes in the rue du Vieux Colombier, Paris. Other makers of toy soldiers existed in Paris during the second half of the nineteenth century, but little is known of them and they had little influence,

Apart from an excursion by Mignot into the manufacture of flats and a traditional industry in the Franco-German border town of Strasbourg, France has, on the whole, kept strictly to the making of solids, but in Germany the story is a different one. With its medieval guilds of lead workers and their centres at Nuremberg and Augsburg, it was inevitable that a toy industry would develop. The tin mines were there, the makers were there. But although war after war had plunged the central states into ruin and bankruptcy, it was during these harrowing years that the *Zinnfigur* had its birth. Only in subject was there a difference between it and the religious groups made intensively in the late medieval period. The initial design was transferred by

Below Typical Strasbourg models of about 1750. Although the craft of tin-soldier making was almost exclusively a German one, Strasbourg produced many thousands of figures such as these

cutting half a mould into a small block of Thuringian slate, one side being blank; another block was engraved for the back, the blocks were clamped together, the alloy of molten tin and lead poured between them and the excess metal allowed to drain off through channels provided. Later, with the growth of industry, the models were faced with bronze to ensure continued clarity of production. The method of production has varied little during successive years.

The beginnings were clumsy and tentative, but fascinating because of their obvious sincerity. The example inspired by 'Der Alte Fritz' found expression in the workshop of the Hilpert family of Nuremberg, which, having begun by manufacturing scenes of peaceful pastoral subjects, suddenly changed completely into the most important centre for the production of 'tin soldiers' as they came to be universally known. They were produced in such masses that they may well be regarded as the first successful commercial venture in the field, and soon every child in Germany, however poor, might have possessed the troops of the great generals in miniature. Not all, however, were intended for the playroom. Hilpert's masterpiece, Frederick the Great, displays a quality of design and execution that makes one feel it resulted from a special commission, as do several others of a similar nature, including the Prince de Ligne and Voltaire. The majority of the figures that have survived are of cavalrymen, fiercely moustachioed, and with murderous curved swords raised aloft.

Now began keen competition from other makers and the catalogues of two toy-dealers, one in Nuremberg and the other in Berlin, in the 1790s, show that there were by then eight foundries in Fürth, with a total output greater than Nuremberg.

Other countries now began production. A few makers existed in Sweden as early as 1760, and Strasbourg had a regular industry before 1790, which lasted well into the 1830s; Switzerland was very active; in Italy the figures were made at least as early as 1770; a few types

Large flats by Schweitzer, of Diessen-Ammersee, originally made about 1820, but recently recast from the original moulds by Caspari of Hof. Painted by the author

Semi-solid 40mm figures, the riders detachable, *c* 1867. Made by Ammon or Allgeyer. Thousands were annually imported into England from Germany

were made in Copenhagen; flats appeared in Portugal in 1773, engraved by Simon Roulle, French engraver in the service of Don José the First; and in Spain (1830–40).

An export service undoubtedly existed, the tiny models being packed in shavings in light, wooden, decorated Berchtesgaden boxes. It is thought that probably the 'Christmas Presents for the Young Folks who have an affection for the Art Military, consisting of Horse, Foot and Dragoons, cast in metal, in beautiful uniforms, 18s a dozen' advertised in the Tory paper *The Royal Gazette* in December 1777 (when New York City was occupied by the British), were imported from Germany, and shipped to America along with the Hessians.

The firms of Gottschalk, Lorenz, Allgeyer, Werhli and Ammon, most of which lasted well into the middle of the century, paved the way for the later tremendous expansion – which, however, was interrupted by the Napoleonic Wars. But Waterloo could not be forgotten and a few years later the legend of Napoleon was born and has never died. An age of expansion began in the

1830s, coinciding with the coming of the railway, the deeper study of history, the newly rediscovered glories of Greece and Rome, overseas exploration and the pacific joys of circuses, fêtes and junketings. Wars were recorded and brought to life again by the tin figures of the soldiers who fought in them. The leading manufacturer of the period was undoubtedly Heinrichsen, whose imagination was extraordinary and whose industry was prodigious. Every possible military event in history was recorded in complete sets, sometimes numbering several hundred different figures, and Heinrichsen specialised in groups comprising a number of individuals on one stand. In the mid-nineteenth century he wrote a book for children on the ways of using model soldiers for the popular *Kriegspiel* or 'war-game'. Up to this time, sizes of figures varied greatly according to the fancy of the maker, Heinrichsen himself adopting no standard at first. He decided that a uniform size of about 28 to 30mm for an infantryman, a mounted man in proportion, would be of great assistance to the *Kriegspiel* and at the same time help the manufacturers. Production of these figures began about 1848, and was an immediate success. For years they remained the standard size, but recently the slightly larger 30–32mm has been proved more popular.

Heinrichsen's chief competitor was Allgeyer of Fürth, whose output was enormous, and whose quality on the whole was superior. The figures made by both firms are still to be found in fair quantities. A number of other firms were in existence at some time or other during the middle and late nineteenth century, such as Denecke, Wegmann, Weygang, Haffner, Haselbach, Söhlke and du Bois, all of whose figures are very difficult to find. Whilst the true flat figure continued on its way, a curious off-shoot began to emerge. This was the 'semi-flat', which took on a stouter bulk, whilst retaining the general outline of the flat. This eventually led to the 'semi-solid', still based on the flat inasmuch as the legs of man or horse are still in alignment in the same plane, but the rest of the body swells out on either side. The riders in equestrian forms are fully formed, with curved legs to grip the horse, and usually have a little peg to fit the saddle. Normally the figures are on the small side. Thousands, made by Haffner, Allgeyer or Söhlke, were exported, and many are still to be found in England and other European countries where crude examples are still found for sale in the cheaper types of toyshops. They have never been popular, as they are essentially a hybrid, clumsy and unattractive, the semi-flats being usually issued unpainted. Their significance lies in that they led to the emergence in Germany of the true solid. The semi-solids and semi-flats were made for the cheapest toy market – the larger and more competently executed solids were much more expensive. There are isolated examples of completely round models from the 1840s, but the first significant maker was Haffner, who between 1867 and 1886 made models of a quality comparable with those of Lucotte. Other, less competent makers were Spenkuch and Dorfler, and by the end of the century the industry was fully established. Thousands of models were exported, especially to England, in beautifully made polished wooden boxes, not unlike the Victorian needlework box, with gothic lettering in gold on the lid.

Typical box in which German solid and semi-solid models were packed and exported

In the mid-fifties of the nineteenth century the Germans were paramount in the production of solid lead models. *Top:* Turks, 45mm with original box; *Centre:* German hussar, 65mm; *Bottom:* Natives, 45mm; all made by Heyde

The most famous maker of solids is undoubtedly Georg Heyde of Dresden, who is first heard of about 1870. Probably no other firm has spread its net so wide, or made its models in such varied poses. Like Heinrichsen, Heyde specialised in massive sets, with the figures in many postures. Various categories are listed in their catalogues, such as 'first', 'second' and 'middle' quality, 'battles', 'parades' or 'groups', and the sizes of models range from 40mm to 6cm with some exceptional larger ones. The figures are usually on a smallish stand, the heads plugged in. Mounted men are detachable, and in the smaller ones the horses are semi-solid. Two collectors, one on each side of the Atlantic, and researching independently, have recently shown that a number of models previously ascribed to Heyde may now with confidence be classed as by other makers, such as Haffner, and Heinrich of Fürth. A critic might say that the majority of the Heyde figures were clumsy, with elongated bodies and stunted legs, but there is no doubt that they are prized by collectors, largely due to the size and variety of the larger sets, which include accessories of all kinds.

The picture in England at the end of the nineteenth century was of a mass of German and French military toys, both flat and solid, ranging from the semi-flat and semi-solid in 40 and 45mm for the nursery, to the massive, better quality figures designed for the older boy. There existed no native industry, probably owing to the Continental monopoly, and the only reliable record we have of model making by an Englishman is supplied by the phenomenal Captain William Siborne with his two Waterloo models, the first containing 190,000 half-inch figures, the second some 3,000 models about one and a half inches tall. Even in this case, we cannot be certain that he did not actually have the figures made for him in Germany, although no records of orders or payments have ever been traced. The only other person is a certain shadowy Mr Bull who, in 1877, advertised models of Napoleon, Wellington and other celebrated characters, but we have no means of ascertaining their size, appearance or numbers.

However, a certain William Britain, an established maker of mechanical toys, decided that there should be a market for a different type of toy soldier: one that was lighter in weight, and therefore cost less in raw materials, than the imported one, and of a quality sufficient to compete with the overseas product. The result of his experiments, placed on the market in 1893, was the 'hollow-cast' which in essence is a thin metal alloy casing enclosing an air-filled space. His decision to reduce the size of the foot soldier to 54mm completely revolutionised the industry, competing as it did with the larger German and French models. The first of a very long line of models, the 1st Life Guards, proved immensely popular, and the quality of the production and the accuracy of historical detail went

Fine commercial models by Haffner of Franz Josef and his staff

Top Hollow-casts made by William Britain in the early 1900s. These figures are today much sought for: *Left to right:* King's African Rifles, Boer, Royal Sussex Regiment (with fixed arm), USA, Montenegrin officer, Australian, West Indian Regiment

Bottom Examples of Britain's early mounted troops. *Left to right:* Imperial Yeomanry, 6th (Inniskilling) Dragoons, Boer, South Australian Lancers, the same, Boer War

a long way to ensure success. The bright, shining figures in their attractive cardboard boxes covered with a quite individual bright red paper evoked a thrill of delight in the boys who received them as presents (and in the fathers who purchased them) and there are many collectors who look back nostalgically to those magical days when the large toyshops were stacked with boxes from floor to ceiling. Perhaps, also, people were tired of seeing German uniforms or models masquerading as Scottish regiments, and Britain, by concentrating on the British Army in its infinite variety, assured himself of a ready market. It is a great credit to the makers that, even with their limited range, these models could sweep the Continentals from the field to such an extent that they are known universally and found in the remotest of places.

The history of Britain's production is extremely complicated, and shows that many changes were made and original models replaced by ones of better design; different sizes and qualities were introduced and new materials used for accoutrements. The moveable arm has always been a feature of a Britain figure, and here again variations occur. Another characteristic is that whereas the Continentals (Heyde in particular) varied the postures of the figures, Britain adhered to a somewhat rigid régime of about half-a-dozen basic attitudes: shooting-standing, shooting-kneeling, shooting-lying, marching, sloping arms, running at the trail and a few others. There were no histrionics or theatrical poses. So, if you wanted your regiment marching, you could buy as many boxes as you could afford, being assured that all the models would be doing the same thing. There were also teams of horse artillery and, later, field ambulances and barrage balloons.

One of the criticisms levelled at William Britain is that apart from a very few excursions into the regiments of other countries and such perennial favourites as Zulus and Wild West figures, he and his successors missed many opportunities of creating models of historic or world interest. It is perhaps ironic that the most beautiful set the firm ever made (and, indeed, perhaps the finest of all commercial models) happened almost by accident. A small concern, consisting of a young Englishman, Roy Selwyn-Smith, and a German-Jewish émigré, Otto Gottstein, collaborated in a series of medieval warriors, and made them in solid lead. They proved unrewarding financially, and on the lamented death of Gottstein, Selwyn-Smith sold them to Britains, who produced them in hollow-cast under the name of 'Knights of Agincourt'. Happily Selwyn-Smith eventually became chief designer of Britains, and it is certainly due to him that their plastic figures are so outstanding in their design and quality.

Sentiment apart, and the above-mentioned set excepted, Britains' soldiers are still toys, but there is a certain magic about them that has endeared them to many thousands of collectors, and indeed it could be said that the British Model Soldier Society at its inception might well have been named the 'Britains' Model Soldier Society'. With the lamented cessation of the making of metal models for the commercial market (of which more later) their popularity with collectors has reached a hysterical pitch, as evinced by the prices which are paid for boxed sets at auction.

Britains inevitably had its competitors, some good, some downright bad. Of the former the best was John Hill & Co, better known as 'Johillco', whose models stand comparison with those of the inventor of the hollow-cast. Others with smaller outputs were Reka, Fry and Hanks, but there are many unsigned models made by small and short-lived firms that still await identification.

The Second World War eliminated Heyde and forced a temporary diversion of effort upon Britains, but with the return to more normal life the model soldier industry took giant strides forward. Britains and Johillco returned to their traditional styles, challenged by new competitors (Timpo, Cherilea, Crescent); Mignot still represented France with their unchanging moulds, together with Cherband, Berne and Figur (semi-solid). Other countries began to break away from reliance on importations for their models, and started their own native production in solid lead. Steinback (MIM) began in Belgium with largish models, the riders detachable; in Denmark, Banner-Model and Andersen's Brigader-Statuette (both smaller in size) and Krolyn (Rode Orm) who made larger models in aluminium. Two firms, Francesco, and Industria Soprammobili Artistici (ISA) hold a place in Italy similar to that of Britains in England, inasmuch as they specialise in the units of their own country. It cannot be said, however, that the quality is comparable. Spain, having relied on importations, began in earnest, and the models of both Almirall and Lucio Saez-Alcocer are commercial products of good quality. The firm of Casanellas was founded as early as 1896 and, despite the crudity of their productions, they were very popular (even though the horses were still semi-solid) as were those of Palomeque and Sanchez. Norway, Sweden, Poland and Czechoslovakia still relied on importation, their own efforts being mainly concentrated on the ubiquitous semi-solid, although a few true solids were made by Santessonska Tenngjuteriet of Stockholm, mainly of 50mm equestrian monarchs.

Across the Atlantic the American toy-shops also began searching for native talent. As early as 1904 an attempt was made by the American Soldier Company to imitate Britains' models, and McLoughlin Brothers (*c* 1900–12) relied on piracy of Britain and Heyde figures. Between 1914 and 1930 the Warren Company, again, copied the Continental method of the plugged-in heads and the removable cavalryman. Others worthy of mention are Barclay, J. L. Wright (Lincoln Logs), Military Miniatures, Metal Art Miniature Co (later known as Moulded Miniatures), St Louis Lead Soldier Company, Minifigure Company and, of better quality, K. G. Bussler, Jack Scruby and Frank Conley, and K. S. Miniatures. The most important name, however, is that of Comet, founded about 1936 under the name of Brigadier. The early figures were particularly crude, but the advent of a Swedish enthusiast and a German refugee transformed the picture by persuading the

Left Authenticast models designed by Holger Eriksson – the first attempt to produce commercially-made models designed by an eminent artist

Left In the United States one of the earliest manufacturers of toy soldiers was McLoughlin (*c* 1900). Here he has been influenced by the German makers

owner of the firm to call in the services of Holger Eriksson of Sweden. The result was a really remarkable series called Authenticast, of a quality seldom equalled in commercial products.

Over the border in Canada, Samuel C. Jackson is making a limited series of highly specialised figures and, in Latin America, there are at least half-a-dozen firms producing figures of varying quality. Finally, in Australia, Peter Wooten is making a worthy effort to commemorate native historical personages.

Meanwhile, the mainstay of the German industry, the flat, was pursuing its steadfast way. However, the quality of design and execution was gradually rising, and the frail metal of the Heinrichsens and the Allgeyers, which had to be handled with the greatest of care, was being replaced by a tougher alloy. The size was fractionally increased, allowing the possibility of more minute engraving, and much more thorough research into history and costume was being undertaken. The engraver now came into his own, and a much closer co-operation between him and the designer, and of both with the producer, is evident. Aloys Ochel of Kiel (Kilia) became the modern counterpart of Heinrichsen, both in scope and variety, and his works form the basis of many collections. Other prominent engravers or producers of the period (many are still alive) concentrated on special periods of history – for example Gottstein, who collaborated with Madlener to produce a magnificent series of medieval combatants; Hafer, intensely interested in the ancient world; Sandow, with South West African troops of 1904; Scheibert, who covered the period 1812–13;

Above Figures from a catalogue of flats issued by Werner Scholtz. Many of the drawings show a combination of arms and legs – *kombination* figures

Below Figures from a list issued by Eugen Blum of flats designed by Madlener and produced by himself

Beck, with the Siegfried sagas; and Scholtz, famous for his 'Retreat from Moscow'.

The French have also had their makers of flats, notably a series issued by Mignot, but on the whole they have remained faithful to the solid. Britain, also, in the persons of W. Y. Carman and Otto Gottstein, began a short-lived series, never repeated, and in Sweden Georg Rössner revived the old large-size traditional figures for some remarkable evocations of the past. These non-Germanic productions are of the highest quality and eagerly sought by the more discerning collectors, but there is no doubt that the Germans hold the field and the number of designers, engravers and 'publishers' is quite astonishing, and constantly increasing.

It must not be forgotten that materials other than lead and tin-alloy have been used at various periods. One of the earliest was paper, and a tremendous industry of printed sheets, with engravings or lithographs intended for colouring and cutting out and mounting has existed since the eighteenth century. Most countries have contributed to the vast total, but the greatest mass has come from Strasbourg, Épinal, Nancy and various Germanic countries. These sheets have as great a fascination in some circles as the dimensional models, and rare and original issues and their variants are highly prized. The original Britains and Heydes were meant to be played with, the sheets being

Above A typical *Image Populaire* cut-out figure, probably printed in Épinal

mounted on tiny wooden blocks, but this resulted in an alarming proportion of casualties. Now the sheets are carefully preserved in albums or port-folios, not even touched by colour. Contemporary sheets are usually colour-printed more or less indifferently, but attempts have recently been made in England at a better quality production. Mr Allan Robinson-Sager of Toronto has issued an impressive oblong folio of seven sheets, illustrating seventy-four cavalry and foot regiments from *Canada's Colourful History* (*1780–1895*).

Wood, of course, lends itself to carving, but apart from the nursery type of ninepin figure has never succeeded commercially, although exquisite models have been created by master craftsmen. Aluminium and even cast iron have also been experimented with, without any lasting effect, and papier-mâché has been used at certain times. This last material, in this context, is (oddly enough) known in France as *carton comprimé*. Mr John Hanington has an interesting set, and another of which we have heard comprises forty French infantrymen, each four inches high, with a mounted captain. The figures have a spring clip instead of a foot stand. Special kinds of plaster have also been employed. A most unusual set of polychrome figures in this material was made of the Emperor Franz Josef and his staff in Austria about 1856. The spurs and sabres are of tin, belts and sashes of embossed gilt paper, and the sabre straps of leather. The late Francis X. Huber possessed one set, and the late Marcel Baldet had another. Baldet told us of another set, this time

Below These present-day paper 30mm cut-out models of the American War of Independence are made by Hathaway, who also makes the plastic cannon

Left Marcel Baldet with his collection of large plaster models of Franz Josef and his staff. (A coloured illustration of a similar set owned by the late Francis Huber can be seen in *The Saturday Book*, number 20)

Below A remarkable collection of *carton-comprimé* models made in France about 1880

of Napoleon III and his marshals, which was exhibited in Paris in 1922. The plaster models of Herbert Hahn are probably hardly known outside his native Austria, but before his death in 1957 he had made many dozens of 40–50mm figures, which had a ready market in Vienna. Today they are undoubtedly collectors' pieces. Contrasted with these in every possible way are the products of O. & K. Hausser, universally known by their trade mark 'Elastolin'. Founded in 1936, the firm continued making military models until 1939. About 6–8cm high, they comprised Wild West subjects, Highlanders, Washington and his troops, and British and German First World War types, complete with armaments, pontoons, etc. They are as unattractive as a model can be: clumsy in design and production, an unpleasant size, and mounted on a thick and ugly base. Yet they are popular with collectors, especially when found in an undamaged state in the original box. Productions of the firm since the Second World War will be discussed subsequently.

More durable, though as clumsy, are the models in conjoint-tin, usually associated with the penny bazaar, and the colour-stamped flat figure deriving from the sardine-tin. That both these varieties enjoyed a certain

popularity is evident from the number that have been preserved in museums, and, indeed, the author can remember some monstrous examples being given him as a sick child in Liverpool in about 1923. They even figure in an article by M. D. Griffith, *The Toy Armies of the World*, which appeared in 1898:

For stamped soldiers, an artist and expert in martial affairs carves out of metal the model to be reproduced. He carves the two sides separately, then follows the stamping. An enormous roll of tin hangs from a windlass, and, by mean of an automatic steel knife, is cut into sheets as easily and rapidly as if it were paper. At the next table the sheets of tin are placed in the matrices and, by means of a rammer, pressed into every cavity. When removed, they are facsimiles of the matrices. In this way hundreds are struck in an hour. Perfect in every detail, even the hair on the horses is accurately reproduced. The two halves are then soldered together (by means of metal flanges) and every superfluous bit of metal is trimmed away, so that the outline of the figure is clean and well defined . . . I [then] visited the modest rooms of the artisans who make common soldiers out of old sardine tins . . . Into a sort of witch's cauldron are flung these old boxes, smelling of oil and grease. When sufficiently heated they become unsoldered, and, when cool, are hammered, straightened, flattened, and sorted to their primitive state, and then converted into common tin soldiers, similar to those sold by toy hawkers in the London streets . . . The enamelled soldiers – a recent invention – are cut by means of a knife, from sheets of metal and afterwards have to pass through three painting rooms, in which two hundred women are employed.

Similar models were advertised in Paris in the 1840s.

The alien material which had has the greatest success and appears to be here to stay is plastic. In itself, it is an unfortunate word, as it embraces many types of material ranging from a hardish substance (as in the case of Malleable Mouldings) through the brittleness of the present day Elastolin productions, the different texture of Mokarex and Café Storme, the more flexible British product, to the terrible rubber-like monstrosities of the American and Japanese trade, and the queer concoctions of Czechoslovakia, Poland and the USSR. Probably the first successful venture in the non-metal range was that of Malleable Mouldings, which was founded by Hans Winkler in Deal in 1947, at a time when lead models were difficult to obtain. A number of Authenticast designs were used, and heads and equipment were moulded separately. The result was a model of quality which proved too expensive to be a viable proposition, and the firm closed down in 1950. The most impressive move was made by Britains who, in 1953, took over the models started in 1951 by M. Zang and Roy Selwyn-Smith, and marketed them under the name of Herald. These had an immediate success and today they still remain the finest of all plastic figures. One feature has been a virtual recreation of the regimental types beloved by Britain enthusiasts and the invention of the interchangeable figure has had a great influence on other makers, none of whom, however, have been able to achieve anything better than clumsy piracies. In England Timpo, Cherilea, Crescent and Charbens have all competed, but apart from Britains the only firm to produce models of any quality is that of Cavendish Miniatures, with a very small range designed by Stadden.

In their particular type of alkathene the American firm of Marx has had a tremendous success, with models in various sizes and specialising in the large sets beloved by Heyde. Many firms in Europe are making plastic models, perhaps the best outside France being those of Reamsa of Spain, whose quality has

'The Wild Geese'. Walshe, Dillon and du Reine regiments. Models in plastic by Segom

Left The ultimate in standard-sized plastic kits. *Hussard premier Empire*, designed and contructed by Eugene Lelièpvre for Historex

Below Tambour de Grenadiers de la Garde Impériale. A further example of the remarkable new type of kit by Historex

improved since the design has been in the hands of Georg Erik, late of Wimbledon. The harder sort of material is admirably produced by Elastolin, who have invented a kind of colouring incorporated in the plastic, and whose range is expanding. Their large models are beautifully executed, although too massive for our taste – we infinitely prefer those in 40mm. Merten, of Berlin, also produce attractive models in the smaller size. Two coffee firms, who include a figure in each tin, are worthy of mention. Mokarex, of France, cover a large range in 56mm models, whilst from Café Storme of Belgium comes a total of over 350 models from Belgian history. The best of the French plastics, however, are those of Starlux – a magnificent range of medieval models being quite outstanding.

We noted that Malleable Mouldings used plugged heads and arms, and the French firm of Segom have gone one better and produced a series of models with

Historex Artillery before painting. The result of hours of assembly

all limbs interchangeable. A further development which has proved a great success is the kit type of model in traditional size made by Historex. Each model is sold as a large number of pieces to be glued together and the assembly of a cavalryman in particular can be a most complicated and exacting exercise, but the result is most rewarding.

From the kit for standard-sized figures to the outsize one is a natural step. The first model of this kind which we have been able to trace dates from about 1935, and is of a Lifeguard. It is about six inches high, made in four pieces, and is extremely crude. The best models of a larger size were designed by E. Meister for Selcol, but smaller models at cheaper prices by other firms

Above left Prince Eugene de Beauharnais, converted from an Airfix Life Guard, 7 inches in height. The bearskin can be placed on the head, the pelisse is free, and the sword removes from the scabbard. Enno Spandauw took seventy hours on this conversion

Above Authentic reproduction in plastic of a suit of armour in the Real Armoria, Madrid (Drawing by Peter Greenhill). Museums are becoming conscious of the potential inherent in small models of their pieces

These tiny models of Wellington's army were made by Grove and Benoy *c* 1945

put them out of business within a short time. These 'do-it-yourself' kits have proved popular, and one enthusiast, Enno Spandauw, of Gröningen, has so successfully converted one figure to another that he has opened a special museum for the display of his conversions. Mr J. W. Hardie, of Brisbane, fills the interior of his converted kits with liquid cement, and then sculpts them to his requirements with electric cutting bits. He has a collection of over eighty conversions of the British Army from Airfix six-inch kits.

The latest effort in plastic is the 'plastic flat', invented and designed by Rousselot and Lelièpvre. First mentioned and illustrated by Baldet, Lelièpvre informs us that he and the late Monsieur Mathiot each possessed a single example only, as production proved more difficult than anticipated, and work has been suspended indefinitely.

The tiniest and most popular plastics are the invention of Airfix. Designed by John Niblett, they are a mere 20mm, and issued in boxes of forty-eight figures at an extremely low price. To paint them is trying but rewarding. There has recently been a growing interest in tiny figures, probably because of the spread of the 'war-game'. This was invented in Germany in the middle of the nineteenth century, and a considerable literature has grown up. A number of societies are in being, and battles are fought on special tables with rules either fixed by societies or the invention of the players. Games may go on for weeks. Terrain can be the simplest or the most elaborate grouping of trees, hills, villages, roads and rivers; troops may be token units or hundreds of individual figures. So much has been written about the war-game that it would be tedious to add to it here, but little has so far been said of the actual models used.

The tiny semi-solids made by Ammon and other German manufacturers at the turn of the century and identifiable with those mentioned by R. L. Stevenson and Lloyd Osbourne were probably not made with any particular war-game in mind, and it is possible that Grove and Benoy's 30mm models (*c* 1945) were the first to cater for this specific need. This effort, however, was an isolated one; the original beautiful models of Stadden (withdrawn) and Niblett (no longer obtainable) were obviously too expensive for purchase in bulk, and Greenwood's tiny models were for dioramas. Nor can the delightful models by Alymer of Valencia (who claims to be the first to make 20mm models) be regarded as war-game figures. However, Scruby in the United States and Gammage in England soon began to produce large masses of tiny figures, followed by Thomas and Bussler in America, and Hinton in England. Surén's and Stadden's later 30mm models, although designed primarily for the cabinet, are frequently met with on the war-game table, together with the Airfix figures, and the slightly larger sizes of Starlux and Swedish African Engineers. In the 30mm range the original models of Eriksson take an honourable place, together with the English Civil War models of Leslie Higgins. Our own interest in the tiny figure is not its use in the war-game, but the beauty of its workmanship, and the very special advantage of size when used in dioramas.

During the last few years growing attention has been paid to the presentation of the model soldier, and with the blossoming of the specialist maker has come the desire on the part of the collector to show his specimens to the best advantage. Whereas in the past the main bulk of a collection was kept packed (albeit neatly and carefully) in boxes, especially by the collector who aimed at complete units, usually in marching order, the tendency today is to have these permanently on display. In order to achieve this object much space is required, and many collectors solve the problem by using open shelves running completely round a room or rooms, or utilising glazed bookcases. For the individual figure, or collection of individual figures, mounting on a plinth of suitable shape and size, with perhaps a neatly printed inscription, is a tremendous asset. It is extraordinary the way the additional inch or so in height increases the visual impact of the model, especially if the feet are standing on imitation grass or earth. Small, well-designed picture wall-frames of two or three shelves are extremely effective for the display of a few specially prized examples, especially if concealed lighting is used. These frames are also ideal for the display of flats and the tiniest models.

Considerable ingenuity can be used in grouping related figures. They can be mounted on a base, forming a conversation piece, or, in the case of flats, placed in a small box with transparent front and sides. Extra interest is given if a scenic background and appropriate terrain are simulated – a style of presentation very popular in the United States. Many collectors, however, are more ambitious, and assemble their models in larger numbers. In fact, what might well be called 'the cult of the diorama' has rapidly grown, and it is not unusual to find a display of models in glass-fronted cases forming an integral part of the furnishings of a room. Brigadier Young's use of this device is magical.

Diorama, *Bir Hacheim*, composed by Madame Métayer and Eugene Lelièpvre

Models of all sizes can be used according to the space available, either a single Courtenay Nefertiti in a simple, beautiful setting by Denny Stokes, a group of a hundred Gottstein flats, or thirty or so Stadden 30mm Scots Greys, or several boxes of Airfix battle-dress troops in a contemporary engagement.

The tendency to contrive dioramas for the collector's private enjoyment is a far cry from the original idea, which was to portray an important historical event in as large a setting and using as many models as possible. Baldet illustrates and describes what must be the first recorded diorama of the Battle of Dettingen made by a 'former Guards officer' in the Musée de l'Armée at Paris. No attempt has been made to individualise the figures, which are merely symbols; but a Battle of Lodi, executed at Napoleon's orders in 1804 by Martin Boitardo used 15mm figures pinned into the ground and incorporated remarkably realistic shell-shattered buildings. Other examples occur in the middle of the nineteenth century, but the glory of the diorama is shown in later models, when literally thousands of Heinrichsen and Allgeyer flats were used to portray such events as Waterloo, Leipzig, Borodino, the Siege of Vienna, Wagram and Sacile. English readers will be familiar with the now sadly dispersed collection of dioramas supervised by Stokes and Gottstein which were the glory of the Royal United Service Institution Museum. They were of the finest quality, and there is small compensation in the fact that now, instead of seeing a pageant of English history under one roof, one has to go to the headquarters of the Staffordshire Regiment to see Ulundi, to York to see Marston Moor, to the Dorsetshire Regiment to see Plassey, to the

Thurrock Museum to see Elizabeth at Tilbury, and to the Glenbow Foundation at Calgary to see Balaclava, Waterloo, Blenheim and Crécy.

The makers of flats are particularly aware of the diorama, and plan their sets, large or small, with this form of display in mind. They even issue the 'combination figure' with an extra number of legs, arms and accoutrements, so that by judicious selection a number of variants on the original figure may be obtained. But within recent years the use of 54mm models in dioramas has been growing, and it is in France, with its long tradition of magnificent modellers, that one finds them used to the best advantage. Two,

Drumming up Volunteers for the 1775 Continental Marines, a typical American-style diorama. Figures made of beeswax, with wood and metal, 8.75 inches high

The Battle of Kennesaw Mountain, a vast diorama composed by the Pfabs for their Kennesaw Battlerama, using hundreds of models which they made themselves

both illustrated in M. Baldet's *Figurines et Soldats de Plomb*, reach a perfection that is quite breath-taking. Eugene Lelièpvre makes his figures in different sizes according to the scale of the diorama, and uses different sizes in the different planes; for instance, a foreground model of 12cm, a middle-distance one of 4.5cm, and a background one of 2cm. It is a truism to the painter that the further away an object is the flatter it appears – but how many dioramists realise this? Lelièpvre achieves this illusion by slightly flattening his more remote models.

In the United States the tendency is to create dioramas with very large models, which, though admirably made, tend to become slightly overwhelming. There is a number of examples, however, of the use of normal-size models, as at Anderson House, Washington, Yorktown and Albany; but perhaps the most extraordinary is that of the Kennesaw Battlerama, at Kennesaw, Georgia, created by Vincent Pfab and his wife, comprising the battles of Kennesaw Mountain and Atlanta, and utilising over twelve hundred models made by themselves.

This, then, is the firm foundation of the hobby: the commercial figure – solid, semi-solid, hollow-cast, flat, wood, plaster, paper-sheet, plastic, the war-game figure and the diorama. So far we have concentrated on the commercial figure known as the 'toy' soldier. The question arises as to how or when or why a tiny military figure changes its nomenclature and becomes a 'model'. One might suppose that the quality of the figure determines its status; but a review of a number of collections shows that a collector is as likely to cherish a chain-store plastic creation as one purchased in Burlington Arcade. Perhaps it is the antiquity of the piece? But many collections, possibly because of financial reasons, consist solely of commercial products, and the collector would be most annoyed if you called them 'toys', as would a collector of veteran cars if they were maligned as 'old crocks'. The majority of collections contain a variety of commercial figures with a leavening of ones of better quality, and the name 'model soldier' has the virtue of embracing all types.

Attitudes among collectors vary. One will take a cheaply produced article and so alter, convert or repaint it that it stands comparison with more expensive specimens. Another would consider this interference anathema, and rejoice in the original paint, even though it were chipped and scratched. Value, after all, is relative. A complete set of first editions of the paperbacks issued by a popular publisher is a book-collector's achievement; a Religious Tract Society's give-away eight-page pamphlet on the Franklin Arctic Expedition something of a rarity; a chapbook published at one penny a prized possession.

There is, however, a number of discerning collectors who desire the best that the model soldier maker has to offer, and it is due to their efforts in the past that so many magnificent models have been created. It is obvious that special models have always been made for wealthy patrons, for instance the Franz Josef sets already mentioned, and all the best commercial manufacturers produced models outside their usual range, for example Hilpert's Frederick the Great, Heinrichsen's set for Nicholas I, and Mignot's seventy-five models made for Napoleon III. The evolution from the mass-produced figure, adequately designed, painted by factory-hands, and recast over and over again in the number required, to the sensitively modelled, accurately clothed and skilfully painted model for the cabinet was a gradual one. It may well have begun in Germany where the efforts of Hahnemann, Biebel, Gottstein and Müller were instrumental in educating the public and the makers in producing better flats than had ever been made before. The accent was on historical accuracy, based on long research, allied to the most skilful original drawing and the most artistic and delicate engraving. One has only to remove the original paint from a Heinrichsen and compare it with an unpainted Sixtus Maier and the proof is there. Indeed, for our part we are often reluctant to paint a beautifully engraved flat, just as we have an Eriksson casting which we leave in its pristine beauty.

A German reviewer of the Leipzig Exhibition of flats in 1930 was rather scathing about solids: 'The tin soldier has its ancestors and even its bastard, the so-called lead soldier . . . the tin figure is no lead soldier either in form or content: it is as far from it as a work of art is from a toy.' The writer, of course, automatically eulogised the flat as the traditional mode of Germanic expression, but there was at the time much truth in what he said. A survey of solid and hollow-cast models in the 1930s shows a somewhat unimaginative uniformity of design and execution, and there was a certain amount of dissatisfaction among English collectors, who were anxious for a better standard of production. It was during this period that societies began to be formed (the French *Société des Collectionneurs de Figurines Historiques* in 1931, the British Model Soldier Society in 1935, and the Belgian *Société des Collectionneurs* the following year) and the members either began making their own models or commissioning promising young artists to produce them to their own designs.

The movement spread and, as the resultant models were seen by other enthusiasts, so they in their turn desired to possess similar works of art. The result was that within a few years there was born an impressive array of specialist makers, each capable not only of producing a standard model of quality, which could be sold direct to the public, but of working to all types of commission.

Vertunni of Italy and Eriksson of Sweden, remote from influence or encouragement, had been pursuing their own intelligent and quiet paths, hardly noticed by their contemporaries. Now in France there appeared the triumvirate of Ballada, Berdou and Bittard, followed by Madame Métayer. In England an ex-naval man named Richard Courtenay began making beautiful models of ancient and medieval figures, soon to be followed by a friend and admirer, Frederick Ping. The original master-craftsmen were succeeded, in France, by Josanne des Fontaines, Lelièpvre, and Fouillé, and in England by the young Stadden, Greenwood, Gammage and Niblett, by Willets, The Sentry Box and Synge-Hutchinson and the Coppins. More recent still are Marcus Hinton, Surén, and Higgins, whilst in America an independent school has evolved, led by Bussler, including such well-known names as Scruby, Conley, Murray, Imrie, Risley, Cooke, Steiner and Kramer.

Outside the lead model field, great progress has been made with figures of carved wood, or wood clothed with natural materials, or composition figures. Normally these are large creations, as evinced by the essentially caricature examples of Arthur and Arquette, but Auguste Pranzetti of Sassari, Sardinia, carves his infantry in 54mm scale. Ernesto Chiappa of Turin carves the heads, arms, feet and legs and uses papier-mâché over a metal armature for the torsos of his models, which stand 11–13 inches high. Cloth is used for the uniforms, leather for the belts and straps. The Risorgimento Museum and the Pietro Millo Museum have examples of his work. He also, like Pranzetti, carves 54mm figures. Models similar to Ernesto Chiappa's larger figures are made by Ernesto Battaglia, of Venice.

A contributing factor to the growth in popularity of the model soldier is the interest which museums and institutions are taking in the display of their own collections. This is in turn complemented by the exhibitions staged by societies. The collections at the Musée de l'Armée and in many German and Swiss towns have, of course, been well known for years, but one now comes across displays, large or small, even a single diorama, in the most unlikely places, and municipal authorities are beginning to commission collectors to commemorate historic local events, such as the Battle of Hastings or the Battle of Lewes. Societies are now to be found in most countries, and their publications form a valuable addition to the body of knowledge of the hobby.

Even as early as the eighteenth century military models were occasionally made to order by master craftsmen. This 15cm-high flat figure of Frederick the Great was made by J. G. Hilpert in 1777, and is signed and dated

The Makers

There comes a time when the collector is not satisfied with mass-produced models. As a first step he will try a simple repaint to distinguish a model from its neighbours. If he is skilled with diminutive hacksaws and soldering irons he will next set to work and re-make the commercial model, transforming it into something nearer his own idea of perfection. Indeed, so thorough and clever are some conversions that it becomes impossible to identify the original. To make matters even more confusing for the interested observer, several different models may be selectively amputated to make one new one. Horses are particularly susceptible to this kind of treatment. Going a stage further, the collector may attempt to make his own models. In this, as in any other pursuit, he may be successful or the reverse, and he needs his wife, if he is married, to be both indulgent and long-suffering. If, however, he is not good with his hands, or lacking in imagination, or a busy man, or just plain lazy (and very many of us fall into at least one of these categories), his efforts at self-expression will inevitably prove disappointing, and he has perforce to turn to the specialist makers for the models he desires. And when other similarly-placed collectors are fired with the same idea, the demand is there, and a school of modellers emerges to satisfy it.

These professional sculptors in miniature can be divided into two classes. First, the supreme maker, working only for the most highly specialised market, and taking only those commissions suited to his taste and temperament. Second, the very good craftsman, whose commissions, rewarding though they are, represent only a part of his annual output, and who will turn his hand to a larger range than his more illustrious colleague. Between them they fulfil the collector's desire for a model which is either unique, or, even if paralleled by those of other collectors, is still a remarkable and highly desirable work of art.

Previous page : Poundridge, an incident in the American War of Independence, by Imrie-Risley

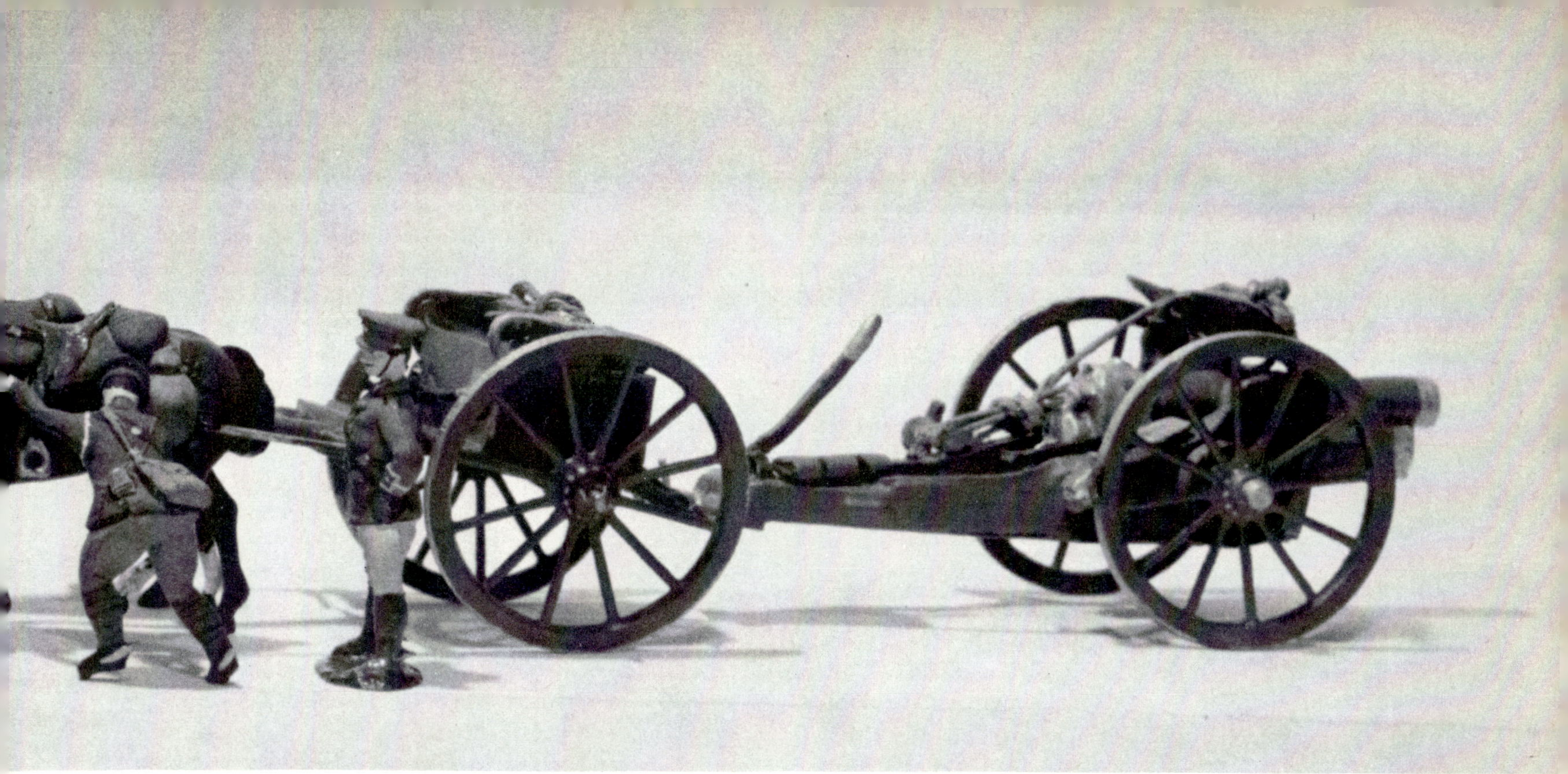

4.5 Howitzer and team, RFA, in the British Expeditionary Force, 1914. An excellent example of conversion by Henry Harris from existing Britains' models. Every man and horse has been subjected to alteration, thus giving animation to the whole

One of the first craftsmen to specialise in models of high quality was Richard Courtenay. His lineal descendant, Ping, carries on the same tradition, and has a more extensive range. Modelling the same medieval period, Niblett executed a number of fine models in 54 and 20mm, but has now turned his attention to the tiny plastic model, with an occasional excursion into the larger size, notably a *Bruce* after Pilkington Jackson. Greenwood, with his partner Miss Ball, specialising in British regiments, was early in the field, executing some exquisite miniatures for use in dioramas built by Denny Stokes. The young Gammage came to notice for his beautiful set of figures for the Coronation of Elizabeth II, and has gone from strength to strength. Marcus Hinton, also, is developing rapidly not only in quality but in range of subject, and there is a small but growing school of younger makers to ensure continuity. Most outstanding of all is Charles Stadden, whose name is as universally known in his field as Britains in theirs.

Among the makers of larger sizes are Pilkington Jackson, in wood (who, however, prefers his models to be called statuettes), Willetts and The Sentry Box combine, together with the short-lived Patmore, and the team of Synge-Hutchinson and the Coppins.

There is a sturdy quality about English models, together with great feeling for the past and a refreshing attitude towards innovation. Because of their dependability they figure largely in collections all over the world. The French, on the other hand, display all the *élan* and feeling for elegance to be expected in the traditional leaders of European culture. A des Fontaines creation is an exquisite evocation of the past, and a Berdou a collectors' treasure. Hardly less eminent are Madame Métayer and, perhaps in a more restricted degree, Ballada and Baldet; whilst Lelièpvre, Fouillé, and Angenot exhibit their great skills in more varied media. As in England, there is a number of new craftsmen waiting to take the place of their elders, notably E. Baptiste and B. Vanot. On the whole the French are more traditionally minded than the British, and their creations appeal more to the collector with the greatest sensitivity to their characteristic style.

Master-makers are not prominent in the Nordic countries, with the exception of that phenomenon Holger Eriksson, the doyen of craftsmen, (and much more recently Søren Brunoe), or in the Germanic block, where Krauhs is the unique exception. In Spain, Valverde's work has formed no school, and in Italy, with the exception of Otello, working in a very limited sphere, interest lies in the creation of models of wood, plaster and natural materials. Across the Atlantic, however, the picture is different. The most eager collectors and the most interested in all aspects of the hobby, the Americans, while appreciating the works of the masters of the Old World, are producing their own craftsmen. Imrie and Risley, and Murray are well known, whilst Cooke appears to be assured of a good future. Stock, Scheid, Bussler, Scruby and Custer have all at one time or another formed a solid background, and new makers are holding their own. With their own special history, it is inevitable that many of their models deal with either the Revolution or the Civil War, but the Napoleonic period and the two world wars are also well represented.

One of the perennial fascinations of collecting model soldiers is to observe the emergence of new craftsmen. Series 77 began to market their models in the autumn of 1970, and by the time this book is published may be household words. In the United States Reg Boutet has so far produced a mere half-dozen models, but one can forsee a succession of fine ones in the future.

There is a whole world of creation involved in the making of a model soldier: whether the figure is commissioned or the fancy of the maker, the problems are the same. The general characteristics appropriate to the miniature having been settled in his mind, the artist begins his research into the general history of the period, and then the specific costume or uniform to be represented. This may well involve the study of rare and erudite works of reference, followed by cross-references to others and perhaps verification from actual specimens in military or civil museums. Not only has the cut and colour of the uniform to be scrupulously accurate, but also the appendages such as the braid, the buttons, the cuffs and the collar. The sword, scabbard, musket, rifle, bayonet, pistol, powder flask, bandolier, pike, slings, and harness have to pass the critical survey of the knowledgeable collector, who is himself very often an expert on the particular subject or period. Other vital details are banners or colours, standards, or heraldic bearings and crests, the correct shape of headgear and the exact type of shoe, the appropriateness of beard or moustache, the hair cut, the breed of horse and its characteristics at any given period of history.

When the designer is satisfied with his researches he normally makes working drawings of the figure, incorporating all the details, and these are then translated into figures of plasticine, plaster, or wood. From these the final specimen is chosen and the mould made, the exact technique being a matter of most personal choice, some using one method, others another. Separate models and moulds may be made for equipment, packs, etc, and, where the artist prefers to work in this way, arms, legs, and heads also. The final figure is then fully equipped with all the necessary impedimenta, which are soldered on. The casting is finally checked for 'flash', which is then removed, and the figure cleaned and primed ready for the next stage.

There is a number of schools of thought regarding the painting of the model. In the early days of

Opposite: Dragon d'Élite, premier Empire.
14cm lead model by E. Baptiste *c* 1968

14
14

Courtenay and Greenwood enamels or oils were normal, with their resultant glossy finish, still much admired by many collectors. Whether one likes this or not depends on the attitude one adopts to the whole philosophy of the model soldier. If he is thought of as a sculpted representation in miniature of a military man in the same way as a Chelsea statuette is a representation, its appearance determined by the material used, then a sheen on the surface is perfectly unobjectionable. Alternatively, if it is to be regarded as a facsimile in 30 or 54mm scale of a six-foot-high fighting man, treatment that simulates the actual texture of flesh, cloth, leather and metal is more appropriate. The emphasis has changed from the first attitude to the second, and with it the style of painting, so that today flat enamels, flat oils, and matt gouache are almost universally used, the shinier media being reserved for such surfaces as would take highlights in real life.

The craftsman at work. Charles C. Stadden working on one of his famous miniatures

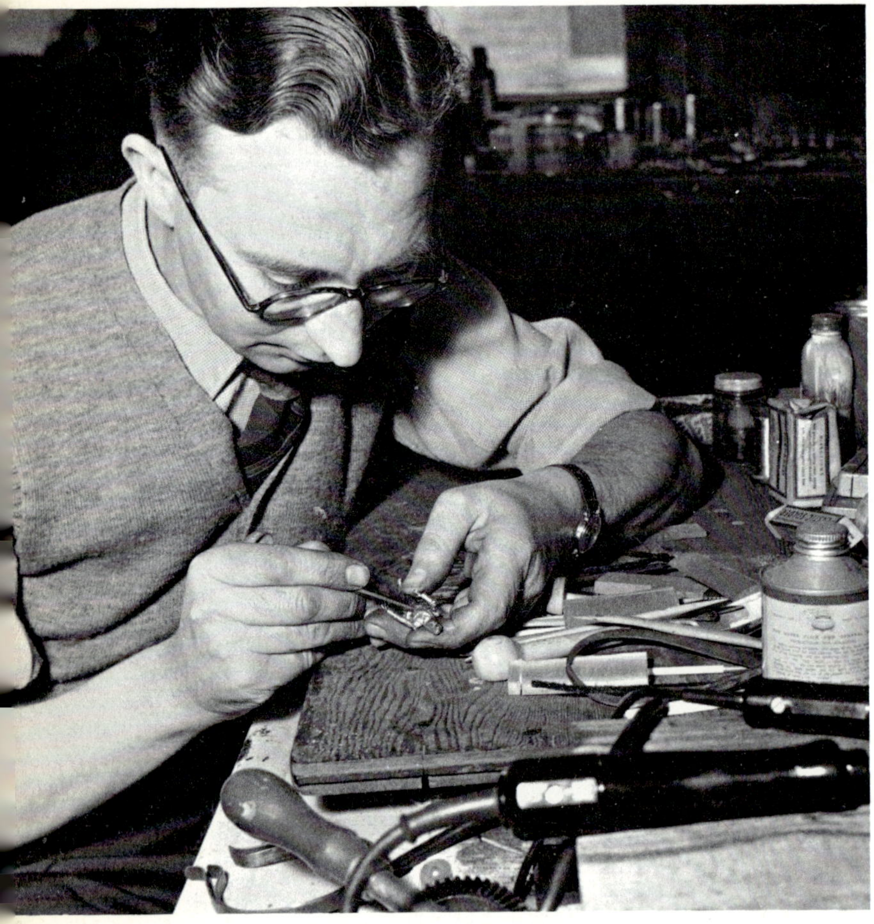

Some perfectionists, however, are not content with a smooth unbroken matt surface, and strive to simulate three-dimensional light and shape by accentuating, for instance, the highlights of the folds of tunic or trousers. In the case of flats, this is essential, if a two-dimensional model is to achieve any degree of reality, but one may well question whether such treatment of round castings is either necessary or truthful. Magnificent though the results may sometimes be, it is doubtful whether a carefully-emphasized crease at a knee or a heavily-lined fold at an elbow can always be correct under varying lighting conditions; whereas the natural emphasis given by strong sculpting or modelling will inevitably be correct under all circumstances. Again, the hide of a horse is not a uniformly coloured and toned thing but full of subtle and subdued lights, which are there owing to the anatomical structure of the underlying flesh and muscle, the fluidity of movement causing the emphases to be on different parts at different times. These highlights are achieved by the very qualities inherent in oils. It is, of course, a matter of personal choice as to whether one prefers to let oils play their natural part (as do Eriksson and Ping) or to simulate material and texture by means of a flatter medium (as do Stadden and Gammage).

We ourselves received a salutary shock. We had adopted the matt-finish method, and repainted a number of our medieval castings which had previously been coated with enamels, taking every care to shade the surfaces, blend the colours, emphasize the folds, and

Opposite: Mousquetaire, 1815. Carved bass-wood, with natural clothing. Unnecessary detail is discarded to express the sense of urgency conveyed by this typical equestrian model by General Angenot

were pleased with the result. Then along came one of the illustrious makers with two groups of his models to be photographed. How insipid our own figures looked! Here was the complete and unashamed use of oils, creating in both sets of models – one a medieval battle-scene, the other an eighteenth-century conversation piece – a vivid and romantic impression that quite dimmed the flame of our matt-finish efforts.

There is one danger common to the painting of all models, whatever the medium used, and that is over-painting. Painters and graphic artists realize that power can often be achieved by omitting detail which would distract attention from the broad design. In the face of a human being one does not normally perceive every eyelash and the striation of the iris; one senses the general effect of the eyes – their proportion, relative colour-tone, positioning in their sockets and so on. Unfortunately too many highly finished models suffer from the ignorance of their painters in this respect, and the typical result is the unnaturally glaring stare of too prominent eyes. There is no logical reason, except possibly as a technical exercise of dubious merits, why eyes should be painted in detail at all. The lengths to which well-meant but essentially futile effort can go in the matter of detail may be seen in many a Society journal, where pages are spent in retailing the methods used by various collectors, even in the painting of flats.

The two sets of models we have just mentioned illustrated the point very clearly. The eyes were skilfully and subtly indicated, made subsidiary to the figure as a whole, and no particular part received inappropriate emphasis. The result was harmonious and life-like, and obviously the work of a sensitive artist. We compared them with a New York Zouave in our possession, gorgeous in resplendent uniform, every fold of the voluminous breeches carefully picked out, with bristling moustache and imperial. It was completely spoilt by a hair's-breadth error resulting in the pupils of the eyes looking in different directions. The unfortunate fact is that these small, unnecessary details tend to become emphasized in photographs, creating an impression of even greater falsity.

One of the outstanding results of the increasing interest in the making of model soldiers is the ever-widening scope. It now embraces all the elements of military history, together with a faint but welcome stirring in the direction of historic portrait models, which, it is to be hoped, will gain momentum. (An example of what has been done in plastic, and could well be done in lead, is the remarkable range of Café Storme.) Arising out of this is the growing variety of stances available. There was formerly a somewhat limited selection of positions, mainly of a parade order, with an occasional excursion into the more active poses. The commercial makers always had their standing-firing, kneeling-firing, marching, and attention positions, but with the advent of new methods of moulding and more tractable materials (and larger sales), fresh and more animated action is possible. Among the specialists today one also finds a far greater range of combat poses, even including casualties, than could have been found fifteen years ago. There is as well an increasing demand for the treatment of the fighting man as a human being in off-duty pursuits, engaged in amorous dalliance, smoking a quiet pipe, playing cards, being greeted by a favourite dog, trying on the plundered uniform of a beaten enemy. There is a growing tendency to combine a few such figures to make a conversation piece, and to heighten naturalism as much as possible by the use of accessories.

The changing interests of collectors naturally influence the craftsmen, and a generally harmonious relationship between maker and collector has developed.

In the part of the work which follows we give short biographical sketches of a number of eminent craftsmen from various countries, working in different media. We indicate their aims, their ideals, and their methods, together with a review of the qualities by virtue of which they have reached their high position.

Austria

Helmut Krauhs, *Salzburg*

Helmut Krauhs lives in a small house at the foot of the mountains overlooking Salzburg. The house faithfully reflects the occupant's background and interests, for everything has been thought out with military precision, and it is full of objects either made or collected by himself, so that it is a veritable museum of folk art and military history. Country-made cupboards and painted wooden chests contrast with flags and weapons which conjure up the *Königliche-Kaiserliche Armee*. Such was his upbringing; but today the sword rests in the scabbard.

Krauhs was born in 1913 in Laschau, of an ancient and aristocratic Hungarian family, and was brought up in a Hungarian fortified castle which had been family property for generations. In his youth he made toy soldiers of wood, cardboard or paper, and early in life he was given a box of Wollner's typical Austrian semi-solids. This firm made their models in six different sizes, size two being the most popular. They also produced three-dimensional carriages and guns. Krauhs recalls that the gift came from an uncle from whom he cannot remember ever having received another present. . . . Later, when he moved to Vienna, he bought many other Wollners, 'number one style, semi-solid, 20mm'.

Leaving the Theresian Military Academy at Wiener Neustadt he was placed in the artillery of the *Bundesheer* and then served as an officer in the German *Wehrmacht* throughout the Second World War. It has been said that a soldier spends most of his time waiting so that he will be twice as quick when action is needed. *Oberleutnant* Krauhs used his waiting time to develop his woodcarving skills, making little military subjects, mostly in caricature – which he gave away.

Helmut Krauhs arranging a group of his models of the Austrian army

In 1945 Krauhs's military career ended, and with it his house, his money and his livelihood. Once again thousands of Austrian officers had to turn their hands to other employment, and he decided to utilise the talents he had hitherto used for relaxation. The first statuettes that he carved professionally were purchased at rare intervals by discerning persons, but gradually, as his technique improved, the rate of sales quickened. Eventually the demands of wealthy collectors, museums and military academies resulted in a constant stream of orders. Today he can afford to pick and choose his clients.

His main interest lies in historic military uniform, but he has also created hundreds of baroque, gothic and Renaissance nativity figures, and is well known for his carvings of peasant costume. The visible flesh of the models is represented by carved limewood, otherwise he employs the materials proper to each part – cloth for the uniforms and costumes, leather for straps, saddles and harness, metal for breastplates, swords, scabbards,

Above The coach of Charles VI of Spain. Papier-mâché figures with carved limewood faces and hands, with natural clothing. The whole made by Helmut Krauhs

stirrups and spurs. The bodies themselves are of plaster. In some instances he has incorporated a metal stand protruding behind the heels to enable the figures to stand upright. All the glittering gold and silver lace, the epaulettes and the froggings, are worked in metallised thread, and the guns can actually be fired – in short, no effort is spared to achieve realism. All his work is done with the help of his wife and one assistant only.

One of his greatest achievements is a set showing the evolution of the Austrian army from 1648 to 1848 (fifty models) for the Heeresgeschichtliches Museum, Vienna. These are not just single figures, like his *Graf Brown* at the National Army Museum, but animated groups of soldiers fraternising in their respective period uniforms, arranged with great naturalism. Other sets include one of twenty-five models of the Papal Swiss Guard (including a portrait model of the Commander) for the Vatican; a baroque hunting breakfast featuring Charles VI; a parade of wine harvesters (for the Danube Museum in Petronell); a cortège of homage of the various corporation officials before Charles VI (in the baroque exhibition in Melk, comprising thirty models, together with horses, vehicles and sedan chairs); hunting scenes for the Haus der Natur, Salzburg; sailors dragging their boats upstream (Donaumuseum, Nieder Österreich); uniforms of the Rainer Regiment

Left Armoured General, *c* 1580. A magnificent large model in papier-mâché, carved wood, leather and metal, by Helmut Krauhs

(Rainer Museum, Salzburg); and the funeral of Maximilian (Stadtmuseum, Wels, Oberösterreich). There are models by Krauhs at the Museo Navale, Venice, and at West Point, and several were presented by the Austrian Minister of Defence to General Eisenhower.

We have seen photographs of some mounted officers in Hungarian uniform which are really magnificent, but our preferences are for the armoured general of 1580–90, in its splendid setting, the remarkable six-horse coach of Charles VI, with its attendants and outriders, and the wonderful evocations of the Mozart family and the creations of Wolfgang Amadeus.

As a relief from his professional commitments he carves for his own pleasure, in various sizes, and makes 20mm *Zinnsoldaten* inspired by Mittman's figures, for war-games (1870, Rome, the Napoleonic campaigns, the Seven Years' War, the Thirty Years' War, the Middle Ages, and the *Landsknechts*). Through the kindness of Dr Kröner we possess a couple of these little gems, one an elaborate *kombination* figure. These he engraves, casts and paints, together with the artillery, houses and backgrounds. One who knows him well says that 'on high feast days', he will sit down and prepare a war-game table. A landscape will emerge, with a town (based on the fortifications of Dinkesbühel, Rothenburg or Nordlingen) with streets, churches and surrounding hamlets. The terrain becomes populated with carriages and guns, townsfolk and combatants. Gathered round are his friends – a lawyer, a doctor, a civil servant – who join him in reconstructing some battle of the past, in an easy-going manner – in a way, as Dr Kröner says, that one would expect from a gentleman of breeding and culture.

His plans for the future? 'To continue to create: it is my greatest joy.'

Denmark

Søren Brunoe, *Copenhagen*

The works of Søren Brunoe may well be virtually unknown outside his own country. It was, indeed, at the instigation of our friend Cornelius Frazer of Amsterdam that we now have the opportunity of examining his figures, and the privilege of introducing them to a wider public.

Brunoe was born in Copenhagen in 1916 and is unmarried. He was educated successively at the Gl Hellerup College, School of Decorative Art, the art school of P. Rostrup-Bouesen, and the Académie André L'Hôte, Paris. He first exhibited as a sculptor at the Autumn Exhibition in Copenhagen in 1943, and in the next year as a painter. During the Second World War he was in the Civil Defence, and is currently attached to the Danish Navy as Admiralty Staff Artist, and sails with various units, painting all the time. Periodically he teaches drawing and the history of art at the Danish Naval College.

Brunoe's first contact with the world of the toy soldier was at the age of six when he was given a box of soldiers and sailors by a friend of his father, an army captain, who was rather grieved at his preoccupation

A Flank Attack. A delightful evocation of the early eighteenth-century. Solid lead figures in 54mm made by Søren Brunoe, who also designed the setting

with toy ships. As with Fouillé, interest in the two combatant arms have clashed ever since. As he grew, so he tried his hand at moulding and casting, without any great success. One of his great interests was in history in all its aspects, and nothing gave him greater pleasure than the great silent movie epics of the time: like *Charles XII* and *Ben Hur*, and he was always miserable if his models did not compare with those in the films.

About 1947, when he happened to be in Paris, Brunoe noticed a poster, advertising an exhibition of model soldiers. He was overwhelmed, as have been many others, by the craftsmanship and superlative quality of the exhibits. So he determined to begin creative work once more. Here his artistic training stood him in good stead. He began to realise that just as the real artist behind a ship model was the shipwright who created the prototype, and that the ship builder had no other option than to follow the blueprint as faithfully as possible, the human figure was the real raw material of models and, therefore, endless research had to be made before a drawing of a human figure could be faithfully translated into the medium of lead.

Brunoe models his prototype in wax or plasticine, but prefers Isopon. The size is mainly 54mm, but occasionally he makes statuettes in the traditional porcelain scale of 22cm, and with these he admits that he has been greatly influenced by the famous F. A.

Bustelli, of the Nyphenburg factory. In making complicated postures, of which he is fond, Brunoe cuts the mould apart, casting the components separately, and soldering them together. A cavalryman, for instance, he likens to a jigsaw puzzle. For painting, he formerly used Humbrol, but later discovered that a wonderful effect was to be obtained by mixing powdered colour with Talenz Matt varnish, thus obtaining matt colours in the rarest and most delicate of hues.

Brunoe has a profound feeling for architectural settings, and constructs these himself, for his own models, and for those of friends and fellow-collectors. Evidence of these is shown in his *Flank Attack*, with its graceful balustrade and semi-nude marble statues, in the solid fortress at the *Siege of Frederikstern*, *Clair de Lune*, and in the *Roman Forum*. He sometimes works from historical paintings, but more often than not discovers that it is impossible to reproduce an artist's figure in three-dimensional terms. He quotes a painting by Cederstrøm of Charles XII's body being carried across the border by his grenadiers, in which the body would be about ten feet long! However, Brunoe acknowledges his debt to the painters of the past, which he uses when engaged on any special period. In these paintings he studies not only the costumes, but the faces, bodies and postures as well, especially those of Gainsborough, Watteau, Fragonard and Reynolds, so that he is able to convey the spirit of the times, which he does superbly. We have in front of us as we write a colour photograph of a most beautiful figure of the French actress Adrienne Lecouvreur (*c* 1742), which has all the grace of a porcelain model, and another of a *bal masqué*, with a superb architectural setting which evokes the Venice of Casanova. His fighting men are purposeful but with the same feeling for period expressed in the tiny models of Surén. The eighteenth century is Brunoe's favourite period, and naturally one finds much of Danish history in his work.

He feels that in all his work truthfulness of detail must not stand in the way of art, and he therefore, when necessary, exaggerates or suppresses, as does Angenot in his very different way. Other makers whose work he admires are Berdou, Baldet, Rousselot and Higgins. Brunoe works mainly for private collectors and museums such as the Swedish Army Museum, whilst models of crewmen of the year of the disaster of 1627, commissioned by the Wasa Museum, Stockholm, are on sale at that institution.

Charles XII *of Sweden at the Siege of Frederikstern*, 1718, by Søren Brunoe

France

General Angenot, *Aix en Provence*

The old-time sailor often, using only a knife, spent his hours of inactivity on the interminable oceans in shaping from stray pieces of wood ships that he had either known or dreamed of. General Angenot modestly claims fellowship with the nautical brethren, but how far removed his creations are from those of the humble matelot can be judged from the illustrations.

We first saw his models, not of ships, but of equestrian subjects, at one of the exhibitions of the *Société des Collectionneurs des Figurines Historiques*, and were immediately struck by the living quality of his horses and by their riders who seemed fused into a composite whole with the moving steed. They opened new vistas in the art of model making, and stood out by their individuality from the otherwise superb but by comparison conventional examples of the cream of French craftsmen.

General Angenot at work on one of his unique models

General Angenot was born in 1893, and served during the Great War as a general of a cavalry division. His army career over, he turned to woodcarving as a relaxation and a hobby, and what more natural than that cavalry should be his prime concern? After a long period of research and difficult, often disappointing, experiment, he evolved a mature process of craftsmanship and at the same time a philosophy of art. Basically, the process is easy to describe. The first essential is the thorough study of the object, numerous sketches being taken from all angles. Secondly, the massing out of the principal bulk and the lines. Thirdly, the adoption of a scale which will determine the relative proportions of various parts of the body – which parts are to be accentuated or neglected or to be retained – at the same time ensuring that the character of the figure, its dress and equipment, will be in keeping. And finally the making of a framework, half skeleton, half clothed, which will impose the correct attitude and carriage on the finished figure. This often starts as a simple silhouette in profile, cut out in duplicate, which will gradually form itself like a foetus with a left-hand and a right-hand part which eventually coalesce. Alternatively, a basic torso or trunk is made; the head, legs, arms, etc, being worked separately and assembled in turn.

So much for basic principles. The next stage is the clothing of the frame, the costume, the equipment and the like, and here every ingenuity can be practised as the materials used will vary as greatly as the objects represented. And the closer one approaches actuality (metal, leather, and those parts which should in reality be flesh) the more one has to improvise. Thus, pasted paper is used for the coat, shabracque and saddlecloth, bookbinders' leather for bridles, swords are cut out of razor blades, buttons are stamped from metallic paper, the manes made from nylon floss.

Now the artist takes over. Angenot firmly believes that to give an impression of life, nothing must be slavishly copied, either from one's authorities or from nature. One must spend a long time observing and collecting one's impressions, and then try to translate as best one can the life and movement of the object. He has completed in the region of a thousand figurines, and so rigorous is his integrity that he has destroyed about three-quarters of them. His collection at present numbers some two hundred. He is a perfectionist, and his only consideration from start to finish is the making of a model as well as he knows how. Not for him, as he himself says, the God Janus: 'One smiling face turned towards art, one severe visage turned towards the initiation and promotion of sales'.

An animal in motion is perhaps the most difficult of all objects to depict, either in sculpture or by the graphic processes, as many an artist knows. Visions of the inspired brain too often become static and frozen when translated into cold reality. Throughout the history of art there have been painters who have eschewed the formal use of the model, relying instead on their powers of repeated observation, and whose sketches have always seemed more vital than more carefully executed exhibition pieces. Angenot is a great rider and a trainer of riders – see his *Célébration du Cheval* (privately printed, Limoges, 1967) – and his horses, carved with great love and *élan*, are obviously each based on a particular animal. To convey the idea of movement he exaggerates, he eliminates, he streamlines and finally achieves a unique sense of urgency. The rider, too, is fined down to the essentials, man and mount making a harmonious unit.

One of the greatest difficulties a maker of models experiences is the provision of a solid base for a horse in movement. It is easy enough for a competent craftsman to balance his horse on three legs, more difficult on two, although Courtenay and Selwyn-Smith manage this admirably. Eriksson and Stadden and Imrie rely on the presence of a convenient clump of foliage placed under a hoof to take the weight; others use various devices such as a supporting foot soldier or the use of the tail as a balancing agent. The results are sometimes effective, sometimes the reverse. The actual area of a hoof is proportionately minute, and when it becomes the fulcrum for the mass of the whole model transmitted down one tautly stretched leg, one could do it only in wood. Angenot achieves his results by using the lightest possible basswood, so that knowing, and being in perfect command of, his material and its stresses and strains, he can carve his figure with complete confidence as to the final balance.

Elegant woodcarving by Angenot, with natural clothing and nylon floss

Marcel Baldet, *Paris*

Marcel Baldet is well-known as the creator of many fine models and as the penetrating and observant author of *Figurines et Soldats de Plomb* and *La Vie Quotidienne dans les Armées de Napoleon*. He is, moreover, active in collecting circles, being the Secretary-General of *Sabretache*, a committee member of the *Société des Collectionneurs de Figurines Historiques*, and a member of many other societies, and adviser to the Musée Militaire de Montreal. Above all, many a collector will vouch for his enthusiasm and readiness to share his wide knowledge and experience.

He was born at Angers in 1898. In 1914 his studies at Saint-Cyr were interrupted by the real thing, and he soon found himself in the infantry of the French army. Four times wounded, he survived the horrors and ended up as a lieutenant and a Chevalier of the Légion d'honneur, with numerous French and Allied decorations. During the Second World War he was successively Captain and Major, being wounded again in 1940.

In civilian life he followed a journalistic career, and is now the head of a reporting service for a French daily. He is much sought after by film companies on account of his knowledge of military matters.

Baldet began making models in 1940–1, being dissatisfied with the existing types, none of which came up to his standards of exactitude. His aim was the creation of numerous different models of as fine a quality as possible, each unique in itself, and quite distinctive in its attitude. This approach precluded, because of expense, the use of a separate costly mould for each figure. Instead a single torso was cast, forming the basis of all the models. The legs are manipulated into the required position, either walking, at attention, running, or 'at ease'. (This is a method adopted by a number of makers, and generally known as 'animation'.) They are then clothed with the appropriate legwear; the arms are moulded separately, soldered on in the appropriate action, and the upper part of the body built up. The hands are 'opened', the thumb being separated from the fingers in the most natural manner.

Above Marcel Baldet holding two of his own models

The various parts of the body are then clothed in layers of the thinnest lead, one soldered over the other in successive operations, and all traces of solder and waste carefully filed off. The solder, moreover, is worked with a graver where necessary, in the way a sculptor chisels marble. Equipment is made from the thinnest possible sheets of brass, then soldered. Soldering irons of two or three strengths are used, and

Opposite The carriage of the Viceroy of India, *c* 1908. Converted from Britains' figures by Major Henry Harris

the file is constantly in operation. In addition he makes use of surgical instruments, such as scalpels and tiny saws.

Painting is done scientifically, using fine quality English oils which remain unaffected by any acid that might remain in the solder.

Baldet's method, therefore, amounts to the moulding – as distinct from simple casting – of metal (similar to Ping's technique) and each piece is obviously unique and individual, the result of much research, and subject also to such varying techniques as the occasion demands. For him, the model soldier provides relief from the ever-present study of military history and at the same time complements it. He is at his happiest when creating models of the military figures of the eighteenth century, both of France and of her allies and enemies. Nowhere are the results better seen than in the groups of famous figures of the American War of Independence (Washington, Lafayette, Rochambeau) he has made for Anderson House, Washington. A wider view of French history is given at the Musée Militaire de Montreal, where the French regiments in Canada and French explorers (La Salle, Champlain, Nicolet) are portrayed in single figures and in dioramas. He is also equally at home in any period of history, and can create a representation of a Greek hoplite or a Roman infantryman, a Knight of the Golden Fleece or a French *poilu*, and examples of his models are to be found in many collections and museums both in France and other countries.

Above Carignan-Salières Regiment. One of a series of models made by Marcel Baldet to illustrate French-Canadian history

Left Montcalm. A splendid 54mm equestrian model by Baldet, made for the Montreal Military and Maritime Museum

Roger Berdou, *Paris*

The summit of the art of the model soldier is reached in the works of Roger Berdou. Nobody, not even des Fontaines, can begin to rival this remarkable master, and it is from him that the elegance and assurance of the modern French model stems. Whether he realised his consummate ability at his first attempt we do not know, but certainly the corpus of the models that he has made over the past fifteen years or so contains so many of astonishing quality that practically any single one could stand as representative of his entire output.

We had, of course, heard of him. Though to the majority of collectors he was only a name, he had been spoken of with awe by a few of the most knowledgeable connoisseurs. What was inexplicable was the number to whom he was apparently quite unknown, at least in England. We were at a loss to understand how a collector familiar with the works of des Fontaines, Ballada, Métayer, Courtenay and Ping could fail to know the greatest of them all. Even on the Continent, Jean Nicollier, in a fascinating book with an unfortunate title (*Collecting Toy Soldiers*, 1967) published in Switzerland, which includes examples of most of the masters, completely ignores him and, what is worse, does not even recognise his work – illustrated though it is by an excellent colour plate, the caption of which does not mention the maker's name. We ourselves knew of him only by repute and from a photograph supplied in 1959 by the late Baron Francis Huber, and it is only recently that we have been able to

Premiers Dragons, 1809. A magnificent 54mm-high model by Roger Berdou, the greatest contemporary French master. He is unequalled in his depiction of horses

view his models directly, and learn the reason for his being so little known in the world of the collector.

One reason for his anonymity is that he never advertises, unlike so many of his fellow-craftsmen. And he works only to commission and then only in the period in which he is interested. The result is that unless one happens to know a Berdou enthusiast one will forever miss the thrill of seeing the work of a genius. We know of four Berdou collections – undoubtedly there are more – and their names were given to us by Berdou himself. One is Elton L. Puffer, of San Francisco, another Lyle Thoburn, of Gates Mills, Ohio, and a third lives in England. This last collector whom, in deference to his wishes, we must call Mr X, is so sensible of their value as works of art that he is apprehensive of theft, and for this reason wishes to remain anonymous. The fourth was the late Baron Huber, half of whose collection passed just before his recent death to Mr X. It was at the latter's house that we saw these, together with other Berdou models which had been independently commissioned. It is impossible to describe here fifty superb pieces of craftsmanship in detail, but we assure you that the overall effect is overwhelming.

There is perfect control over the minutest detail, yet no detail is allowed to obtrude. At first sight the fifty horses are identical except for colour; closer examination reveals subtle differences. It is just credible that another master maker might be able to match the quality of the riders, but no one could touch the superb artistry of the horses. Even the painting of these is breathtaking. The hairs of the manes are made of single strands of the thinnest lead – not an impossible achievement for a capable craftsman, but what other maker could shade the manes with such delicate sensitivity?

One has become so used to seeing models representing violent action that an assembly of fifty horsemen all standing quiet might well be thought monotonous. The art of Berdou, however, is such that each model has a separate identity, allied to an inner fluidity, which is conveyed whether it is standing by itself or grouped with others. A handful of other artists achieve this inner tranquillity on occasion: Ping, Eriksson, des Fontaines, Leliêpvre, but Berdou can do it each and every time.

His chosen period is, of course, one of the most colourful in history, and the uniforms then worn the most complex and varied; here is scope enough for the display of mastery over material: the scarlets, the crimsons, the light and dark blues, the whites, the greens, the glittering gold lace, a painter's dream. But how often has this very riot of detail and colour appeared tawdry and meretricious? Even granted success in both departments, there remain the horses, to which we inevitably return. Many an otherwise finely conceived and executed equestrian model has missed real greatness because the creator cannot match the level of skill employed in making the rider by that employed in making the steed. Here, above all, is where Berdou is the supreme master. Happy the possessor of a single model by him.

He was born at Versailles in 1907. At school there he showed great aptitude for drawing and painting, and took a course in art at the *atelier* of Albert Gallandre. He was not the only one of his family with similar inclinations, for his father Charles was a master painter, sculptor and gilder, earning a *médaille d'honneur* for his life-long work on the restoration of the chateau at Versailles. His military interest was fostered by family history – his father was a corporal, his grandfather a sergeant-major (also a calligrapher and stone engraver); a great uncle (Commandant Horca) and two uncles, both servicemen who distinguished themselves in the Great War, gained the Légion d'honneur, the Croix de Guerre, and the Médaille Militaire respectively. Roger himself served as a second gunner at Mayence during the occupation of the Rhineland in 1928.

His preference for cavalry dates back to a meeting with Jean Dillet, Lieutenant-Colonel of Aviation (died

Opposite A group of models typical of Berdou's artistry. *Left to right: Garde Impériale, Mameluk; Lieutenant Porte-Entendard* 1806–10; *Mameluk*, 1807–68; *Timbalier* 1810–12; *Trompette* 1805–10

1950), at that time President of the French model soldier society. Learning that Berdou was working in oils and pastel (as he still does) he introduced him to his collection of 30mm flats of the First Empire period, which he was in the course of assembling and painting. Berdou had already admired the drawings of Edouard Détaille and Meissonier, and the military watercolours of Maurice Gallandre, of Versailles; and now, in the house of Dillet, he was able to study the works of Bucquoy, Rousselot, Leroux, and Lelièpvre.

He assisted Dillet in painting his flats, but contact with Ballada soon brought him to the realisation that he could create his own models, but he chose 54mm solids, and his first efforts, based on Ballada's data, of cuirassiers and trumpeters of the First Empire, appeared in 1945. He tried repeating these, in order to form a series, but soon found that he lost interest if he had to reproduce the same model several times. During this period of experiment he was able to sell several models to dealers, which was a great encouragement.

He has remained faithful to the First Empire, as it is probably the best documented of all periods, and offers so much scope for individuality with its multifarious uniforms, that each model becomes a new challenge. At the same time he acknowledges that pre-Revolutionary and Second Empire models offer great possibilities. However, he is now in a position to accept or reject commissions as he pleases, and he finds that most of his clients favour the period he has made so magnificently his own.

Lyle Thoburn, however, induced him to make a series of models (twenty-five or so) illustrating various units of United States cavalry from 1775 to 1940. He also made a number of horses so that Imrie might provide the riders. This was a happy combination of client and two very dissimilar craftsmen, but Berdou does not make a practice of it.

Characteristically he will never commence a new model if one is already in hand, with the result that a visit to him to see his productions would be attended by some disappointment – all that he would be able to show would be the model on which he was currently working.

His starting point is a wax model, from which he makes a mould made of dental cement. The resultant cast requires, he says, a great deal of trimming and adjustment. Each part is made separately. The horse, for example, is in seven pieces: the head, the four legs, the pedestal, and the tail. The space for the saddle is hollowed out and the saddle inserted. The saddle cover (sheepskin or panther) is made of thinnest sheet lead, the crupper, bit, neck ornaments, halter, breast-strap and martingale of copper, the mane and hair of single strands of lead. For the rider, many materials are used, appropriate to the articles to be represented. Plumes have a core of brass, busby pennants are in lead with pompon and shako cord separately inserted; stirrups, stirrup-leathers, spurs, sabretache with the straps in copper, the sword with its hilt and the rings in copper; the left arm holding the reins, the right arm holding the weapon in the clenched fist; the crossbelt for the cartridge pouch and the shoulder belt are added in sheet lead, with the hook for the blunderbuss and the withdrawal strap for same. The pelisse is made in sheet lead, the arms of the pelisse inserted, the cord of the pelisse in copper, and all items, such as reins, whip, etc, soldered on. The minutiae, such as buttons, frogging, medals, are also soldered on. It becomes, therefore, a series of superimpositions, each having to be absolutely accurate before the next move can be attempted, and a complete model may therefore consist of a very large number (an average of seventy) of separate constructions and solderings. The collector can attempt this for himself if he purchases a Historex model, but he then has the considerable advantage of having the individual parts provided for him in advance.

When Berdou is satisfied that every detail is impeccable, and that all soldered parts are absolutely perfect, he begins the painting. An undercoat of special finish,

Douzième Hussards, 1804–12. Scrupulous accuracy and great artistry is conveyed by this master work by Berdou

'Novemail' or 'Renaulac', is first applied to protect the subsequent paintwork from the lead alloy. This layer reveals any slight blemishes that might have been overlooked, which can then be corrected. For the painting proper the finest oils only are used – 'Lefranc', 'Linel' or similar – mixed with best quality turpentine. He begins with the face of the rider, then transfers his attention to the horse, following a prescribed scale of colours, working from dark to light, and constantly blending touches and tones with a squirrel brush. This he regards as the most difficult part of the whole operation, much of the time being spent in attempting to reproduce successfully the exact shades and gradations of the horse's coat. The figurine itself of course, also requires great care, countless touchings and retouchings being given before Berdou is satisfied.

Each model is mounted on a thin base, with the description neatly inscribed by hand on the upper side. He has a most elaborate series of charts describing the position of the rider, and the legs, head and tail of the horse, for each of the models. No two collectors ever have an entirely similar model.

Once a collector has purchased a Berdou, it is difficult not to commission another, and the collections we know of consist of anything from fifty to a hundred models each. Here, again, is an enigma. One would suppose that for a masterpiece of this kind one would have to pay a commensurate price, obviously a high one. However, we learned from Mr X that this is not so; indeed, the figure he named seemed extremely modest in comparison with the prices charged by a number of his contemporaries – for much less worthy models.

As the models are all of one period (except the few designed in conjunction with Imrie) we do not propose to list them individually. To do so would only provide a roll-call of the various units of the Napoleonic army. Inevitably, of course, Napoleon himself figures in the list, not only in his heyday, but at various other times of his career, together with all his marshals and his relations. And it would be invidious to single out any one model for special commendation. Each in its own way must be regarded as a masterpiece, and to praise one is to praise all. It is better to let the photographs speak for themselves.

Berdou, as befits a great artist, is modest and full of praise for his fellow makers. They, in turn, speak of him in the highest and most affectionate terms. Collectors fortunate enough to have visited him have happy memories of the welcome accorded them by him and his wife (who died two years ago) and the enthusiasm for his art that bubbled forth, often for a whole evening. He is still pursuing his art in his chosen manner, so that each year another collection of Berdou models is born.

Vive Roger Berdou!

Josianne des Fontaines, *Bouloge-sur-Seine*

There are certain artists in all spheres especially noted for their versatility. Whatever they turn their hands to results in something miraculously perfect. Where flamboyance is required it is managed with consummate skill; where simplicity is the ideal, it also is achieved.

As we have seen, Berdou works to a self-imposed pattern and we can admire only the models which go from his workshop to a small clientele. But we have greater access to the works of Josianne des Fontaines, a fellow-compatriot.

It is difficult to say much about her as a person. This feminine artist is not easy to approach, being full of shyness and reserve, and so we know little of her aspirations or her failures, or of her beginnings in her chosen field. What we can do, however, is to assess des Fontaines' achievement in the light of those models which we have seen or had described to us. It is doubtful whether we shall say anything new, but at least we will be able to show a few of the models that this remarkable woman has made.

As a preliminary to modelling she goes to work to find out – like a conscientious actor preparing his part – all she can about the figure she has in mind. She reads biographies of the subject, discovering all those little personal idiosyncracies and quirks of human conduct that stamp him as an individual. Portraits from all periods of his life are carefully studied so that an exact portrayal at the chosen time may be made. She would, for example, if commissioned to do a model of Beethoven, decide whether he was to be, for instance, the young man conquering the world with the *Eroica*, or the creator of the last quartets, bowed, ill, tormented by creditors, ear-trumpet in hand, but still indomitable.

National characteristics are, of course, given full attention, the nobility or lack of it in faces given full play, and the relative height and physical proportions of the nationality duly considered.

Officer, *Régiment Agenois* in the American War of Independence. A fine model by des Fontaines

When all details are settled, the model is made up from a number of parts, each cast separately, and assembled on a nude torso. The face is moulded and sculpted, and the costume cut from the thinnest sheet lead, piece by piece, and built up to the requisite design, and all the accessories made separately and soldered on. In the actual casting she is assisted by her father.

She works to commission only, and in this way preserves her freedom of choice. Her work may be seen in the flesh, as it were, in Paris and Montreal, and a number of photographs of her models are included in the books by Baldet and by Blum. (See, in particular, the miraculous medieval hawking pair in the latter.)

It is with the greatest pleasure that we are able to illustrate a few examples of her work that may be unfamiliar to some readers. The model of Murat, which is illustrated on page 68, is a remarkable study in theatrical magnificence, displaying an extraordinary insight into the character of the subject. In the hands of a lesser artist the effect of the multifarious decorations, the plumes, the trappings, the tinsel splendour, might well be disastrous, but the whole conception is so breathtaking in its breadth and delicacy, its sure grasp of form, and its mastery of material, that this must indeed be one of the finest models ever made.

The model of Prince Eugene de Beauharnais (Custer collection) is also one of resplendent beauty, but quieter in tone, befitting the subject. In this case the distribution of colour is such that the slightest jarring note would be instantly apparent. (Philip O. Stearns has a different version, equally impressive.) Similar in

A resplendent Murat, by des Fontaines. A masterpiece of the model-maker's art

context and period is a Napoleon at Eylau. Here the Emperor is shown in his winter travelling apparel and is comparatively austere in conception, proving an admirable foil to the more flamboyant turnout of his marshals. In the same vein are the kettle-drummer of the *Chasseurs à cheval de la Garde*, 1810, and the French Carabiniers, 1800, both of which are illustrated in Blum's book.

Duguay-Trouin and Montcalm are more sober, purposeful creations (dare we say that we find the faces perhaps a fraction large?) and it is obvious that she delighted in creating Washington and Lafayette (Blum collection). It is surprising to see among these figures the medieval mounted models (Stearns collection). These, again, convey the whole spirit of the period in the poise, the trappings and the colour, which, however, do not obscure the iron will of the ruthless fighting man.

Most of these models are in the hands of American collectors, though Brigadier Peter Young had, apart from others, a magnificent series of models of the English Civil War which Mademoiselle des Fontaines had been making for him until he disposed of them to Philip O. Stearns.

Georges Fouillé, *Chatillon-sous-Bagneux*

The author first heard of the work of this remarkable French artist from his friend Henry Harris, who had come from a visit to an exhibition held by the *Société des Collectionneurs de Figurines Historiques* in Paris. The second time he came to our notice was at the publication of *Adjutant's Call* containing a colour-plate of a magnificent Napoleon. The quality of the work was such that we were constrained to seek out this master craftsman – it proved to be Georges Fouillé.

Born in Paris in 1909, he is married and has a daughter in the early twenties. His parents came originally from the south coast of France, and he attributes his love of everything nautical to the fact that he passed much of his childhood by the sea. He found in early life that his leanings were towards the arts, especially to the painting of marine subjects, and he soon turned to the making of model ships.

These activities culminated in 1947, when he was appointed Official Painter to the French Navy. During the Second World War he had made the acquaintance of Eugene Lelièpvre, who introduced him to the art of creating model soldiers. He devoted several years to making marine subjects ancient and modern, in 55mm scale, for private collectors, at the same time making numerous dioramas for the Musée de la Marine de Paris.

In 1955 he conceived the idea of creating a collection of models of larger scale to illustrate uniforms in greater precision and detail. At first he had doubts

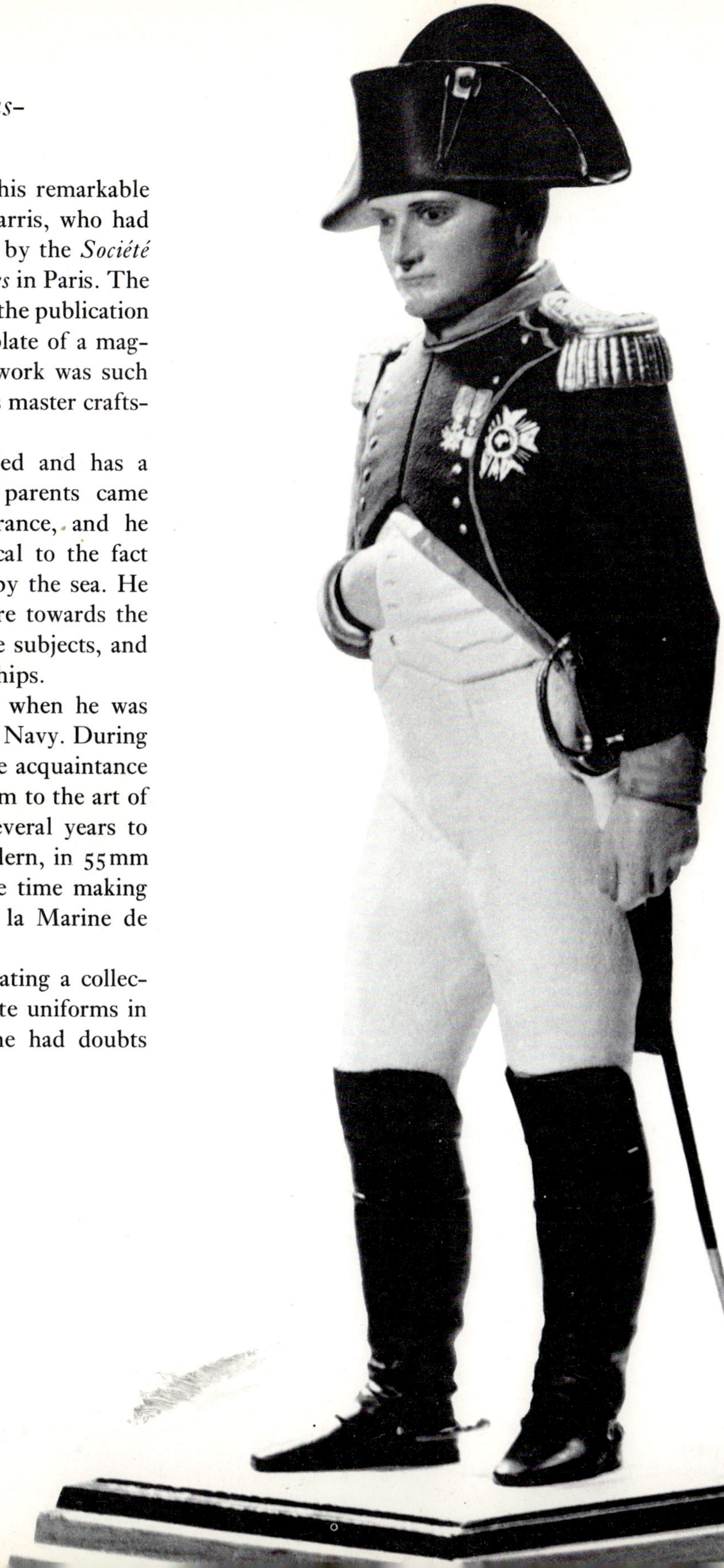

A 6-inch-high, solid lead model of Napoleon in characteristic pose. Made by Georges Fouillé, who specialises in figures of this size

about the wisdom of changing to larger models, but the results have shown his decision to be the right one. Little by little, at the request of collectors, he began to make models of the First Empire and also of the *Ancien Régime*, and in particular the standard bearers of the pre-Revolution regiments.

The 55mm figures are built up of thin sheet lead in the traditional manner on a nude torso, some models consisting of as many as forty-seven separate parts, and then painted in matt oils. Later Fouillé changed his method to the technique of separate pieces made specially for each model and assembled by solder, especially in the larger models. Each part is painted first, then the hair is fixed to the head, the arms and legs to the body, and the various accessories are added one by one in their natural order.

The prototype is first modelled in clay, a plaster version follows and the final model is in lead. When it is satisfactory, plaster moulds are made of the various detached pieces. The large figures are roughly six inches for the foot-soldiers, the cavalry in proportion. There is no doubt that the size helps the artist to express detail to the full, and an extraordinary impression is created.

The range is necessarily small, as Fouillé works at these models in his spare time, and his only assistant is his wife. His figures include Napoleon, mounted and on foot, *Grenadiers de la Garde*, *Chasseurs à pied de la Garde*, *Hussards*, *Chevaux-Légers Polonais de la Garde*, *Mameluks*, *Cavalerie Lourde Premier Empire* (all on foot) and *Artillerie*, *Chasseurs*, *Lanciers*, *Mameluks*, *Hussards*, *Chevaux-Légers* and *Chevaux-Légers Polonais de la Garde* (mounted).

In all these figures there is a wonderful sense of steadfast purpose; resplendent in blue or scarlet, glittering with gold braid, there is always a fighting man beneath the trappings. No one particular figure will receive attention here, but those that seem to us to epitomise the French military tradition are the trumpeter of the *Artilleur de Cheval de la Garde Impériale* – a tense, eager figure mounted on a magnificent horse; the *Mameluk*, a symphony in scarlet, green and gold; and the drummer of the *Grenadier Garde* – a model which could stand as a symbol of the whole of French military history.

Fouillé's work may be seen at the Musée de la Marine de Paris, where in several dioramas he has employed his 55mm models to remarkable effect. Another outstanding example is a model of the stern of an eighteenth-century galley of the line. Here the models are miraculously combined with the structure of the ship, and all the details – woodwork, lanterns, flags, and so on – are scrupulously accurate and worked with the utmost skill and artistry.

Fouillé's real love must not be forgotten – his passion for all things nautical. His work includes a long series of illustrations for the *Grand Dictionnaire Larousse*, and *Ships: a Picture History in Colour*.

Left : Drapeaux. Splendid examples of Fouillé's work in 54mm

Opposite Fouillé is noted for his wood-carvings of naval subjects. In this study of part of a galley the 55mm lead models blend beautifully with the elaborately ornate and wonderfully carved woodwork

Eugene Lelièpvre, *Montrouge, Seine*

The magnificent dust wrapper of Baldet's *Figurines et Soldats de Plomb* was our first introduction to the work of Eugene Lelièpvre. The elegance of the mounted figure, the grace of the gilded gates, and the architectural beauty of the setting denoted the hand and mind of a master.

Eugene Lelièpvre was born in 1909 and at an early age evinced a particular passion for drawing and painting horses, a passion which he still possesses and expresses in the media of graphic art and the model soldier. As official painter to the French army he has ample scope for the exercise of his skill, and his spirited hand-coloured line drawings are well known in collecting circles. His official duties naturally absorb most of his time, and model making is in the nature of an artistic relaxation. Beside making individual figures in large and small sizes, he has employed his talents in the making of dioramas, either entirely by himself or in collaboration with other artists, notably Métayer.

In creating models for dioramas he bears in mind the effects of perspective, making the figures in various sizes to accord with diminishing scale, thus those in the foreground may well be 12cm, those in the background 20mm, and the intermediate ones scaled accordingly. All the figures are round, the nearer ones fully, but as distance is reached the roundness of the figures becomes less pronounced. For this reason he does not use the 20mm war-game figure, which does not allow for this optical effect, or the flat which, however three-dimensionally painted, does not achieve the same result. Scales vary greatly, depending on the surfaces and the décor which he has to animate, and the effect to be obtained. But as each figure is made separately, it is easy to vary the size in the process.

Materials vary as well, and are often the result of impulse rather than of reasoned decision. He makes figures both large and small, sometimes in wood, sometimes in a mixture of paper, glue, and plasticine, sometimes just a paper model, sometimes tin, cut and shaped, and wrought if necessary. He claims that once the model is in place it is impossible to determine what it is made of. The miscellany of materials used to create the illusion of reality in a diorama is treated with the same care: tanks, wagons, vehicles, boats and the like are made in different scales and materials according to inspiration. The effect in the end justifies the means.

Eugene Lelièpvre has made many large sized models in various materials. This, 38mm in size, is one of a *Trompette des Gendarmes de la Garde*, 1745

Lelièpvre's larger figurines are fully articulated, and clad in cloth. They vary from 25 to 38cm from head to foot. The horse and the rider are of plaster, or modelled in wax, then moulded, and painted with exquisite delicacy. The horsemen are made upon an

Opposite above Georges Fouillé at work on some of his colourful 9 inch solid lead models

Opposite below A diorama by Madame Métayer, *Suffren à l'Isle de France*

Delightful carved wood figure, with natural clothing, by Eugene and Madame Lelièpvre

armature of steel wire, and the clothes are shaped and sewn so that they fit like a glove. The hands are of carved wood, each finger articulated so that they may actually grasp a weapon. Hair and moustache are of silk threads, and the materials of the horse equipment correspond with reality – reins of leather, bits of metal and so on.

Lelièpvre is emphatic regarding the necessity of documentary accuracy, a necessity imposed upon him by his work as military painter. He maintains that the scaling of figures offers little difficulty, but has found by trial and error that basic structure is essential to the rightness of the figure.

The making of the smaller figures is carried out in the traditional manner: a prototype in plaster, then arms, heads and legs alike cast separately in typefounding metal and soldered onto the torso. The clothing is of very thin sheet lead, cut exactly to pattern – the only method, he maintains, of creating the exact fold of a garment.

The models he is best known for in England are the ones produced by Historex (R. Gillet Aeros SA) of Paris from his designs and masters. The firm of Segom was the first to popularise the standard-size model in plastic which could be assembled from component parts; Historex has gone a lot further. The figures are made of white polystyrene, the parts assembled and fitted to the torso. There are about forty pieces to each mounted figure, with a wide choice of the appropriate headgear, details of uniforms and accoutrements, and a series of about thirty different horses. Every unit of the Napoleonic army will eventually appear. Complete colouring charts are issued, and advice given on conversion. For this it is necessary to have a pyrogravure (a kind of very small soldering iron fitted with a thermostat) for heating material, thus making it possible to mould the figure and change various parts of the body. The writer bears witness to the extreme complexity of assembling the models, and to their beauty on completion. (Stearns's *Murat*, after Géricault, is an absolute masterpiece.) Lelièpvre has, by designing these figures, added a new dimension to the hobby.

Another project with which he has been associated is the designing of 'plastic flats'. In this he collaborated with his friend Monsieur Mathiot, but too many difficulties having been encountered, the idea has been temporarily laid aside.

Lelièpvre is a modest man, with a strong vein of self-effacement running through his correspondence. Indeed, it was with the greatest reluctance that he spoke about himself and his work. He realises, he says, that many other craftsmen work in a similar manner, that he has been influenced by other French artists, and that he will continue to strive for perfection.

A model such as the coach of Louis XV made for the

Mathiot collection is a remarkable work of art. Entirely of wood, carved, painted and gilded, it is accompanied by forty cavaliers of the *Garde du Corps* and *Mousquetaires* in lead in 54mm size. Of the large figures we like particularly the trumpeter of the *Gendarme de la Garde*, 1745, and the cavalier of *c* 1680. The two mounted cavaliers in Blum's collection in 54mm scale are equally attractive, full of that particular elegance typical of French models.

Monsieur Mathiot was the possessor of the largest collection of Lelièpvre's models, many of which were made specially for him, but at his death they became dispersed among eager collectors. Photographs unfortunately convey only an approximation of the work of this profound artist.

A measure of Lelièpvre's greatness is his attitude to enthusiasts. We ourselves have benefited much from his unstinted assistance, and he is always keen to encourage newcomers in the craft of model-making. An example is shown by the history of Léon Hames, a young Belgian modeller of whom more will be heard. A sample sent to him by Hames for assessment brought forth an eight-page letter of advice and encouragement, followed a few years later by a meeting. The result is that Hames has benefited greatly, and has been brought to our notice by his patron.

L. Hames is a young Belgian artist who works in modelling plaster which when painted becomes akin in appearance to porcelain. This 15cm figurine is of a *Timbalier de l'Escorte Royale de Belgique*

Madame Fernande Métayer, *Paris*

Officier d'Académie (1953), *Diplome d'Honneur à l'Exposition Internationale Artisanale de Florence* (*Italie*) (1954), *Chevalier du Mérite Artisanal* (1956), *Médaille d'Argent de la Société des Arts-Sciences-Lettres* (1956), *Fellow du Mérite Educatif* (1956), Fellow of the Company of Military Collectors and Historians (USA) (1957), *Chevalier de l'Ordre Nationale du Mérite* (Conferred by General Koenig). The above surely indicates an artist of outstanding merit. The recipient of these honours is again a shy, retiring woman, who is reluctant to speak of herself.

Madame Fernande Métayer was born a few miles out of Paris. Her father was a doctor, and during her adolescent years she was schooled, as was the custom of the period, in what she calls '*les arts d'agrément*' – music, embroidery and painting in watercolours. Her great love, however, was for painting miniatures on ivory, a liking which she must have inherited from her grandfather.

Battle of Fontenoy. 54mm models by Madame Métayer (Philippot collection)

After a few months of married life she suffered two blows – first the death of her husband and then of her father within a few months of each other. It was then that her skill in painting stood her in good stead, for an antiquarian friend introduced her to a collector of flats. This was at the time that Mignot was entering the field of flats and commissioning the designers and the collectors and engravers Hamel, Rousselot and Armont (Petrocochino) to produce what proved to be a magnificent series. Madame Métayer was introduced to them by the author, Léopold Marchand. With the group she learned engraving, casting and painting specially commissioned models. The painting of a flat requires a rigid self-discipline. The normal commercially painted specimen consists of two or three bold colours only, with no attempt at shading or figuration: a flat painted by an artist is a miracle of miniature painting.

This led, by a natural process, to painting solid or *ronde-bosse* models for collectors, many of which offended her sense of artistry. It seemed absurd, she says, to spend hours painting precise details on figures lacking good proportions or historical sense. So she decided to make her own models, and the *Petit Soldats de France* were born. Her spell of service with

Hamel, Rousselot and Armont proved of very great service, and her new models quickly gained recognition. Her interests were naturally concentrated on Napoleon's troops, but she has also produced outstanding models of the era of Louis XV and XVI, and later periods.

For an infantryman of the first Empire she requires seven moulds: one for the head, one for the torso, two for the arms, the cartridge box, the knapsack, and the sword. After trimming each part she solders them together, and the whole is painted in oils. She bases her information on the meticulous drawings of Rousselot. The majority of her models are static. We were fortunate enough recently to see a collection of about a hundred, formerly the property of Francis Huber, and, arranged on shelves above twenty-five Berdou's, to which they proved a perfect foil. They were in groups of four: an infantryman, a colour sergeant, a drummer and an officer, all at attention, and all in the varied uniforms of the French *Grande Armée*. The faces, at first, seem identical, but are, on closer scrutiny seen to be very slightly different, and the *drapeaux* are especially well done. Madame Métayer makes no concessions to the current fashion of elaborately painted folds – her colours are perfectly flat, allowing the moulding to fulfil its purpose.

There are those who have been fortunate to see the Louis XVI models with the Lelièpvre background, reproduced in Baldet's book, and she has collaborated notably with the same artist in the diorama of Bir Hacheim.

By her exhibition work Madame Métayer has gained clients from all over the world and now works strictly to commission.

The corpus of her work is solid if not extravagantly adventurous, and there can be few collections, especially in France, which do not contain examples of her meticulous craftsmanship.

Madame Métayer fills the little time for leisure which is left to her in reading books of history, memoirs and biography, which she enjoys, in gardening and in bird-watching.

Germany

Werner Scholtz, *Berlin*

Putting a maker's name to a traditional German flat figure, or *zinnfigur*, can be a frustrating exercise compared with doing the same with respect to a round or solid model. It is not that the actual making is more involved, but those who design, engrave, and market the figure all have an equal claim to recognition. In England, if we mention a Herald model we mean the marketer, if a Stadden we indicate the designer, and in the United States a Murray model may have been designed by Greer or Custer or Murray himself.

With the flat figure, however, we would be equally correct in saying that a certain model was by Madlener (designer), Maier (engraver) or Ochel (distributor). The difficulty is compounded by the fact that every designer and every engraver works for a number of what the French call *éditeurs*, which in our idiom is 'agent' or 'distributor', as the lists of different publishing firms contain different works written by the same authors. In relation to flats, we see that Ochel, Neckel, Donath, Mignot and the like market models designed by

Werner Scholtz

Madlener, Rousselot and others, which in turn are engraved by Frank, Lecke, Maier and others well known in their profession, both designers and engravers offering their services to a number of *éditeurs* at one and the same time. The simplest way out of the difficulty to our mind is to classify flats under the name of the distributor, as Heinrichsen, Ochel, Mignot, even though they represent only the final stage.

As typical of the vast and overwhelming *zinnfiguren* industry, we will concentrate on one maker, *Berliner Zinnfiguren Werner Scholtz*. Scholtz was born in 1904 in Horstmaas, Hollstein, Germany, the son of a chemist. The family moved to Berlin two years later, where, as a small boy, Werner first began to collect flats, and he has remained there ever since. He joined the firm of Roskopf, and assisted in the making of their miniature gun models, which are just the right size for use with flats. In 1934 he produced his first flat, engraved by Sixtus Maier – the first of a long series. Later he began to experiment with the larger sizes, and in 1961 came the first one in 7.5cm size, The Congratulator, after Spitzweg, engraved by Rössner.

Gradually he built up a circle of engravers and designers, himself designing many of the accessories, and he is proud of the nickname 'Father of the Berlin Tinfigures' given him by his friends. It was during this time that his small establishment was known as the 'Spitzweg Shop'. Always striving to increase the appreciation of the tin figure, he planned and advised for several films and conducted classes in Charlottenberg for the painting of flats, an occupation that earned him other nick-names: 'the Father of the Berlin Drawing Courses', and 'The King of the Tinsoldiers'. When his first catalogue was published, he issued it complete with painting instructions, an admirable practice, adopted since then by several makers of solids and plastics, but not to our knowledge by any other *éditeur* of flats.

In all his work, Scholtz carries on the tradition of the old Berlin *zinnfiguren* firms, such as Söhlke and Haselbach. Other makers whom he mentions, of whom we had not previously heard, were Broker, Bohler and, in 1919–20, *Deutsche Zinnfigurenwerkstatte in Berlin*. Scholtz seeks constantly to issue fresh models, so that, as he says, 'the busy man can find rest and recreation in the romantic realm of the tinfigure'.

Scholtz's productions figure prominently in dioramas in many parts of the world, and his range of subjects is so vast that it would be difficult to think of an historical period that he has not covered. He plans his groups in the Heinrichsen tradition, with anything up to four hundred or so separate models, so that even as great an undertaking as the *Retreat from Moscow*, with all its detail of the carnage of war and the elements of nature, is fully represented. Here is the *Grande Armée* indeed; not now resplendent in its pride of aggression, but staggering home, broken, the fancy-dress creations of Murat stripped of their tinsel, the wearers weary puppets.

There is a terrific series of troops of Frederick the Great in a variety of engagements, equalling the Napoleonic range in its magnitude, which has earned him yet another *sobriquet*: *Friederichianer*. A great number of additional models can be added in either

Landsknecht standard-bearer
A monumental flat by Scholtz,
painted by the author

A group of Maximilian-period knights in 30mm flats by Werner Scholtz. In this unpainted state the beauty of the engraving is conveyed. These models offer great scope for skilful painting

series, using the numerous permutations of the many 'combination figures', a speciality for which Scholtz is justly famous.

He has a range of fine mounted knights of the Maximilian period (which fit in well with the series by Ochel), Huns, Greeks, Romans, Sumerians and Egyptians, social life and prehistoric monsters. In the anthropological and social series particularly outstanding are the primeval animals and their hunters; the Greek athletes and bathers, the desert folk, the town and country types from the eighteenth to the twentieth century. Many are treated with refreshing humour.

Perhaps the series of which he is most proud is the vast range of *landsknechts*. These are in standard size, but he has had one made in 8cm which is a masterpiece. Engraved by Lecke, it portrays a standard-bearer, and is the epitome of this particular era.

Scholtz's own collection consists of his own figures, and those of other makers, old and new; solids, wood, paper, plaster, composition, original boxes and thousands of references.

Great Britain

Major Alan Coppin and Patrick Synge-Hutchinson, *Purley and London*

Major Alan Coppin was a commissioned officer in the Devonshire Regiment during the Second World War, and his son David (now in his early thirties) naturally became interested in military matters. In 1948, when he was nine years old, his father bought him a box of Britains' Peninsular War British Infantry. This decided them to make other period models by the conversion of Britains' standard figures. A few years later they were able to display some two hundred models of all periods, both mounted and foot, and David in particular exhibited great talent in this direction, winning several competitions at the meetings of the British Model Soldier Society, to which they both belonged.

Opposite above Russell Gammage specialises in the making of models of periods not easily obtainable. Here is a grouping of his Gauls and other barbarian tribes of the Dark Ages

Opposite below Prussian Cavalry units. 54mm models by Stadden

Models in plaster and natural materials, by the Coppins and Synge-Hutchinson.
Left to right: Post Captain, RN, 1805; Major, Royal Marines, 1805; Vice-Admiral, RN, 1805

The skill and detailed accuracy these conversions showed recommended them very highly to a very old friend of the family, Patrick Synge-Hutchinson, who suggested an amalgamation of talents in the production of larger-scale models, which would give greater scope for detail, and would prove a more satisfactory outlet for historical research allied to creative pleasure. Synge-Hutchinson had studied sculpture at the Royal College of Art, at the Central School of Arts and Crafts, and as a pupil of Albert Toft, and had exhibited at the Royal Academy at the age of eighteen and in subsequent years. His work includes busts of G. K. Chesterton and Rudyard Kipling (the original is now at 'Batemans', Burwash). A replica of the latter was owned by the late Sir Winston Churchill. Since the Second World War he has devoted a great deal of time to the study of art history and is a frequent contributor to such journals as *The Connoisseur*. (Indeed, it was the Editor, Mr L. E. G. Ramsay, who first drew our attention to him.

Synge-Hutchinson designed a number of figures of plaster treated with shellac, on a scale for the foot soldiers of 1·25 inches to the foot, and slightly larger for the cavalry, and handed them over to the Coppins, who completed the uniforms, the accoutrements, and the painting. Contact with Regimental museums was made, and commissions obtained.

They work mostly in sheet-lead of varying thicknesses, wood, and wire, and make tailor's patterns of paper before cutting and fitting the lead coats or jackets. They use matt paint for cloth, skin, etc, semi-gloss for the horses, and gloss for polished leather, and no detail is merely painted on. The smallest button, the stripes and badges of rank, the stripes on trousers, and other details too numerous to mention are all applied

individually. The features and physique of the figure are altered to suit the rank and character of the model portrayed, and when campaign medals are placed on the figures, a check is made to ensure that that particular regiment actually took part in the campaign – the kind of detail sometimes overlooked by modellers.

Production is necessarily slow, as the team goes to immense trouble with research to ensure that every detail is absolutely correct, which, as every researcher knows, entails searching through Dress Regulations, Royal Warrants, picture galleries, museums, old books and prints. The elusive detail may take months to find, but those acquainted with the finished models will agree that the results justify the efforts.

The first model they made was an officer of the 4th Queen's Hussars, to the order of the CO for presentation to an officer who was leaving the Regiment, and since then they have made a large number of single models and groups for various regiments, notably the group of twelve figures of the King's Dragoon Guards at the National Army Museum (formerly at Sandhurst). Coppin senior has an amusing story to tell regarding these particular models. The KDG's regimental carpenter made a large case to measurements supplied to him for packing the models, which were to be taken down by Coppin by road, and sent the case by train to Paddington, where the modellers collected it. As they accompanied it on a porter's trolley down the platform, they received a number of sympathetic looks, and even some hat-raising from onlookers. They then suddenly realised how much the box resembled a coffin!

One of their most interesting commissions began as a speculation. They made a model of a Royal Marines private, 1805, and offered it to the Royal Marines depot at Deal. No funds being available for the purchase, they then took it to the National Maritime Museum, where Commander May, the Curator, put it before the Trustees, who not only accepted it, but ordered eleven more of the Trafalgar period, ranging in rank from Able Seaman to Admiral. When they were completed, another twelve of the 1749 period (when naval officers' uniform, as such, was first introduced) were ordered, and they are now engaged on a series of 1910 naval types. Coppin and Synge-Hutchinson consider themselves fortunate in that Commander May, besides taking an enthusiastic interest, has gone to endless trouble to help with details from his immense fund of knowledge, and (but rarely) when this proved inadequate, to find references either in the library or from the actual uniforms in the Museum.

Opposite Typical medieval combatants by Richard Courtenay

Above King's Dragoon Guards, 1815. A model in plaster and natural materials. By the Coppins and Synge-Hutchinson

After the first models appeared at Greenwich, the Curator of the Canadian National Maritime Museum saw them and commissioned a set for his museum, and these were collected by a Petty Officer from a Canadian destroyer on a visit to Portsmouth.

Their favourite periods are the eighteenth and early nineteenth centuries, but they get great enjoyment in working to any period. At the time of writing David is not available as a member of the team, as he is in the Services in the Middle East, so work has slowed down somewhat. It must be emphasised that this is team work, as all the participants particularly stress. The results are certainly remarkable, and lose nothing by comparison with others in the same medium.

The late Richard Courtenay, *Slough*

Perhaps no modeller ever made such an impact within strictly self-imposed limits as did Richard Courtenay, probably the first of the specialist makers of model soldiers, and his creations hold an honoured and unique place in model soldier collecting.

After a brief collaboration with Doran, which resulted in rather undersized figures of no great quality for the commercial market, Courtenay branched off on his own. The earliest models include a Viking, Roman gladiators and a mounted knight, all of which were later withdrawn (although the Viking mould is still in existence). Although these early models, especially the mounted ones, are spirited, they lack the sure touch of later models, and the smaller size is not representative, although the painting is fine. A later development is shown in plate 60 of the author's *Model Soldiers: a Collector's Guide*. He recalls seeing this first in an issue of *The Studio*, when his interests were not connected in the slightest with model soldiers, but even so the appeal of a beautiful decorative group was there.

About 1931 Courtenay met a fellow-modeller whose interest, intelligence, integrity and sensibility matched his own. Frederick Ping had been collecting Courtenay models for some time, attracted by their workmanship and the period which Courtenay was making peculiarly his own. At that time they were both living near Slough, and in their conversations Courtenay disclosed that he had served in the Merchant Navy

Thomas, Lord Roos and Piers Sieur de Sancergnes in combat. A rare Courtenay pair of combatants

Three spirited and rare Courtenay models

(another tie in common, Ping having been in the Royal Navy). Courtenay had a profound sense of history, with special emphasis on the medieval period and this, coupled with his knowledge of heraldry and artistic ability tended to make him concentrate on the fourteenth century and, in particular, the Black Prince and his companions. He compiled lists of the men who fought in the wars of the period, and, whenever possible, traced their coats-of-arms. He had an extraordinary instinct as to where to look for his information, and Ping spent many hours searching libraries and museums, on hints given by Courtenay, where he might find perhaps just one name or, with a stroke of luck, a whole retinue or list of characters. Not only English, but Scots, French, Flemings, Germans and Spaniards figured eventually in the lists they compiled of those who fought at Crécy, Neville's Cross, Poitiers, Najara and other less well-known actions. Nor would a coat-of-arms be included if it was at all doubtful.

All the time he continued to add new moulds until at his death in 1964 there must have been two or three hundred. On rare occasions he made moulds for private orders and these seldom found their way into the collectors' market.

It is more than likely that Ping's influence was responsible for the remodelling and converting of a number of early figures, and Ping was certainly the direct inspiration for the Crusaders and the archers.

Courtenay is, of course, best known for his reconstruction of the medieval scene: kings, knights, both on foot and mounted (occasionally two on a stand); archers, crossbow-men, men-at-arms and esquires. The mounted knights are varied in their action, the horses standing, galloping or rearing. We are fortunate in having been able to examine the large collection of moulds and the resultant castings made under Ping's careful hands, and we were able to see that, contrary to the general belief, Courtenay cast his riders separately and soldered them to the horses. Some of these were altered slightly to give variation before soldering to the base. There are a number of detachable helms, and these again are more varied than one realises, and many of the visors are movable as are a number of sword arms. Swords, scabbards, misericords, banners and shields are cast separately. There are some bald-headed and some bare-headed warriors, and even one with an eye-patch.

Remembering Courtenay's interests, it is not surprising to find that there are a number of figures of Edward III and the Black Prince, both mounted and on foot, in knightly attire or in Garter robes and at various periods of their lives, together with John II and his son, Joan of Arc, Xaintrailles, La Hire and Dunois. With these are a set of Garter knights and their ladies, Knights of the Star and of the Golden Fleece (made only for a firm in New York). A Scots knight with a double-headed axe is another model not generally on sale, and he even essayed a six-inch Black Prince but, as he himself said, the effort of casting it proved laborious.

Two of Courtenay's beautifully modelled ancient peoples: Cleopatra with a slave girl

The many knights and the computations of heraldry are too numerous to mention (some idea is given in the review of the collections of Mr Bevan Rees and Mr Faulkner) but whether in jupon or cyclas, wielding axe or brandishing sword, proud in victory or humbled in defeat, each is a worthy specimen, beautifully wrought and meticulously painted in enamels. Much of the richness of colour derives from Courtenay's use of gold leaf, in preference to the more normal yellow to denote *or*, but of course he adheres to the convention of white rather than silver owing to the tendency to tarnishing of that metal.

Egyptian figures were probably among the first to be put on the market, and Nefertiti, Seti I, Cleopatra and the Slave Girl are beautiful models. A Nubian bowman and a Shardanu bodyguard, a running officer and two footsoldiers, Assyrian and Babylonian mounted soldiery and a priestess of Ishtar, a court lady and a male fan bearer, may well have been for private clients, although the moulds of the last two are in existence. A Persian footsoldier and a Greek lady are also little-known models. Famous personages from the sixteenth through to the twentieth century complete Courtenay's work. He was not fully attuned to the later periods, however, and the models are not characteristic of his achievement.

Courtenay was a quiet, mild man, never pretentious: he loved his work and lived with his characters. Never coveting large rewards, although he had plenty of opportunity to commercialise his work, he preferred to remain the complete individualist. Details of his life are scanty, and his biography is in his models.

Russell Gammage, MSIA, *Charlton, London*

The name of Russell Gammage is one to conjure with. Ever since this still-young modeller began producing miniature figures, collectors have looked forward eagerly to his new ventures, for Gammage has a mercurial way of producing every now and then an unusual figure or two among the more normal lines. He will begin a series which may extend over a number of years, and which is obviously sound commercially, and then switch suddenly to an entirely different period. The result is that each new idea is exciting for the collector and, obviously, to Gammage himself. It is, however, infuriating to the poor reviewer, and we must have had more trouble (but also great enjoyment) in trying to present a just appraisal of his output than in that of any other maker!

Gammage served in the Royal Navy during the Second World War, but was invalided out. Following up a long-standing interest which he had continued during the war, he decided to become an art student. He therefore took the National Diploma in Design in Illustration at a London College, and then studied for a further year for the Art Teacher's Diploma. During this time he experimented in sculpture and three-dimensional work, and in 1950 competed for the display work for the Cotswold Tradition in the Festival of Britain. Having obtained the commission, he applied for a year's absence from college and, this being granted, carried out the work for a very successful display. After completing his studies and while working as a free-lance designer, he was asked to design model figures for the firm of Graham Farish, and eventually took over the management of this side of the business. When the firm decided to cease model making for a more profitable line, Gammage left to continue free-lancing, but then began to receive letters from people all over the world who had bought some of the beautiful Coronation set he had made and who wanted more. When Lord Greenway asked to have the Pakistani and Gurkha bands made and painted as they had appeared in the Coronation procession, Gammage decided to go into the model soldier business in a small way, and has since pursued a hard-working and intelligent career, ever willing to accept suggestions.

Meanwhile he was still teaching art part-time and building up his industrial design work (he is a full-time member of the Society of Industrial Artists and Designers), but both design and model soldier making grew so rapidly that he had to give up teaching, and eventually to employ extra help. This proved a difficult period, as the first assistants were gifted amateurs who offered their services, imagining that working at their hobby full-time would be an idyllic existence. But to the dismay of all concerned the opposite proved the case, for the very good reason that the standard achieved by the amateur can be very good at times, but to work continuously at an economic project is something that the amateur modeller is unaccustomed to, so that the standard started to decline from the top quality which has always been Gammage's hallmark.

Eventually he realised that he could not rely on model soldier collectors for his staff, still less could he apply to the Ministry of Labour for model soldier makers. So he decided to employ people with an interest either in history or modelling, and who were skilled in work which could be directed along his own paths. After a few failures the business has now settled down, and everybody has found their place in the main scheme, which is to have staff who are specialists in one field, but who know enough to appreciate the problems of the others, and who can also take over in another department for a short time in case of emergency. This makes for greater flexibility and also smooth progress of the models through the various stages of manufacture. By having a spell of casting, for instance, the model maker appreciates more fully what can and cannot be done on a figure without causing problems for the mould makers and casters.

Unlike some other modellers, he has not gained his reputation as a maker within any special period, but owes it rather to his excellence in whatever he sets himself to produce. A review of his achievement discloses figures of Greek hoplites (including one with the Homeric figure-of-eight shield), Romans, including musicians, Egyptian soldiers, Normans, English bowmen of two periods, men-at-arms (one returning from foraging) and the English Civil War. Then come representative units of the 'old French War' and the American War of Independence, Frederick the Great's armies, English and French of 1795–1815, the Royal Navy of the eighteenth century, Germans of 1880 to 1914, British County and Highland and Lowland Scots Regiments of the same period, Russians of 1914, the Second World War (British, Germans, and Japanese), Gurkha and Pakistani Pipe Bands. Portrait models of Montgomery, Wavell and Rommell, and a French Tambour Major are excellent figures, whilst the set of Waterloo artillery with cannon and limber, with a companion French set, are quite outstanding, and invite comparison with Imrie-Risley's similar group of half-a-century earlier. To our mind nothing in all these models exceeds the excellence of the British 1914–18 line troops, which are the epitome of resolute courage, combined with the sculpturesque quality of Sargent Jagger.

Gammage's most recent venture, which has achieved outstanding success, is a series of ancient peoples. Here are a number of nude male and female figures (with an assortment of wigs according to type and period) which with the minimum of addition can be easily adapted to a variety of uses. (These should not be confused with an earlier nude of malleable metal, which could be animated and clothed.) Together with these is a series of Egyptian slave girls, dancing girls, acrobats and musicians, beautifully modelled and a challenge to the

Below Splendidly modelled 54mm figures of Romans, created by Russell Gammage

Above Prussians of the time of Frederick the Great. An imposing collection of models by Gammage

painter, and undeserving of the occasional facetious and unworthy remark made by model soldier enthusiasts of lesser intelligence. With them are the goddesses whom they attend and, to round off a fascinating series, a magnificent war chariot, a masterpiece of artistry and construction.

His 'Connoisseur' models are made primarily because he himself is interested in the subject, and is as yet necessarily limited in range. They include a Light Dragoon officer (though it may be legitimate to criticise the proportions of the horse's head in this otherwise outstanding model), a *Cheval-Léger Polonaise de la Garde* (*Lancier* and *Trompette*, 1807–1814), a Prussian Cuirassier, a German Hussar with lance, a *Chasseur à Cheval de la Garde*, 1800–15, a British Lancer 1880–1914, a guidon bearer of the Royal Scots Greys, 1815, a trooper of the 2nd North British Dragoons, 1758, a Napoleonic Hussar, and a German *Garde du Corps* officer, 1880–1914. They can be purchased painted or as castings.

Gammage co-operates to a remarkable degree with his clients, catering for the collector who wants an excellent model, or one who buys in bulk, and expects to pay a proportionately lower price. An example of the 'super' model is the Light Dragoon officer mentioned; the Napoleonic, British and ancient world models are the normal range for the average collector, and the 'Cabalt' figures are so reasonable in price that they can be purchased in worthwhile numbers.

The majority of Gammage's models are refreshingly static, without the violent action seen latterly in the

Gammage is probably the only contemporary maker who can convey such a feeling of sturdy dependability as is portrayed by these British Infantrymen of the Great War

work of so many makers. Many collectors, however, like more animation in their models, so Gammage experimented for some years in an attempt to find a metal amalgam which would be durable yet malleable. His first success was the pair of nude figures already mentioned, where the legs and arms could be bent to a reasonable degree. The demand for an actual clothed figure with similar qualities led to the 'Cabalt' lead model, where a uniformed casting could be bent at the knee and elbow, so that a new stance could be adopted, a head capable of being twisted. This led in turn to a better quality figure with the same adaptability, hence the 'X' type model. Another collector's foible was catered for when he brought his ingenuity to bear on producing a casting of good quality which was malleable enough to be bent into a number of positions and with studs on the feet for use in a baseboard or diorama. These 'Q' models, which displaced the 'Cabalt' range, incorporated a series of different heads and a set of arms in six positions.

He was also one of the first in the field in the production of 20mm models specially designed for use in the war-game, and has a long list of different figures to his credit.

Gammage works on the Continental method of a basic model with head, arms, and equipment plugged in or soldered onto the figure. He makes a wide variety of headgear, and reins and sabretache slings are made of a special metal which does not become brittle as does copper.

Quite early in his career he became interested in gold and silver work, having been commissioned to design some figures in the former metal. He felt the need for more technical training in these materials and did two years' evening classes at the Central School of Arts and Crafts in London. The result of this training shows in the detail and proportion of the later 'Rose' models, some of which are so finely finished that he is currently producing them in gold and silver, especially for Wilkinson Sword of London. He is also a skilled woodcarver, and has executed many commissions for large statuettes, clothed with natural materials.

Due to his training and design work, he has always been concerned with the presentation of his catalogues. He was one of the first to produce a fully illustrated catalogue, which was greeted with joy by many collectors in out-of-the-way parts of the world where books of reference are almost unobtainable. It was more of an illustrated handbook to the craft, and invaluable to convertors. In addition it stressed the extreme flexibility of the models, with their separate heads, arms, equipment and the like.

Above all, Russell Gammage is an enthusiast, and transmits his enthusiasm to others.

Opposite An unpainted casting of a model, a *Grenadier de la Garde à cheval*, by Gammage, showing the sculpturesque lines. Various items, such as the reins, are soldered on later

The late John Ambler Greenwood and Miss Kathleen Ball, *Scarborough*

John Ambler Greenwood was born in 1893, and died in Ayton, Yorkshire, in 1971. His work links the first productions of the renaissance of the model soldier with the present-day flowering of the craft. He was a pioneer in more ways than one. It is mainly due to him that the true 54mm size has been so universally adopted (although there are signs today that makers are increasingly exceeding this most attractive and sensible measure). Furthermore, he made 20 and 28mm models of unbelievable quality whilst others were merely groping in the same direction, and finally, he convinced the makers of dioramas that solids had as vital a part to play as flats in this important aspect of the model-soldier scene.

Greenwood was a quiet, retiring man, and of his early background little is known, except that he served during the First World War with the Manchester Regiment, and saw action at Gallipoli and in Flanders. It has been said that he became a commercial traveller, and undoubtedly his frequent visits to London would have brought him into contact with Morrells (now Hummels) in Burlington Arcade, where he would meet model soldier collectors. In 1935 Greenwood became one of the first seventeen members of the newly-formed British Model Soldier Society.

He must have had a feeling for the craft well before this, as, when he was about forty, one of his chess-playing friends suggested that he make a set of medieval-style chessmen. He became so interested in the idea that he not only did this, but began tentatively to produce other models. Soon he turned to the making of what was to become his speciality, the British Army. At this time the British Model Soldier Society was composed mainly of collectors whose main occupation was the assembling of the models produced in mass by

Below and opposite Various units of the German army. 54mm models by Greenwood and Ball

William Britain, and it is not difficult to visualise their enthusiasm when Greenwood began to make a model that was not only in solid lead, but better proportioned and more historically accurate. No longer would they have to convert and repaint Britains! And when he was joined by Miss Kathleen Ball (now Mrs Nathaniel) whose skill in painting has become a legend, the lasting popularity of his work was assured.

Greenwood's method of working was, for those days, revolutionary. He cast in a metal of such pliability as to allow arms, legs and heads to be 'positioned', or, in present-day jargon, 'animated'. This was a great advance on the rigidity of other contemporary models. Not only this, but weapons and equipment were not moulded with the figure, but cast separately and soldered on. His skill was used to good effect during the Second World War, when, as commander of a local Home Guard detachment in Wellington, Shropshire, where he was living, he made models of German paratroops for use in the identification of enemy troops.

After the war Greenwood began his equally famous range of 20 and 28mm figures which eventually spanned history from Roman times to the present day. Again his craft appeared at just the right time. The famous Otto Gottstein was in the throes of supervising the outstanding collection of dioramas in flats which used to grace the walls of the basement of the Royal United Service Museum. As many a collector knows, to try and convince a 'flats' man that a solid is as good for a diorama is akin to asking a Socialist to agree with a Tory. But such was the quality of Greenwood and Ball's work that Gottstein was completely conquered, with the result that he commissioned the partners to make the figures which fit so admirably into Denny Stokes's terrain for the *Battle of Flers* and *D-Day*, which were the subjects that concluded the series.

The collaboration did not end there: Gottstein, eager to enlist world sympathy for the plight of the Jews in Nazi Germany, projected a series of dioramas for display in the United States, where they made a profound impression. They may be seen at the Jewish Theological Seminary in New York, and an illustrated catalogue entitled *Proclaim Freedom* was issued. Stokes again made the settings, and Greenwood and Ball made about three thousand-odd figures, a feat spanning four years of work. This series of thirty-five dioramas ranged in intensity from bloody warfare to quiet theological discussion.

Other commissions from industrial and mining concerns followed, together with a set of six for the Grenadier Guards, and a D-Day commissioned by Sir Winston Churchill for the Inter-Allied Museum at Arromanches. Of more recent date is Crécy, at West Point, which is illustrated in Blum's *Military Miniatures*. Stokes at one time commissioned models from Greenwood and Ball for his own dioramas, which he exhibited from time to time, and had a collection of figures which were left over. One of these he gave to the author – a most lovely Cromwellian trooper.

Later still Greenwood became interested in the wargame, and the models he made for this pastime were as beautiful as the larger ones. Enthusiasts were welcome to battle at his home in Scarborough, where he had moved from Wellington in 1959. In 1966 he sold his business interests, but continued to cast for private clients and for his own enjoyment. During the time that he and Miss Ball were associated he was responsible for the designing and making of the original models and the casting and positioning of the figures, whilst his partner concentrated on the work of soldering on the weapons and accoutrements and painting the more important models, the remainder of which were delegated to a devoted team of four specially trained young female artists.

Greenwood figures will be found in many collections, and impress by their sincerity and serenity. They are ideal medium for the representation of the history of the British Army. Greenwood's models continue to be produced by William F. Pearce.

Marcus Hinton, *Taplow*

Rapid expansion after a tentative beginning seems to be a feature of the model soldier world, and an outstanding example is Marcus Hinton. In 1956 he began work with Simon Hunt, but only a few months after the formation of the partnership the latter resigned so as to be able to devote all his time to music. However, nothing daunted, Hinton continued on his own under the original name of Hinton Hunt Figures, and he was soon actively assisted by his wife. Hinton's interest in model soldiers and military history began as a hobby, and he is happy to say that turning the hobby into a profession has not dulled his enthusiasm. Being a collector of actual military equipment has stood him in good stead when the making of a model is concerned.

Studying maps during the Crimean War. Two impressive 54mm models by Marcus Hinton

It seems inevitable that his main range is of the ubiquitous Napoleonic period, with its tremendous appeal of fanciful uniforms and the seemingly endless permutations of *grenadier* and *chasseur* and *lancier* and *tirailleur* and *fusilier* – to say nothing of their subdivisions. Some idea of the range of Hinton's models may be gained from his catalogues. Of the Imperial Guard we have the Old Guard, the Middle Guard and the Young Guard; *grenadiers à pied*, *chasseurs à pied*, *grenadiers Hollandais*, *fusilier-grenadiers*, *fusilier-chasseurs*, *tirailleur-grenadiers*, *tirailleur-chasseurs*, *conscript-chasseurs*, *flanquer-chasseurs*, *voltigeurs*, *Garde Nationale*, *artillerie à pied*, *génie de la Garde*, *marins de la Garde*, and the mounted troops: *chasseurs*, *grenadiers* and *dragons*. Next we have the infantry of Line in all its many branches, then foreign troops in the service of France: Polish *Légion du Nord* and *Vistula*, *Régiment de la Tour d'Auvergne*, *Irlandaise*, *Isenburg*, *Prusse*, Swiss *Bataillon de Neuchâtel*, *Valaisan*, Italian *Légion Piedmonteuse ou du Midi*, *velites de Turin et de Florence*, *Vétérains Romains*, and *Tirailleur de Po*. Added to these are Sardinia, Holland, and the German States.

Napoleon's adversaries are represented by an impressive range of British troops: Foot Guards, infantry of the Line, Grenadiers, Light Company, Fusiliers, Light Infantry, Highland Regiments, Royal Engineers, Royal Artillery (including Rocket Corps), and Hussars. In the service of Britain are the King's German Legion and the French émigré troops. Britain's allies are represented by the Austro-Hungarian Empire, Imperial Russia, Prussia, Spain and Portugal. They are all constantly being added to.

Other periods covered are the American War of Independence, pre-Revolution France, Wayne's Campaign against the Indians, modern British troops, and Rome and Greece (including musicians). The section showing most expansion is that dealing with the American Civil War, which is second only in popularity among collectors to the Napoleonic era. Creeping up in

In wartime a soldier is not always on duty. This amusing composition of Hinton models displays also the additional items such as baskets and riflestands that he makes, which prove so useful in the construction of dioramas

public demand is the once-despised Crimean War, for which Hinton is making models of the three principal protagonists. The latest addition is a representative selection of models of the Risorgimento and of the Middle Ages. Prominent among the latter are fine portrait models of the Black Prince and the Dauphin, a crossbowman with pavise, an archer with sharpened stake, and a group of the twelfth century to 1485. The armour is skilfully delineated, and in the case of the Black Prince the leopards and lilies are engraved on the jupon. A welcome addition in this range is a herald, with tabard and long trumpet.

Hinton is as well known for his 20mm models as his figures in standard size. There are beautifully made miniatures worthy of the highest admiration when given serious and careful painting. This achieved, they are quite outstanding. The American Civil War range is welcome, as also is the so-far small selection of the English Restoration and the Battle of Senlac.

Finally, there is a most invaluable collection of accessories – sentry-boxes, gun racks, camp tables and stools, stretchers, sections of pavé, treasure chests, despatch cases, chevaux de frise, wine bottles, cups, rifles, muskets, pikes and lances. These are a great help to the diorama maker or those who like to arrange their models in small groups.

Marcus Hinton's own enthusiasm for the Southern cause in the American Civil War leads him annually into the extravagance of dressing up in uniform and running up the flag on Gettysburg day, much to the astonishment of his neighbours in the peaceful countryside where he lives. He is aided and abetted in all his ventures by his equally-enthusiastic wife Cynthia, who is an expert at painting the models, and who has been known on occasions to dress up as a cantinière.

Their own enthusiasm extends to the acquiring of uniforms, helmets and equipment, and their pleasant riverside house is full of them. The owners themselves provide a welcome gaiety which is sometimes lacking in the model soldier world.

Newcomers: Edward Surén, *London* The late Leslie Higgins, *Northampton* J. Tassell and P. H. S. Bird, *Gravesend*

The models of Edward Surén commanded immediate attention when they first came on the market. They have a rare grace and elegance, which is even transmitted to his catalogue, the phraseology of which is reminiscent of a by-gone day. We first saw his 'Willie' 30mm models at the Waterloo Convention held by the British Model Soldier Society in 1965, and were impressed with their excellent qualities. The range at the moment of writing is small, but will obviously expand. Starting with the Romans and the Gauls, the periods covered include the seventeenth and eighteenth centuries, the Napoleonic and Boer Wars. There are, moreover, 'personality' figures. A number of well-designed mounted models are available.

Perhaps the most interesting (because the most unusual) is the selection of Civil War pikemen and musketeers. These have in most instances been modelled on the original copper-plate engravings illustrating the elaborate drill of the times. The pikes,

A Royalist Pikeman, 1642. A fine 54mm model by Higgins

incidentally, are of the authentic terrific length. Elegant eighteenth-century officers include the Duke of Cumberland, the saddlebow complete with removable holsters. The Napoleonic era has started well, and one can expect numerous additions. The 'personalities' include Richelieu, Napoleon, Wellington, Charles I and Queen Henrietta Maria, and the Lionheart. The 'Charles' is a fine, vain figure and, indeed, the whole range of models owes a great deal to the illustrations of the times, conveying a sense of period not always found in other models, backed by scrupulous accuracy. It is therefore surprising to find that the scale of the horses of the mounted Normans at the Battle of Hastings was not uniform, but we understand that Surén is in the course of amending this. (We exempt from this criticism the mounted Saxon, whose cob is historically accurate in being of a smaller size.)

Surén's aim is to make the 30mm model what the 54mm has been to collectors. He feels that it is perfectly possible, granted the requisite skill (which he has in abundance), to produce as much detail in the smaller size. His figures are made up on pre-animated 'dollies' with modelling plasticine, from which models are ultimately produced by the usual centrifugal casting process. Very little animation, if any, is done once a figure is cast in metal, as he feels that chopping and bending about at this stage are bad for the qualities his work is valued for.

Another craftsman whose figures have come to notice recently is the late Leslie Higgins, a sculptor by profession, who designed for commercial firms. One could buy from him a Norseman, a Grenadier of 1745, a Cameron Highlander (1900) and a beautiful little set of about a dozen models of the English Civil War, all in 20mm size. The set consists of a standard bearer, a drummer, an officer with raised hat, an officer presiding at a drumhead conference, an harquebusier, three combatant figures, and Cromwell and Charles I, all on foot. In quality they stand comparison with Niblett's better-known figures, and, indeed, fit in well with them. Higgins has also experimented with the same period in 54mm size, together with models of Henry VII, Henry VIII, Elizabeth I, Mary Queen of Scots on the block, and Charles I. Added to these are an English Puritan and a Restoration gallant. His models are beautifully designed and cast and painted, and he captures the atmosphere of each period, as for example, his Parliamentary drummer, gaunt and purposeful, and the Restoration gallant, oozing luxury and lechery. His death was a sad blow as his potential had not been fully realised in his models.

One of the delights of the model soldier enthusiast is the discovery of new talent. We have been fortunate in that we have had perhaps greater opportunities than most collectors in this respect, inasmuch as a collector will draw our attention to a rising star, or we will receive a model from a maker of whom we had no previous knowledge.

We have had some exciting moments in this connection, in the main with 20 and 54mm figures and flats, so it was a welcome surprise to receive from the makers a small collection of large models labelled 'Series 77'. Subsequent correspondence revealed that they emanated from the firm of John Tassell and P. H. S. Bird, of Gravesend.

Tassell served in the Queen's Company Grenadier Guards from 1954 to 1959, when he married and became a painter and decorator. He took up model-making as a hobby during this period, and, like Spandauw, tried his hand at the conversion of Airfix 7-inch plastic kits. In 1961 he began working for Norman Newton Ltd, and his first models were a French Grenadier of the Guard, an Empress Dragoon and a British Foot Guards' officer in 7-inch size. He also helped to animate the various models made for the firm by other artists. As he himself is six feet five inches tall, he may well have been subconsciously attracted to the larger size. Over the last ten years he has made tanks and armoured cars, as well as military figures in various sizes, and recently began a range of

Delicacy and grace is the keynote in these 30mm solids made by E. Surén, who specialises in models of this size

Right Pioneer, British Infantry of the Line, Napoleonic Wars. An outstanding figure by Series 77. Note the attractive two-tier base, with distinctive lettering and simulation of natural materials

54mm figures and equipment of the Second World War, marketed under the name 'Lasset'.

Bird has been involved in all types of military modelling for some years, especially dioramas and painting for Norman Newton Ltd. One large one in particular, depicting an incident during the Napoleonic Wars, of a skirmish around a windmill, may be seen at Piccadilly, bearing his name. He, like Tassell, is in his middle thirties, and also married.

The size of the model is 65.5mm, which allows for much greater scope for detail than the smaller ones. They are cast from improved hand moulds and furnished with large, circular, two-tier stands. They are beautifully proportioned and excellently sculpted, with great attention to minutiae, and an air of elegance. It is possible that a purist might find the legs disproportionately short and stocky, but this does not detract in general from the overall effect. The painting, done by Bird, is exquisite, with a touch of reticence that one applauds in Ping. Although the eyes, as happens so often, receive an inordinate amount of attention, the size of the figure tends to absorb the over-painting (although, as usual, this tends to become emphasised by photography).

The range is fast growing, with emphasis on the Napoleonic period. New ideas are emerging, as Bird has taken over the entire business, John Tassell having recently (1972) left the combine. The result so far is an impressive series of *landsknechts*, very gay and swaggering, as may be imagined, one fully armoured figure having a detachable sallet. Bird tells us that he intends to remake a number of the original figures to bring them even more into his own scheme of perfection.

Overleaf Light Brigade-Crimea, 1854. A group of 54mm models made by Charles C. Stadden. A period of history that was once despised but now finding favour with collectors

Frederick Ping, *Salisbury*

It was in the collection of L. H. Cox of Brighton that we first saw models by Frederick Ping: ten figures of Celtic, Saracenic, Mayan, Saxon and Grecian warriors. There was an integrity and serenity about them that attracted immediate attention, even in the company of Courtenay, Greenwood, Stadden and Gammage. Apart from the subtlety of the modelling and the scrupulous accuracy of the painting there was an inevitability about their whole conception which sprang from a tremendous feeling for period.

The impression was confirmed when we saw further specimens of Ping's work in the medieval field, a series of models from M'Ian's *Clans of the Scottish Highlands* and a set of English Kings and Queens of outstanding quality. His range, as listed in the old Hummel catalogue, runs from the ancient world through the Dark Ages to the Norman Conquest, the Middle Ages, Asiatics, Incas and Aztecs, the Tudor Period, the religious wars of France, the Thirty Years' War, the Polish campaign against the Turks, the American Civil War and the Napoleonic era. However, the listed figures convey little, for Ping prefers to work to commissioned orders and his complete achievement can only be guessed at, as his models are to be found not so much in catalogues and agents' windows, as in connoisseurs' collections all over the world. And many and varied are the models he has made, not only the normal military and historical ranges, but more unusual and exotic creations such as sets of *The Mikado* (for Peter Cushing) and *The Beggar's Opera* (for

The World's Greatest Generals The choice was Shamus Wade's, and he commissioned Frederick Ping to make the set

Brigadier Peter Young), General Wade chasing an *inamorata* (Ping has only recently discovered the identity of the collector for whom he made it!), tradesmen (also for Cushing), modern politicians and their wives. The one person he refuses to immortalise is Hitler.

Ping tells an amusing tale of his first successful venture into the commercial field. Having seen at a Sussex public library a copy of M'Ians' *Clans* (even in those days an expensive book) he was fired to create miniatures based on the colour plates. He therefore approached his local public library with a request that they obtain the work for him to study on the premises. After a long time the Librarian informed him that they could not trace a copy but, upon being informed as to where Ping had seen a copy, not only did they immediately procure it, but sent it to him post free with an unlimited borrowing time. While the book was in his possession, the local library was damaged by heavy bombing!

He made his notes, and returned the *Clans* to the library. He made a few models and offered them hesitantly to Hummel's, who, to his great surprise were immediately impressed, and ordered the complete set. They are probably the best known of Ping's models, as they have proved so popular that the maker has had to repeat them many times.

Ping had, of course, been making models prior to his seeing the *Clans*, but mainly for his personal pleasure. One of his earliest contacts was with Richard Courtenay, and there is no doubt that these two men, with similar ideals and interests, influenced each other, and Ping's own collection, destroyed, alas, by enemy action, was mainly of Courtenay's rare and early models. When, later, he began to place his own medieval miniatures on the market, rather than competing with Courtenay they were complementary. Courtenay's knights are full of action, whereas Ping's figures are conceived rather as a quiet projection into the past, and more static, but not less vital, with a native dignity.

Examples of Ping's *Kings of England* series: *top right* is Edward I; *top left*, Edward II; *bottom right*, Edward III; *bottom left*, Richard II. The painting is meticulous, and no detail obtrudes

Warwick the Kingmaker and his attendants. 52mm models made by Frederick Ping. One of a series which illustrates the important personages of the English medieval period

Every model he makes is an original because, contrary to general practice, he does no casting. Each creation is based on a standard torso, is animated and then built up by thin metal and solder. The resultant model is slightly under the standard size. One of the characteristics of a Ping model is the facial likeness that he achieves. One can readily recognise a Henry VIII by any modeller but, in Ping's case, whether it be Henry V or Richard III, or Buckingham or Sir Thomas More or Brackenbury, the physiogonomy of each is entirely based on authentic contemporary portraits.

One of his absorbing interests is the mystery that surrounds the character of Richard III. In this more open-minded age the balance of historical evidence has tipped strongly in favour of Richard, and Ping is one of his most staunch supporters. It was with the greatest pleasure, therefore, that some years ago he received a commission for a model of the much-maligned king. Since then he has met his patron, Miss Jane Taverner, of Martinsburg, West Virginia, and has made a large number of models for her and her friend Miss Nadia Elins. Both these ladies share his sympathies with the last of the Plantagenets, and the models he has made well present the king's complex character and many rôles.

There are models of Richard in armour, on foot, and mounted on 'White Surrey'; in a black doublet edged with fur and in a gold brocade tunic (as in the painting in the National Portrait Gallery), in coronation robes with Anne Neville; as Duke of Gloucester, together with his esquire, trumpeter, standard bearer and the banner of England. Surrounding the central character are a number of the principal personages of his reign: his father and mother, the Duke of York and Cecily Neville; Clarence and Isabel; Margaret of Anjou; Henry IV and Louis XI; his brother Edward and his banner; Elizabeth Woodville; Warwick the Kingmaker with his trumpeter, esquire and banner; the young Princes; 'the Cat, the Rat, and Lovel our Dog', together with billmen, crossbowmen, archers and handgunners.

The Taverner collection is not yet completed, but enough has been done to indicate its scope and achievement. Not content with the period of Richard III, Miss Taverner and Miss Elins have a series by Ping of other English figures: Cerdic, Harold, William I, Geoffrey of Anjou, Henry II and Becket; Boadicea, Empress Matilda, Matilda of Flanders, Eleanor of Aquitaine, the Fair Maid of Kent and Rosamund Clifford. No figures later than Richard III are contemplated. Other outstanding portrayals of Richard and his court are in the possession of H. C. Faulkner, where, under the review of his collection, they are fully described.

Ping's excellence of painting and his profound knowledge of heraldry may be seen on many a Britains' 'Agincourt' figure; these are often passed to him by collectors who recognise his eminence in this field. At the same time he makes subtle changes in these excellent models, adding a crest to a helmet, or providing a couched lance in lieu of a sword, so that, combined with the beautifully painted heraldic bearings, the figure achieves a new dignity.

The greatest tribute to his integrity and skill was the handing over to him of all Courtenay's moulds and castings on the death of that great man. No one knows the history of each model as well as does Ping; no one but Ping has such profound sympathy with the creator and his period. This does not, however, prevent his indulging in judicious improvisation, so the models that one now sees in Hummel's are really by 'Courtenay–Ping', in the same way as Gottstein's flats became 'Gottstein–Blum'. A model that one thought one knew so well now attracts a second look – it has a different visor, that duo of combatants is new – or is it? No, it is two separate Courtenays joined together. New banners and standards are appearing; riders are sitting different horses; the action is being increased; some of the early models of which Courtenay tired are being recast. All this, however, is done in a spirit of reverence, with no lessening of quality of casting or of painting.

It is difficult to talk of the man himself with anything but affection. He is quiet, diffident even, and modest. It takes a long time to get him to talk about himself. He would far rather discuss King Arthur or Maiden Castle or Badbury Rings, or Froissart, or Monstrelet. It is good to know that he has at last decided to replace his own bombed collection, and has been carefully building up a beautiful series of English monarchs, many throned, a Crécy action group, and a few other favourites which he intends to keep. The names of those within his circle of friends and collectors – and his models – tell you more about the man than he will himself.

'The Sentry Box'
Miss Yvonne Edmonds and
Dr Lovel Barnes, *London*

Just after the close of the Second World War a number of flats and 54mm hard plaster models of historical portraits appeared on the English market. These were the result of the joint efforts of W. Y. Carman, Dr Lovel Barnes and Otto Gottstein, and were known as 'Carbago' models. After the death of Gottstein (who had been responsible for the flats) a number of the figures were renamed 'Argosy', and were redesigned by the sculptor, Raymond Briton Riviere. Eventually Barnes and Riviere added a military line but the only ones in current production are the historical models, now remodelled and cast in lead ('Matchlock').

Barnes was eager to produce a larger type of model, and, in the early 1950s, went into partnership with Nancy Wynne-Jones for the production of 12cm figures. Some of them, notably the first Indian Cavalry model, were modelled by Barnes, while others were done by various artists, the foremost of whom was Briton Riviere. What distinguished these models from others was that they were of plaster, and the author can remember the impact they produced on him when he first saw them standing elegantly on display in a large store in Brighton.

After some years, and as a result of difficulties encountered owing to a certain understandable fragility of the material, it was decided that they should be made in metal.

Apart from Riviere the artists whom they had employed had had no particular interest in military models and whilst this did not matter greatly in the days when the models were in plaster, where the detail had to be minimal, it quickly became apparent that a much higher standard would be required for models in lead. Riviere's responsibility lay with the production of the original plasticene conception and, although an artist with a flair, he tended to neglect detail. When the huge task of attempting to convert the plaster figures to metal ones began, the moulds had to be remade several times, all with an eye to their improvement, and each one had to be cut up into pieces. Very little, therefore, was eventually left of the Riviere models.

Barnes had long been interested in model soldiers. Now in his sixties, he remembers the days when he drove shopkeepers mad by insisting on looking through the entire stock before making a purchase. Actually he knew from the beginning what he wanted, but he just had to see everything. He was one of the very first members of the British Model Soldier Society, and belongs to a number of military societies both in this country and abroad. His scope is pretty catholic, with a particular liking for the Napoleonic period. As a busy doctor he has never had a great deal of time for modelling, certainly never as much as he would like.

Miss Yvonne Edmunds appeared on the scene at the beginning of 1954 as secretary and business manageress. She confesses that at the time she knew nothing whatever about military matters, but although concentrating on the business side, the analysing of documentation and the checking of detail, she soon became fascinated by the whole business. When the change-over to metal began, with the attendant necessity for adaptation of the models, she progressed in easy stages from telling others what she wanted done to showing them, and then doing it herself. To speed up the process of converting the plaster models to metal ones she decided to try her hand and was soon cutting up and changing detail, though as yet not attempting original work.

About five years ago, when the work of getting all the old foot figures into metal was just about completed, Miss Wynne-Jones, who had been a sleeping partner for a long time, decided to leave the firm, and Miss Edmonds became a partner. Since then she has done more and more modelling and now she does most of it. Because she prefers to build up, rather than carve away, and is not very good at soldering, she at first found difficulty in working in metal. However the introduction of new materials for modelling has helped her a lot, and she has now found one of the many plastic cements which suits her admirably. Her way of working is to start with a basic part with no detail, and then 'dress' it. When this is complete it is cast in lead and then given its final trimming and polishing to produce the finished master.

Because of the size of the 12cm figures they have to be cast in many parts, and for the larger parts the life of the moulds is rather short. This means that quite a lot of re-making has to be done, particularly with the more popular figures. Every time a mould is remade more work is done on the master, because neither of the partners is ever really satisfied with a figure and

Large, solid lead model of an officer of the Blues, present day, by The Sentry Box

they can always see something they would like to change for the better.

Since they began to sell figures unpainted and in kit form, they have been particularly anxious to improve the fit of parts (and the detail) to make it easier for the amateur to assemble and paint them. Because of the amount of remodelling and remaking which has to be done all the time, the number of completely new figures which can be produced is somewhat limited.

Mounted models have proved particularly troublesome, and for some time no effort was made to get these into metal. However they are now coming on to the market in increasing numbers, and it is hoped that several more will be on the market shortly. Neither Miss Edmonds nor Dr Barnes feels capable of modelling a horse, and the two which are available were commissioned from trained sculptors, the partners being responsible for the riders and accoutrements.

The general method of work on a new model is as follows. Dr Barnes will have an idea and start working on it with his usual enthusiasm, probably during a weekend at home. He will then take it along and discuss it with Miss Edmonds who is the more practical of the two. Sometimes as a result of these discussions, the idea will be abandoned, but usually it will go ahead with some modifications, and Dr Barnes will continue to work on it until a good basic figure is produced. He will then turn it over to Miss Edmonds to dress up and convert into metal, after which he will have it back for the final cleaning-up and polishing.

When it is a question of remaking an existing figure, however, Miss Edmonds will usually do nearly all the work on the master. Sometimes, particularly in the case of the earlier ones, this means stripping the whole thing down and starting again, while at other times it just means trimming up and adding some more detail here and there, and perhaps improving the fit.

Dr Barnes, having been interested in military matters for longer than Miss Edmonds, has a much greater knowledge of uniforms generally, although she has pretty well caught up with him on the British uniforms of the twentieth century. Consequently he does most of the reading and research, and provides most of the documentation from which she works, while Miss Edmonds, having more time to devote to The Sentry Box, does most of the practical work. Each criticises the other's work freely and this often results in Miss Edmonds working on a figure while Dr Barnes stands by giving advice and encouragement – which as a psychiatrist he is so well qualified to do. Neither of them has had any sort of artistic training, both having learned the hard way, by trial and error. Like most other workers in the field, they look back at some of their early efforts with horror. Some of the very detailed work, such as the trumpet banner, and designs for shabracques have been commissioned, though Miss Edmonds is finding that she can do more and more of this work herself. Those things which are more of an 'engineering' job, such as a basic drum, are also commissioned from a specialist in that field.

The painting of the mounted models is done by a lady specialist who has been working for The Sentry Box ever since the firm started, and most of the foot soldiers are painted on contract by a studio which was set up specially for this purpose and which, although they do some other work, is mainly devoted to the painting of The Sentry Box models.

Dr Barnes is an enthusiast, full of ideas, but not so

Three superb, large lead models by The Sentry Box. *Top left :* Piper, Royal Scots; *centre :* Drummer, Royal Scots Guards; *bottom left :* Trumpeter, Household Cavalry

good at turning them into reality. Miss Edmonds is more practical, and they therefore make a good team, each keeping the other from going too far. Both would love to have more time for modelling, but Dr Barnes has his medical practice, and Miss Edmonds, as well as doing his medical secretarial work and keeping the practice running, also does all the organising, selling, packing and mould making for The Sentry Box; in fact everything that does not come under the heading 'casting, assembly and painting'. At one time she even did the casting and assembly as well, but with the growth of the business this became too much for her and that part of the work is now put out. The painting she has always refused to attempt because she says that, in self defence, there must be something she doesn't do. As it is, The Sentry Box has become her whole life, and she regards the work she does for Dr Barnes in his medical practice as her hobby. She has not taken a real holiday for seventeen years and her only relaxation is television. She has indulged herself to the extent of hiring a colour set, but usually works even while she watches. She did have a 'busman's holiday' recently when she went to see the film *Waterloo*, and she always takes a day or two off at Christmas. Once, she recalls, she had time to make fitted carpets for her whole flat, but those days are past and a little knitting or essential sewing is all she can find time for. Gardening she does 'because the garden is there', but she grudges every minute she spends in it, and has had most of it paved over to reduce the work load.

Dr Barnes has never, since his university and hospital rugger days, had any hobby other than model soldiers. Nowadays he relaxes from psychiatry and The Sentry Box by making up and painting Historex models for his private collection. He also buys lots of other models, but seldom finds time to do anything with them. He takes a holiday every year, but combines business with pleasure by visiting foreign military museums and members of foreign societies, as well as overseas customers.

Such is the quality of the models that the creators are members of the Guild of Model Soldier Manufacturers, and there can be few collectors who are not familiar with their work. The range is predictable – the favourite and most colourful British regiments. Here are the Household Brigade, the Dragoon Guards, Hussars, Lancers, Royal Artillary, the Highland Brigade, the Indian Army, the Territorial Army and Yeomanry. Besides these, there are units of the Peninsular War and of Waterloo, and also of the First Empire. Each model is available in a number of positions. In the mounted range the horses are hollow-cast, the riders solid. Models are also obtainable in kit form, and crowns, 'pips', stars, medals and chevrons can be supplied separately.

The mounted Officer of the Royal Scots Greys, 1897, is a colourful model, beautifully sculpted, whilst those of the present day 'Blues' and of the 15th Hussars, 1815, are full of a quiet dignity. We particularly like also the piper of the Scots Guards and the State Trumpeter of the Household Cavalry. Each shows scrupulous attention to detail and the modelling and painting are beautiful.

Officer, Royal Scots Greys, 1897. Large solid lead model by The Sentry Box

Charles C. Stadden, *Rustington*

Of recent years there have been a number of craftsmen whose work has progressed swiftly, and whose creations have received recognition in all countries. Perhaps the most remarkable of these is Charles C. Stadden, whose rise may well be called meteoric – indeed he has become a household word among collectors of model soldiers. One of the most versatile of all makers, he seems equally at home in all periods; added to which the variety of the action and posture of his models have enabled him to create an amazing number of figures. His industry is astonishing: an average of from four to six fresh 54mm figures a month, with perhaps a number in 30mm, appears to be his normal output.

One had expected to find a highly geared man, keenly sensible of time and motion, possibly with a highly sophisticated system of endless belts and short cuts as aids to production. Nothing could be further from the truth. We found a normal, intelligent, and most likeable man, taking his time, eager to talk and relax with his family in their pleasant bungalow in suburban surroundings. He was born in Leytonstone, East London, in 1919, and from his elementary school won a scholarship for art, but was not able to take advantage of it. He did, however, continue with evening courses in drawing and painting which stood him in good stead later in life. Joining the army in 1939, he served throughout the Second World War in France, the Middle East, and Italy, and was demobilised in 1946. Service with the Territorial Army included periods in the mule transport, RASC, Cyprus regiment, Royal Fusiliers, and at the moment he is a keen member of the Royal Sussex Regiment.

After the war he started work as a freelance commercial artist and gradually his interest in military matters began to assert itself. About this time also, he began carving models in wood, an interest that still survives. In his home he has a very fine two-foot-high carved and painted figure of an eighteenth-century grenadier which is a joy to behold.

In 1948 he joined the British Model Soldier Society, and there renewed contact with a great friend, C. B. O. Hingle (late Royal Marines) and their mutual interests decided them to join together as a team. Stadden recalls with some amusement the rather puzzled reception given to his woodcarvings when he showed them at society meetings – most of the members at that time were conservative in their collecting and Stadden's figures were alien to the tradition of 'Ancient Britains'.

Stadden and Hingle began working professionally in 1950, in a couple of rooms in Whitechapel where Stadden made all the masters and moulds, and Hingle painted the main colouring, with Stadden filling in the finer detail. At this time they worked in the $1\frac{1}{2}$-inch scale; but in 1951 Stadden began to make the standard 54–55mm size, and Hingle gradually mastered the finishing technique of the painting. The turning point in Stadden's career was reached in 1953, when he met Roy Belmont-Maitland, who, as sales promoter, took over the burden of paper-work and the constant worry of sales, and thus enabled Stadden to concentrate on the production of master-figures, and to experiment in techniques. By this time Hingle had become expert at painting, so the work of the partners fell neatly into place. They employed out-door labour to help with production under Stadden's supervision, and it is interesting to relate that girls proved the best painters and, not unnaturally, made working conditions agreeable. In 1957 Hingle left to take up a post with a firm of chartered accountants, to be replaced in 1959 by Alex Griffiths (ex-Gordon Highlanders and Commandos), who took over the workshop, which at that time was situated in Holborn, the sales department being in Shepherds Market.

Stadden was now entirely free to design the models, and decided to do this in his own home, in the pleasant company of his wife and children. Since 1959 production has gone up by leaps and bounds, and shows no signs of diminishing, and it is more than likely that Stadden is the best-known name in model soldier collecting circles.

In his early days he worked from sketches, drawings, woodcarvings, or clay models, but today his accumulated knowledge of uniforms enables him to eliminate much of the preliminary work and start directly on the model. (The fact that his father was a tailor has given him an uncanny knowledge of how a jacket should hang.) Most makers use distinctly different techniques to achieve the desired result. Many of the English, French and Americans build up from a torso, adding heads, arms, legs, and at last clothing with thin layers of lead. One whose work is familiar to many uses a completely nude figure, and adds clothing and equipment by means of solder only. One or two carve their figures direct from soft metal. One of these is Eriksson, another is Stadden. Eriksson leaves the chiselled planes standing out, Stadden smoothes them off – *chacun à son goût*. A Stadden model consists of a complete figure: facial expression, headwear, clothing, cuffs, buttons and decorations all carved direct, and on the sole of each foot a small projecting peg. When the figure reaches the London factory the arms and legs are 'animated', or eased into different positions, and the equipment, such as pack, scabbard, waterbottle and the like soldered on; the pegs on the feet are soldered to thin metal stands, the residue filed off; the model passes to the painting rooms, and eventually finds its way to the shop in Piccadilly. (The only exception to this process appears to be the 'DYK' models, where the rider is in one piece, the horse and furniture in parts.)

Stadden's own consuming passion is the British Army, 1660–1914, which he believes has been on the whole sadly neglected, a state of affairs he is speedily rectifying. Over a number of years he has built up a mass of information, so that he has most of the details at his finger tips. Most of the data on the uniforms of foreign troops comes from Belmont-Maitland, who has a reference library and a knowledge of the German Army second to none. Maitland decides on what figures are to be made, based on his knowledge of the selling possibilities, and the idea is then taken over by Stadden, who designs the model, decides the technical details of casting, and works closely with Griffiths. For his own pleasure Stadden is working on a Brigade of Infantry, 1751, in 33mm size as a centrepiece to his own collection, which will consist of models showing the change of uniform of the British Army from 1660 to the present day. He is also making twelve-inch-high woodcarvings, of the Sussex Regiment and the Royal Fusiliers, regiments in which he himself served.

A review of Stadden's models is difficult. The lavishly illustrated catalogue issued a few years ago by Norman Newton Ltd. (and continued by *Tradition* and Lieutenant-Colonel Nicholson's *Model Soldiers*) lists about a thousand figures, from a Roman to a British private of 1944, but since its publication the models have continued to pour forth, and there are, of course, many that are not listed because they have either been withdrawn or the stock is exhausted, and others again, have been completely remodelled. Most notable of those not now obtainable are the 1½-inch masterpieces which were too expensive to persevere with (including Cromwellians, of which Charles Sweet, Jn, has a collection). To these should be added the models made to special order which are to be found all over the world, notably in the collection at Blenheim Palace. The range and output are so bewildering that all that can be attempted is a general survey.

To many collectors the name Stadden is synonymous with the Napoleonic Wars – indeed he has long outstripped the French themselves in sheer quantity and variety. There seems, as far as we can see, no aspect of the *Grande Armée* unrecorded, whether in 54 or 30mm size; and more recently the smaller has had much success, especially of Napoleon and his staff. Looking through the catalogue, one finds impressive illustrations of the Imperial Guard Artillery, Dragoon, Foot Artillery, Officer and Gun Team and the many bandsmen.

Household Cavalry, Life Guards and Horse Grenadiers, *c* 1750. A group of fine models in 54mm by Charles C. Stadden, who is particularly at home with this period

Cardinal Richelieu and Musketeers.
A fine group by Stadden

There are some collectors who are a little overwhelmed by the carnival-time riot of French military costume, and whose tastes turn rather to the less extravagant British uniforms. It is here that, in our opinion, we see the best of Stadden. Whatever the period, whether the Line Infantry Private of 1748–68, the men of 1742–68, units of the British Army of the American War of Independence or any of the magnificent series of Abercrombie's, Moore's, or Wellington's men, it is not difficult to see what lies nearest to Stadden's heart. If forced to make special mention of any of these, we would choose the Royal Horse Guard; the Drummer of the Light Infantry; the Trooper, Light Dragoons, 1806; the Private, Light Infantry; and the Standard Bearer, Foot Guards, 1700–10.

To these main groups may be added the various Prussian and Bavarian units, the German troops of the Georges and the Germans of the Kaiser, American Revolutionaries and Unionists and Confederates, Royalists and Parliamentarians, Caesar, Frederick the Great and his army, and medieval knights with removable creasted helms, both on foot and mounted.

Stadden is a perfectionist, always seeking, as he says himself, to better his technique. He refuses to take himself too seriously, however, and thinks collectors in general are over solemn in their approach to their hobby. Nor does he resent criticism, if honest and constructive. No man can turn out a perfect figure every time, and occasionally we find what to our minds (though maybe not to others') seems an alien or over theatrical gesture, as in his model of Murat; or slight anatomical clumsiness, as in Rommel; or an uneasy fit of headwear, nor, we think, are his horses always successful. One has only to look at the horse of the Polish Light Cavalry, which detracts from an otherwise impeccable model; or that of the British Gunner, Royal Horse Artillery; of the French Artillery, or the Falling Prussian Hussar. One automatically compares them with Eriksson's mounts. However, these are minor blemishes on a range without parallel, and these were early models. In the majority of cases he has solved his difficulties and produced a fine animal – outstanding in grace and beauty are the figures of the Prussian Army, Beauharnais, Royal Horse Guard and, above all, the Royal Scots Greys' Standard. We learn also, that many of the earlier models are being replaced by ones more nearly perfect in design and execution.

The slightly larger size of many of his latest models has disturbed some collectors, wedded as they are to the usual 54mm size. When we asked Stadden the

Above Extra-mural activities for the army. A delightful conversation piece by Stadden

reason for the increase in height he told us that a special figure was needed – a rush job. After casting, it was found to be somewhat taller than usual, but it was too late for alterations to be made. The figure was despatched, and the result uneasily awaited. The client was delighted, and ordered more in the same size. Gradually other clients came to look with favour on the change, and the extra fraction of an inch has its own adherents.

He has recently returned to the 20mm figure, this time specifically for war-game use, with a little exploited period, the Crimean War, and going to the other

Left Examples of Stadden's fine Romans

extreme, he has created the magnificent 'Shoulder-Knot' statuettes, twenty centimetres of solid lead, painted, on three-inch-square bases, of selected military types. In between these comes the miraculous 30mm series.

Stadden himself is a master of painting, as his commissioned models show. The standard he sets, however, is hard to match in commercial models, and one feels at times that those figures not directly from his hand have a tendency to that over-elaboration of detail discussed elsewhere.

Stadden's work does not end with the models we have just reviewed. He is also kept fully occupied in making masters for many companies who produce plastic toys, kits, dolls, animals, model-railway accessories, ships and cars, and has worked with many other well-known artists, such as Roy Selwyn-Smith and George Erik.

Examples most collectors will recognise are the set of four 1748 figures and Henry VIII and his wives (both for Cavendish Miniatures), and (but not so generally known) the range of colossal figures of the last war for Louis Marx and a beautiful set of chessmen for Triang. The most extraordinary thing we saw in his studio was not a 'Super Stadden', but a plastic OO-gauge mother and child. This also can be seen in most model-railway shops, and it will be remembered that the mother has the child by the hand. The remarkable thing is that the whole group is made in one piece. The margin for error is fantastically small.

Howard Francis Willetts, *St. Ives, Huntingdonshire*

Howard Francis Willetts was born in 1905. His father was a member of a large Midlands building firm (a family business) and his mother a teacher. He had three sisters and a brother, and the whole family moved about the country wherever Willetts senior's business took him – London, Birmingham and Basingstoke. They were at Basingstoke at the beginning of 1914, and it was the sight of some infantry regiments in training that began Howard's interest in military matters and inspired him to collect lead soldiers.

Willetts's first job was in the drawing office of an engineering firm, but he left this to join the Workshop Training Battalion of the Tank Corps. A victim of 'Geddes's Axe', he transferred to the engineering branch of the Civil Service, and when the Second World War was declared he was moved to Administration to serve as a lecturer on Leadership and Administration and as a Liaison Officer in the RAFVR.

As a result of a breakdown in health in 1947, entailing many months of illness and convalescence, his interests turned to heraldry, painting, and history and when, in 1950, he was invalided out of the Civil Service his doctor (indeed a friend in need, and over a number of years a source of inspiration) suggested that a living might be made by the use of these new-found talents and interests. So Willetts decided to try making military and historical models, starting from scratch, learning the production of moulds and casts, the painting, and the many other things necessary. Trial and error proved good taskmasters, and eventually, after working for a short time with a sculptor whom he regards as the finest artist in the field of military model design, he realised that his craftsmanship was now of a high enough standard to enable him to compete with others in the same field. He had already decided that the larger model offered more scope for the display of his particular talents, and he soon found that the size of his 'Matchlock Military Models' was appreciated.

He has never tried to mass-produce the models, nor has he built up a staff of assistants. He realised early on, however, that a better result is obtained when the skills of a professional craftsman are employed rather than when trying to do everything oneself, and so in 1952 he engaged Joseph Grassi as a master maker of casts and moulds, and since 1954 T. Allen has collaborated with him as painter.

Howard Willetts at work on one of his models

Willetts's idea is that the model should be viewed as a whole – all parts, design, modelling and painting being complementary one to the other. Remembering that the model has to stand close scrutiny whether placed in a cabinet or taken in the hand, the painting must complement and not supplement the modelling (a point often forgotten), therefore the painting-in of high-lights and shadows is avoided; the sculptured figure must take the shadows and lights from its moulding and position.

Another important aspect of the model is the stance. Some regiments call for a relaxed pose, others for postures which will show off to the full the most colourful pieces of uniform or equipment, for example, the Highland regimental kilts and shoulder plaids. Before deciding on the pose of the model, photographs of the particular regiment are exhaustively studied and, after selection has been made of the pose that is most comfortable for the wearer of the uniform, and at the same time displays the uniform at its best, a drawing exhibiting the model from all angles is made. Attention is given to such details as the position of the sword hilt according to regimental tradition.

The model is then roughed out in clay, and from a temporary mould two or three casts are taken (in a commercial plaster which allows the carving of fine detail) for the making of the master-model. Satisfied that the master is correct in every detail, Willetts then covers it with protective lacquer in preparation for the making of the working mould. The next stage is the making of a plaster case for the actual mould, the case being made in two portions round the master. After the case has hardened, the master is placed in it and the case secured to prevent the two halves from parting while the moulding material is being poured through the channel left in the top of the case. During the pouring the mould is agitated to rid the material of air bubbles. The mould is then dried at a moderate temperature for some hours. After thirty-six hours the mould is ready for use and the master is finally removed.

The castings are made in a specially hard and very fine plaster, which has passed stringent laboratory tests, one showing a compression strength of over 7,000lb per square inch. Before pouring the plaster into the mould a heavy gauge galvanised wire armature is inserted, running up the centre of the arms, legs and head, so that the cast is reinforced from head to foot. The plaster is then poured, again the whole is agitated, and finally the cast is removed.

The finishing details such as the pouch and belt buckles are now carved in, all edges are checked to ensure clarity and the clothing folds approved to avoid the necessity of over-painting. Particular attention is paid to the chemical constituents of the dry pigments to be mixed together, so that long life of the colours is assured. The painting begins at the top and works downwards, the slowly-drying oils being regulated by the artist as matt, semi-matt, or gloss, as required, and up to a dozen different models are painted at the same time.

The model is completed by the final addition of the sword sling, the sword, cap-lines, etc, the swords and other weapons being made of the appropriate materials. A limited edition of seventy models is made from each master, each one bearing a certificate giving its number, and the master is destroyed. Approximately seven inches high, they have black and grey bases carrying the designer's name.

The models so far produced are of officers and other ranks of the British Army covering the period 1900 to date. This period has been chosen to pay tribute to the soldier in the glory of his scarlet, blue, and gold-laced uniforms, and to remind us of his passing. The details are taken from the Army Dress and Clothing Regulations, and from Willetts's own large collection of reference books.

Besides the regiments of the British Army, we find representatives of the Royal Air Force and Royal Navy, Royal Canadian Mounted Police, Air Training Corps Cadets (made as a trophy), the Honourable Artillery Company, Yeomen of the Guard, Princess Patricia's Canadian Light Infantry, the Royal Marines, Indian Army, Jaipur State Forces, 8th Punjab Regiment, King's Point (Merchant Marine Academy, USA) and Valley Forge Military Academy.

A special group comprises the Royal Scots Fusiliers, South Wales Borderers, Duke of Cornwall's Light Infantry, Middlesex Regiment, South Lancashire Regiment, Seaforth Highlanders, 9th Deccan Horse, 12th (POW) Royal Lancers, Middlesex Yeomanry, and an Admiral of the Fleet.

Equestrian models include Lancers, Hussars, Dragoons, Royal Horse Artillery, the Highland Regiments, Guards, Royal Scots Greys, and Queen Elizabeth II as Colonel-in-Chief of the various Guards Regiments. There is also a portrait model of Prince Philip as Admiral of the Fleet.

Examples of Willetts's finely detailed and painted 7-inch-high hardened plaster models

There has not been much time left to Willetts for other activities. Before the war, and after until his health let him down, he ran a boys' club, but had to stop in 1947. He has now retired from active model making but still keeps a few original moulds. Nowadays he lives quietly, reading history, listening to and watching selected programmes on radio and television, and pottering in the garden. Whilst having a properly justifiable pride in his achievements he refuses to take himself too seriously. He frequently glances at a motto that he has illuminated and hung in his workroom: *The work of one day is gazed upon for a thousand days.*

Italy

Ernesto Chiappa, *Turin*

The quality of Ernesto Chiappa's models is instantly apparent. Although he works at times in the 54mm scale, he feels that he can express himself better in a larger size. He finds 30 to 35cm ideal for his purpose. In this size he builds up a torso of papier-mâché on a wire armature, and carves the heads, legs and arms from wood. The body is then clothed in material simulating the original, and accoutrements are made from leather and metal. He specialises in the old Piedmontese Army and Italian Naval uniforms, 1775–1918.

Elegance is the keyword for Chiappa's models. The delicacy of the carving of the hands is to be noted, and indeed, we cannot express anything but profound admiration for the wonderfully composed officer of the 1st Hussar Regiment of the Italian Republic.

Understandably, Chiappa's works are to be seen in public places, notably at the Risorgimento and Pietro Millo Museums.

Officer of the First Hussar Regiment, Italian Republic, 1802. A colourful 30cm model, made of carved wood and papier-mâché, with actual materials for the clothes and accoutrements, by Chiappa

Lord Cardigan. A spirited model, 15cm high, by A. Pranzetti

Augusto Pranzetti, *Sassari*

Pranzetti is a skilled woodcarver who works in various sizes, ranging from 54mm to 60mm for the foot soldiers, and up to 15cm for the equestrians. One of his most important contributions is a series of fifty-four Italian army soldiers from the constitution of the Kingdom of Sardinia to modern times. This was completed in 1951 for the Municipality of Sassari.

We have seen photographs of very life-like models of Her Majesty Queen Elizabeth II as Colonel of the Grenadier Guards; a fine officer of the Blues (12cm); Lord Cardigan in spirited action; a 6th Light Dragoon of 1830; and one of the 18th Hussars, all mounted. Of the foot soldiers, a Grenadier Guards colour bearer, an officer of the Blues, a Grenadier Guards drummer, an officer of the Scots Guards and another of the Gordon Highlanders, and a piper of the 60th Light Infantry are specially worthy of mention. Perhaps our favourite is the drummer-boy of the Sardo-Piedmontese Army (1848). Here is fine action combined with realistic portraiture.

Sweden

Holger Eriksson, *Karlstad*

In all branches of art there are those who, working within self-imposed limits, achieve unobtrusive but nevertheless distinctive mastery. John Sell Cotman is remembered for the perfection of his translucent watercolours; only when he forced his talents into alien fields did his sure touch falter. Joseph Crawhall's tiny paintings on holland still remain miracles. Many others will come to mind.

Among the artist-creators of the model soldier there are a few who work within similar self-chosen limits, and whose figures are all the more distinguished for it. Holger Eriksson is one of these, and those familiar with his work would not wish it otherwise.

Eriksson is one of the older school of model-makers, and has pursued his quiet way in comparatively remote Sweden. Married, with one daughter (a son died in 1962) he is the head of a drawing-office, and for years has used the familiar monogram HE on drawings and later on the base of his models.

He has been interested in model soldiers since boyhood, and cut his teeth, so to speak, on the flats, semi-solids and solids of the Swedish firms of Tenngjuteriet Schreuder and Ohlsson and Mars, and on importations from Germany. The urge to create flowered about 1934, and he seems to have quickly mastered his craft, for in 1936 he joined the British Model Soldier Society and the French society and gained contacts with other collectors and makers.

By 1944 his talents were being recognised far outside his native Sweden, and he was approached by Curt Wennberg to make a large number of designs for 40 and 54mm models for a newly-conceived venture by the American firm of Comet, who intended founding an industry in Eire. Wennberg's chequered career has been discussed elsewhere (in the author's *Model Soldiers; a Collector's Guide*), but whatever his inconsistencies we must surely be grateful to him for bringing the work of Eriksson before a wider audience. Generally speaking the master craftsman is a lone wolf, making and painting and marketing his models in necessarily limited numbers: here, for the first time, the model soldier world saw an amalgam of artist and commercial company prepared to give him unlimited scope and to guarantee distribution *en masse*. Commercial firms are usually more intent on best-selling lines and large production than artistic merit (Herald and Starlux are among the exceptions) but here was a class of model not only beautifully designed and adequately cast, and available at a reasonable price, but in two sizes – of which the 40mm was the more immediately popular and has, indeed, remained so.

So the Authenticast figure was born. It lasted until 1949, running concurrently with work for Malleable Mouldings of Deal. It would be a difficult task to list all the original designs produced, and Mr Judd possesses a number of which we had not previously heard. Moreover, Comet informs us that they still have all the original moulds, together with a number from which no figure has ever been cast. In any collection of models these Authenticast creations are easily recognised; even if the casting and painting are at times clumsy, the design and conception is so original as to be unmistakable.

Wennberg now started his Swedish African Engineers (SAE) venture and Eriksson designed a large number of models in 30mm size. Here, however, the

Holger Eriksson with a selection of the beautiful models in different sizes which are a delight to the collection. On the far left are some of the large carved wood Swedish Hussars

production was very clumsy. Even so, the high standard of design is apparent, and the figures had an immediate success.

Today Eriksson works only for collectors and museums as a relaxation from his normal work, and issues his own catalogue, which lists some two hundred models in 30mm, twenty-five in 40mm, and a hundred in 54mm. Naturally, the emphasis is on his own native Sweden – cuirassiers and infantry of the time of Gustav Adolf, all types of troops of the period of Charles V, dragoons of 1778 to 1886, and cavalry of 1900. Other periods and countries represented are Romans, knights, Danes, Cossacks, the Indian army, English Life Guards, Mounties, Uhlans, French Napoleonic and 1870, Americans of the Civil War and 1876, cowboys and Indians, and Finnish troops. His portrait models include Hannibal, Coleoni, Gustav Adolf, Franz Josef, Charles XII and XIV, Oscar II and Gustav V.

He works from his own drawings, models the figures, makes the moulds, casts, and paints the resultant model. His passion is for horses, and he has studied and drawn and carved them in wood from an early age. (Some examples of his carved wood 90mm figures are shown on page 125.) This devotion to horses accounts for the extraordinary beauty of his equestrian models. Whether standing, walking, trotting or at full gallop the illusion of movement is amazing. One has only to cite the 30mm models of the Lifeguard and the Swedish Horseguard (walking), the 40mm Swedish Horseguard of 1814 and of 1900 (galloping), Napoleon and Elizabeth II, the Swedish Lifeguard and the Swedish Hussar, both of 1814 (all standing) and the German cavalry officer (1935) and the Viking (galloping), to show the different approach to each action. The foot soldiers are equally impressive, the marching infantryman being perhaps the finest of all representations of the purposeful fighting man. The 30mm models of eighteenth-century Swedish troops are sheer delight.

The models are conceived sculpturally, and obviously worked with a chisel, emphasising the planes, which gives structural strength and truthfulness. Charles Stadden is a great admirer of Eriksson's work, and agrees that it is this emphasis on planes that gives an Eriksson figure such distinction. He paints his models in oils, and leaves the planes and contours to make their own contribution without having recourse to shading. But to our mind the full beauty of an Eriksson model is in its unpainted state, when the sculptured surface is, as one fervent admirer puts it, like regimental silver.

Eriksson makes no concession to glamorous uniforms and seems indifferent to the more popular or extravagant periods. He brings instead a welcome touch of refreshing Nordic austerity. His appeal is to the intellect – his achievement is subtlety of form and thoughtful and exquisite craftsmanship.

Napoleon I and Queen Elizabeth II.
Models in 54mm by Eriksson

Equine fluidity of motion is expressed in these two 54mm models by Eriksson of a German cavalry officer *c* 1935 and a Viking. Note his device for supporting the hoofs

United States of America

Norman H. Cooke, *Chepachet, RI*

A letter from David Winter contained an enthusiastic reference to a maker previously unknown to us. Contact with Norman Cooke ('Lance Historical Miniatures') brought not only a speedy reply but a delightful model, packed in such an ingenious way as to defy all efforts of destruction by the postal authorities, a point not without its significance.

Like many makers, he is also a collector. His interest in things military dates from as far back as he can remember, but about 1940 the crucial transition began, and his lead soldiers ceased to be regarded as mere toys – a trifle late, he regrets, to save some of those now rather rare pieces so common in American shops during the thirties. After that it was a matter of improvement in painting technique, learning the art of conversion, building up a good reference library, and finally making his own figures. This came slowly, as a consequence of service in the 104th Division during the Second World War and the subsequent pursuit of a PhD in history.

'Lance Historical Miniatures' was born in 1958, and is in fact a joint operation in which Norman Cooke and

Units of the American forces in the War of Independence. 54mm models by Cooke

his wife Lisle work in partnership; indeed the trademark is an amalgam of their names. Luckily Lisle was a maker and painter of figures long before they married, so no coercion was necessary!

They belong to the ranks of the dedicated makers in that they make no attempt to produce in large quantities, nor do they think they ever will. The only models they make are those in which they themselves take a personal interest because of either style or period. The figures are hand cast (no rubber moulds) and without exception in 54mm scale. A high proportion of the accoutrements and all the weapons are cast separately or cut from foil.

The French and Austrian armies of the late eighteenth century are their special interest, for instance, the French Regiments of *Bearn*, *La Reine*, *Royal Roussillon*, *La Sarre*, *Lyonnais*, *Garde Française*, *Grenadiers de France* and Lally's *Irlandais* in the Seven Years' War, together with the Regiments of *Touraine*, *Auxerroix*, *Foix*, *Saintogne*, Lauzun's *Légion* and *Deux Ponts* serving during the American Revolutionary War. Standard bearers of regiments also in America during this period include those of *de la Marck Deux Ponts*, *Touraine*, *Soissonnais*, *Foix*, *Auxerrois*, and *Bourbonnais*. Austro-Hungarians of 1798–1814 include staff officers, adjutant-generals, and artillery officers: the Bavarians and Prussians (1806–12) follow, and there is a fair-sized group of French on foot and mounted, serving during the Napoleonic wars, including a Mameluk trooper and drummer, and a portrait model of the little Emperor as painted by Meissonnier, together with a sprinkling of Russians of the same period.

As is only to be expected, the largest group is of American troops during the Revolution, including specimens of Haslett's Delaware (five positions), Washington's Life Guards, 2nd New Hampshire, 6th Pennsylvania (Irvines), Smallwood's Maryland, an officer of the Rhode Island Train of Artillery, Butler's Rangers, standard bearers, and a single British infantryman. They have made a few American Civil War models, and will occasionally, when pressed, accept orders for nineteenth and twentieth century and other subjects (a winged Polish Lancer of 1683, for instance, is a very colourful figure). They also do a certain amount of diorama work, and hope to develop this side. Much of their commissioned work involves special portrait figures based on such sources as Knoetel, Teuber and Ottenfeld, Lezius, Philippoteaux, Lefferts and the like.

Many of their figures are conceived in relaxed attitudes, either standing at ease with the gun in various positions (the author's Brunswicker is enjoying a quiet pipe), but the American Revolutionary War troops are more varied in action – marching, running, kneeling and standing firing. A Cooke figure is made with integrity and painted with precision. It is refreshing to find that the colours are allowed to speak for themselves, acknowledging that the shadows form naturally from the contours of the figure and the lighting in which it is placed. It is sincerely to be hoped that the Cookes will continue on their present course, resisting the ubiquitous pressures of commercial competition.

William Imrie and Clyde Risley, *New York*

William Imrie's models are so familiar to many of us that it comes as a surprise to realise that they first appeared in New York no earlier than the 1950s. First there was a preliminary period of specialisation in hand-made models called 'Imrie Custom Miniatures' in 20 and 54mm, and four-inch scale items for museums and private collectors. Each model was thoroughly researched so that scrupulous accuracy was achieved, and eventually Imrie became recognised as an authority on military uniform, being elected a fellow of the Company of Military Collectors and Historians.

In 1956 his wife Helen, artist-trained at the Cooper Union, joined him in a commercial venture called 'Hellenic Miniatures' – a series of unpainted castings of Napoleonic subjects. The range was greatly expanded in 1960, utilising the many sculpting and casting techniques by then developed. The miniatures have become so popular that for the last four years or so it has been impossible to make any more 'Custom' miniatures. The business moved into larger premises in 1961.

In 1962 Imrie was joined by Clyde Risley, who brought with him a wealth of technical knowledge of human and equine anatomy. Risley is also an artist, trained at the Pratt Institute, and for fifteen years he worked in advertising as art director of an agency. Having always been interested in both military history and art, Risley has assisted several American makers of miniatures with his finely designed horses and men. In 1963 he was made a Fellow of the Company of Military Collectors and Historians for his research, illustrations and models of the American soldier. Nor have we exhausted the range of their work, for Risley's wife is also a graduate of the Pratt Institute, and was responsible for the painting of all the figures for a *Fallen Timbers* diorama exhibited by John Scheid at West Point Museum several years ago.

Imrie and Risley together create the figures, each

model being entirely original, and make the moulds, the models then being cast in a centrifuge. They also manufacture their own paints, premixed to the correct shades for most military uniforms. In many cases the heads and arms are cast separately, thus enabling a number of variations to be obtained; in fact, 'diorama' packets are issued, comprising packs, muskets, camp kettles, axes, hatless heads, caps, cocked hats and assorted arms. Many of the models are drawn delightfully by Risley, and appear in their catalogues. More of these appear in an interesting work of great use to collectors, Risley and Imrie's *The Model Soldier Guide*, 1964.

In all their work they like to see movement and alertness, even if the figure is merely standing. Proportion, also, is a factor they watch with great care, and naturally accuracy of detail should also be present. Added to this is that indefinable something that makes a figure breathe; a quality which they hope they have achieved in the range of mounted French hussars.

Three-figure diorama of an incident in the American War of Independence, made by Imrie-Risley, and painted by Donald Burgess. A present-day tendency is for a few related figures to be grouped on the same stand

Their largest series is of the popular Napoleonic Wars, the models being marketed in an assortment of postures: advancing, marching, firing, loading, wounded and at ease. The officers are given variety by the sword being held in a number of ways. Drummers and musicians are sitting, at ease, running, or at attention. An important feature is a twelve-pounder field-piece, together with the necessary crew and equipment. A number of the mounted models are particularly attractive, and we would cite the 7th and 9th Hussars in the Blum Collection as being worthy specimens.

Naturally, the wars of America bulk large. There is an impressive range of Civil War figures, in a variety of poses, and here again, the mounted figures are impressive, especially Lee with aide-de-camp (Blum), Lee and Jackson before Chancellorsville (McDonnell) and the Confederate Cavalry bugler (Blum). Horses and riders in violent disturbance of equilibrium are difficult to express with conviction, and it is not disrespectful to say that they are no more successful with their falling Union Cavalry leader (Blum) than Stadden is with his Prussian hussar in a somewhat similar position. A figure in comparative quietness, and full of character, is the Confederate general (Blum) which is akin in spirit to Hinton's Crimean War general with map.

To our minds, the American War of Independence lies nearer their hearts. This unhappy conflict offers magnificent scope, with its wealth of uniforms and the number of separate and distinct companies which constituted the armies of the combatants, and they can be seen to advantage in the numerous dioramas of Brandywine, Trenton and Valley Forge created from Imrie-Risley models by C. Ashton McDonnell and, in particular, the Poundridge skirmish made for Blum. In this range there are over sixty positions available, but we would certainly place high on the list the Congress's Own drummer boy – a figure of great insight and charm; Washington (standing) and the Feld-Jäger of Hesse-Cassel. The mounted figures are vital

The Civil War naturally attracts American collectors. Here is a fine example, 54mm high, of a commanding officer, by Imrie-Risley

and spirited, the Trumpeter, First Troop Philadelphia City Cavalry, being a masterpiece. Another outstanding achievement is the Revolutionary gun team (beautifully illustrated in Blum) with six-pounder gun, limber, and lead-horses and civilian drivers. The heavy draught horses, with correct harness, are perfect in their strength, and considering the complexity and detail of

the gun, it is surprising to hear that assembly is easily performed.

Imrie-Risley's Second World War models are also outstanding in this somewhat neglected period. The equipment and dress are remarkably accurate, and the figure of the German paratrooper quite memorable. But the figures that remain longest in our memory are the four-inch-tall private of the 27th Foot, 1757 (albeit the facial colour is unharmonious), and the 1776 Minute Man (to whose features, however, the same criticism can be applied) and, above all, the Champlain, which to us seems *the* perfect model.

Trooper, Troop A, 107th Cavalry, Ohio National Guard, 1935; the rider was made by Imrie and the horse by Berdou

Opposite This magnificent 4-inch model of Champlain was photographed at the lake which bears his name

British cannon and team, Waterloo period. A group by Imrie-Risley. They have made a number of other groups for different periods of military history

William H. Murray, *Kenilworth, NJ*

One fascination of model soldier collecting is the emergence of the new maker. Unheralded, he emerges gradually, experimenting, mastering the tools of his craft, putting out a tentative figure here, a reasonably good creation there, until his efforts are crowned with success, and his models are considered desirable to acquire.

William H. Murray is one of those who entered the field quietly. Born in 1930, he is married and has two children. He attended the University of Louisville, Kentucky, served in the US Army during the Korean War and is a designer and model maker for a Newark plastics firm. He is a captain in the Army Reserve.

His first introduction to model soldiers was at an early age when he began purchasing hollow-casts of the US army 1914, at five cents apiece. These were followed by Mignots and Britains.

He was just beginning to discover that really fine model soldiers were obtainable when he was sent to Korea (marrying first), but on his return from active service he and his wife had too little money for collecting, so he decided to attempt the intricate art of creating model soldiers himself. Over a lengthy period of time, and with much heart-searching, he managed to acquire a small but representative gathering of fine models to act as a guide, and took the plunge.

After many failures he mastered the art of sculpting, moulding and casting, and was gradually able to add the resultant figures to his collection. Meanwhile he had become an *habitué* of Polk's Hobby Store in New York, a firm well known for the sale of native products and imported models. When it became known that he was modelling, Polk's approached him with the suggestion that he might care to make a line of figures for them to sell. At the time there was a dearth of medieval period figures, and Murray was commissioned to do several of these. We have seen photographs of an archer and a man at arms from this group, and Murray will agree that they are not particularly outstanding.

Murray's interest at the time was the ancient and medieval world, and whilst he seems to have temporarily abandoned the latter, he has created a notable series of Romans – on sentry duty, in parade order, advancing, throwing the pilum, and fighting with the sword. The most remarkable model to our mind is the legionary in full marching order, an unconventional figure, complete with two pilae, a pack pole with two packs, ration bag, cooking pot, wine bottle, and 'acquired' chicken.

At the insistence of the late Henry Becker, he decided to expand his range, and began with an American Civil War gun-crew as accessories to a series of cannon which Becker was making. This was followed by a small selection of Confederate infantry.

As an active member of several American societies, he had noted many very fine models by private makers. Since few of them had any facilities for producing figures in quantity, he decided to approach some of these gentlemen with the idea of producing and selling their models. Two collectors to whom he put this proposals were Sergeant-Major William E. Greer, and Eugene Custer, who both agreed. Since then Greer has been his active associate and devotes as much time to models as his army duties will allow. Custer has been a tower of strength and a mine of information, besides supplying Civil War figures. Greer has concentrated on the American War of Independence, but recent models also include a South Carolina Zouave (1861), a British Soldier (1800) and a fifteenth-century Knight in full armour.

Murray has also been fortunate in the acquisition of a painter of outstanding ability, Alan LeGloahec, who was born in France in 1929. He studied art at Brown University, and is an advertising artist by profession, and a painter in oils and tempera for pleasure. With this background it seemed natural to turn his talents to the painting of model soldiers. His period interests are varied: Ancients, Napoleonics, French and British of all periods.

Murray's most ambitious venture to date is his detailed study of the Russian infantry from 1805–15. Included is the Infantry of the Line, Infantry of the Guard, and the Russian-German Legion. With all the types, uniform changes and positions involved, there should eventually be over nine hundred figures in this group alone. In addition to the above, Murray is expanding his line of Ancient World models, with new Roman types well to the fore. Some interesting representative portrait figures are planned as well as a complementary line of mounted models.

Murray's method of production is traditional. The original figure and the component parts are sculpted in clay, then coated with liquid latex to form the master mould. After several coats of latex the mould is allowed to dry. Prior to opening the mould for the removal of the clay figure, a plaster mother mould is formed round the latex one, to prevent distortion. The master figure is then cast in a small centrifugal casting machine, and then touched up prior to making the production moulds. Into the production mould (formed in a vulcanising press under high heat and pressure in a large centrifugal casting machine and spinning at several hundred rpm) molten tin alloy is poured. The resultant models are cleaned, trimmed and undercoated preparatory to painting.

If one looks even casually at photographs of Murray's models, one is immediately struck with the impression of inordinately thick and squat legs, and startling whites of eyes. The photography of model soldiers, however, is a tricky business (as the author knows to his cost) and very often relatively unimportant details attain a magnitude out of all proportion, thus conveying

Opposite Murray at work on one of his models, showing successive stages

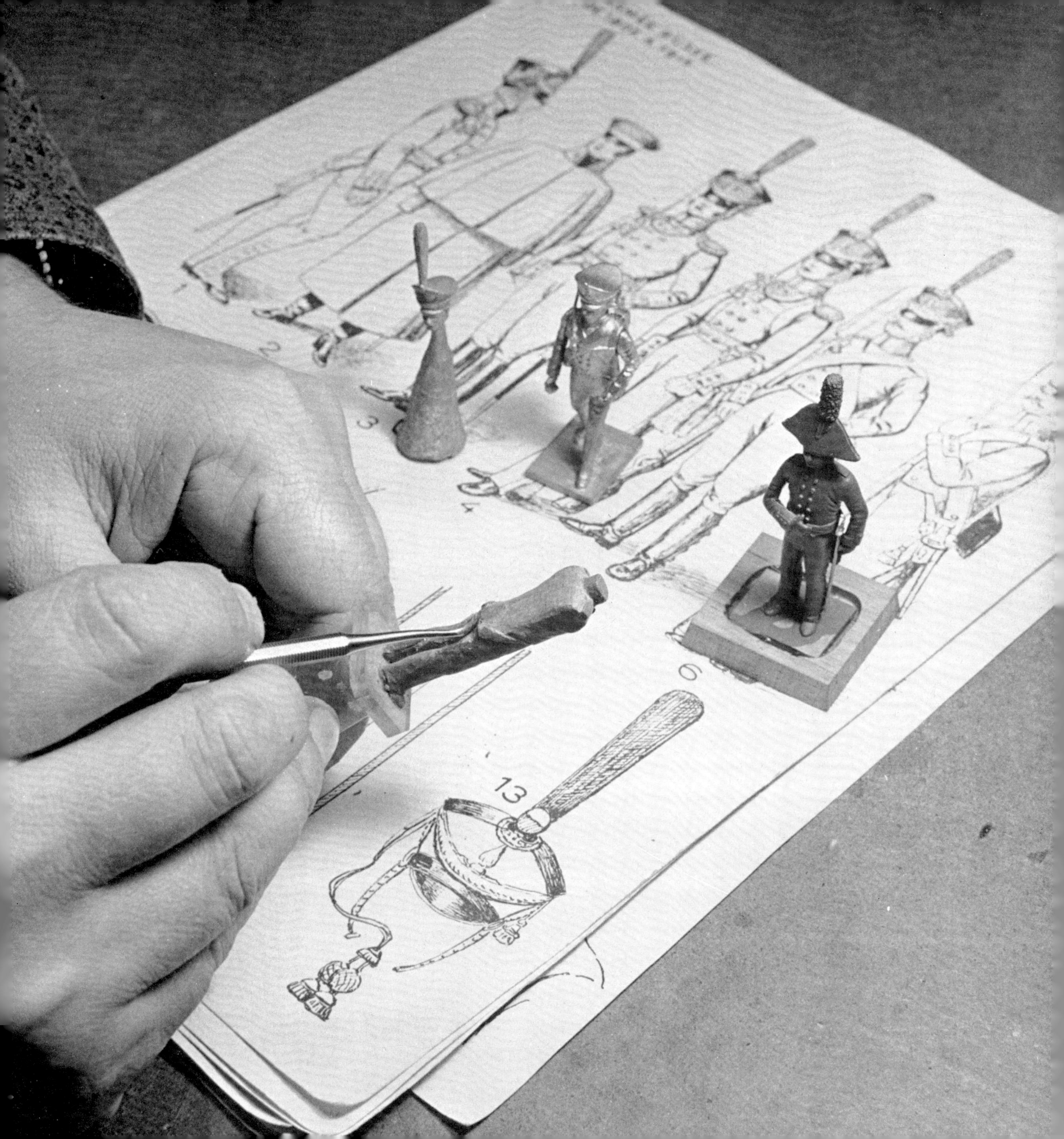
6
13

Above William Murray is engaged on the making of a vast number of models of the Russians of the time of Napoleon. Here are three examples. As is often the case, the photograph does not do justice to the figures, the central one, for example, a copy of which is in the author's possession, being a fine model

an entirely false impression which can only be corrected by examination of the actual models. If one compares the original model of a Russian Imperial Guard NCO of the Semenovski Regiment (1812) presented to the author by Murray and LeGloahec with a photograph of the same model, it will be seen that the whites of the eyes do not appear to be over-emphasised, and the legs, though sturdy, fit perfectly into place. The feet, however, both in the original and in the photograph, appear on the small side, a fact explained by the bringing of the simulated grass too far over the instep, thus completely hiding the toes.

Newcomers: C. R. Broman, *Evanston, Ill.* and Martin L. Kaufmann, *Brookline, Mass.*

C. R. Broman, who trades under the name of H-R Products Inc, is a professional caster of equipment for the architectural model field, and produces model soldiers as a sideline and a hobby, and he has certainly succeeded in bringing an approach long wanted, that of humour. His Central American generalissimo (*c* 1835) is a masterpiece of caricature. The other models he has so far produced are more traditional in approach, although at the same time they include some rather unusual subjects and treatment. Several deal with Indians – a Blackfoot brave and dog, a Wyandot wampum runner, a Mandan chief (after Bodmer's painting) and Osceola, chief of the Seminoles. An Ojibwa hunter is transformed into a Hudson's Bay trapper by the alteration of equipment. The others so far are a Zulu chief, a Bulgarian officer (1914–18), von Richthofen, a German officer and a Japanese officer (both Second World War). In a number of these models a feature is the incorporation of local colour on the stands of the figures, which are issued unassembled.

Martin L. Kaufmann, trading under the name of Cockade Miniatures, has made an impressive start. His models are in 54mm size, and his range is rapidly progressing. Each figure is serially numbered, and his interests are wide. A group of swashbuckling *landsknechts*, puffed and slashed, one drinking from a wine cup, another caressing the hilt of a huge two-handled sword, is welcome, and a Desert Rat and a Mexican Cavalryman (*c* 1845) are useful additions to the usual range. He has completed an entire set of NATO troops of all countries, and also has a Luftwaffe officer and dog. An ambitious venture is a set of four Aztec bearers with a central figure seated in a litter. Limbs, arms and equipment are made separately for fixing to the torso, and each figure is issued with complete painting instructions. We anticipate many more models of interest from him.

Above left Unusual models by Broman of a Mandan warrior and Osceola. They are issued in separate parts, so that the collector assembles and paints them
Above right Colourful *landsknechts*. Kaufmann makes these 54mm models in a variety of postures

Overleaf Purposeful Romans. 54mm solid lead models by William Murray

The Collectors

The object of this section of the work is not so much to catalogue the private collections of the world (an impossible task with an indigestible result in any case) but rather to indicate the scope and variety that makes up the solid core of the model soldier collecting world. One collector may be omnivorous, and, having embraced every period and every maker, every style and every material, acquiring his models in the grand manner, by block purchase, may then, like Alexander the Great, look round for further worlds to conquer. Another, perhaps at the threshold of manhood, may, like Cortes, have looked 'with a wild surmise – silent' – not on a peak in Darien, but in Burlington Arcade outside the agency for Stadden, Courtenay and Ping. It may be years before one or two of these models become his and in the meanwhile the Britains, the Mignots, the plastics supply their place. Maybe these are disposed of later; perhaps they are retained, or even added to. For many are the paths open to the collector of model soldiers. There are the commercial makes to be collected set by set or model by model, together with their variants and piracies; there are the continental flats in their infinite variety; there are the plastics of England, the United States, and of Europe (there are even the atrociously bad productions of the Iron Curtain bloc); there are the paper sheets in their thousands; there are the carved wood figures of France and of Italy; there are the models by the master-makers whose works we have just discussed.

No two collectors have the same aim. There are those who like their models in battalions, rank upon rank, marching round the shelves with drums and colours and artillery (sometimes to an appropriately martial gramophone record). Others have what they call a 'type' collection: at least one figure by every maker irrespective of quality or period. Some concentrate on the development of one particular arm of the services, another will collect within that arm. One of whom we know concentrates on one battle alone; there are many whose sole consideration is the work of one maker. Finance and space are important factors in the building of any collection, and there is an infinite variety possible in the manner in which the collection is displayed.

An eminent Austrian collector has drawn up a list of a large number of collectors, mostly continental, and an analysis shows an extraordinary range of occupation: students, clerks, men of medicine, architects, artists, policemen, civil servants, actors, manual workers, booksellers, men of God, bank clerks, electricians, engineers, teachers, mechanics, farmers, men of law, commercial travellers, chemists, bookbinders, locksmiths, goldsmiths, builders, typographers, sociologists, and, of course, but not necessarily predominating, members of the armed forces. The gentler sex do not as yet figure very prominently on the list, but we know from our experience that there are many wives and daughters who take a keen interest in their menfolk's hobby.

This same Austrian also investigated the size and scope of a number of collections: size expressed in numbers from 1,000 to 50,000, kind of collection by flats, solids, units, types, series, dioramas, war-games, regimental units, and specialist figures. A third section dealt with the periods or epochs: ancient times, middle ages, *landsknechts*, seventeenth-century baroque, Seven Years' War, Louis XV, the French Revolution and the Napoleonic Wars, the nineteenth century, the two world wars, colonial empires, portrait figures, and the civilian world.

With a hobby of such universal interest it would not be true to assume that national pride plays the most important part in a collection. True there are the diehards for whom the indulgent sun has never set on a British Empire, or for whom the Battle of Waterloo ended in a French victory (after all, such an eminent author as Hilaire Belloc wrote a book on the war in Spain without once mentioning Wellington). It is interesting to note, for example, that the main period of interest of the British Model Soldier Society in 1968 was undisputedly the Napoleonic War, followed by

Previous page This 54mm group is from the author's collection

A collector's work-bench. A corner of Mr Hanington's studio, showing models of all sizes and materials, some painted ready for fixing to bases, some castings waiting for painting, and others undergoing conversion. In the case on the left some oval, original, old German boxes will be noted

British troops of pre-1914, then the two World Wars, and the American Civil War.

English collectors have made attempts at various times to create a really representative collection of the British and allied troops at Waterloo to stand as a memorial to that famous battle and to act as a foil to the Mond Collection of Lucotte Napoleonic models formerly kept at the Museum of the Royal United Service Institution as part of the British Model Soldier Society Collection. In 1935 the members of the society tried to achieve this, but in spite of the enthusiasm of W. Carmen and R. Clendennin the project petered out. Many of the members made sample figures, some of which may still be occasionally seen (including a 40mm standing Scots Grey by Selwyn-Smith) and Carman went to great lengths making torsos, heads, caps, packs, etc, in plaster moulds. Britains supplied a small number of models with detachable arms and packs, and Don and Honey Ray made a few figures of a similar nature for Horlicks in 1939, but again the project came to nothing. The nearest approach (but of a transient nature) was the society's exhibition in 1960 at the Royal United Service Institution entitled 'Men of Waterloo'. Many collectors and all the best commercial and private makers in Britain combined to form a most impressive collection of models, filling one Austrian visitor with wonder. Collectors indeed are influenced more by types of material than what they represent. In England and the United States there are few collectors of flats, although the interest in these appears to be growing. Among English collectors Stadden appears to be the most popular, closely followed by Gammage, Britains and Hinton. There is also a following for Elastolin, Greenwood, Hill, Mignot, Heyde, Ping, Courtenay and Airfix. Probably because of the cost few collectors in England possess the masterpieces of Berdou and des Fontaines. In Germany, Austria and Switzerland it is the reverse, with the native flats predominating, but with a growing awareness of the productions of the better makers of solids. There is practically no interest shown in Germany for their own Heyde, popularity being found in England and the United States. France has adhered pretty rigidly to its Lucottes and Mignots and its master makers are unaffected by its brief excursion into the realm of flats, whilst Italy and Spain, though maintaining interest in their native products, are intensely aware of Britains' ranges. Holland and Belgium and the Scandinavian countries, with few examples of their own (apart from the remarkable Eriksson and more recently, Brunoe), enjoy the products of all types and countries, with perhaps a leaning towards flats. The Americans are perhaps the most catholic of all collectors. Having a history of competent commercial makers of their own, they easily assimilate the works of others, particularly Heyde, Mignot, and the ubiquitous Britains, together with the lesser-known products and styles, and a sprinkling of the connoisseur models.

Plastics and papier-mâché compositions are pretty universally collected, but the larger models of wood, or wood with natural materials, seem to find favour more readily in France and Italy than elsewhere; and the collecting of paper sheets, apart from a few enthusiasts in America, appears to be confined to the western European countries.

The greatest single event to have a profound effect on collecting tendencies is the Statutory Regulation 1967, which prohibited the manufacture of any toy soldier having a coating of paint that contained lead. It is also unlawful to make a military toy in lead as there is, as Roy Selwyn-Smith, joint managing director of Britains Ltd, says in an extract from the *Bulletin of the British Model Soldier Society* of April 1970: 'very real danger in lead if it falls into a child's hands. It is now virtually impossible to obtain the type of labour to produce the type of lead soldier for which Britains were famous. The manufacturing technique is now out of date, and unacceptable as a manufacturing process in this world today'. Where Britains led, others followed. When Britains ceased to produce for the home market, the other firms gave up making hollow-casts. Overnight as it were, the hollow-cast vanished, not with a bang but a whimper. In England an honourable tradition came to an end: but Britains still export, and Mignot continues to make lead soldiers. Presumably children of other countries are immune to lead poisoning. What of the thousands who handled Britains and Heydes and Hills and Mignots for over seventy years before the Statutory Regulation 1967 came into being? Did any boffin draw up a table of known deaths of children from lead poisoning due to having played with little lead soldiers?

The result of this was that in England one could no longer buy a commercial hollow-cast lead soldier: the makers used the same moulds for the production of plastics, or redesigned their original models (as did Britains) for the new material. The best of these are very good indeed, and excel the hollow-cast in all ways except in the feel and the tendency in some cases for the paint to flake off.

What now was the collector to do? If he was of modest means the normal commercial channel was barred to him, apart from the purchase of Mignot models, and this was difficult. He had perforce to turn to plastics, and explore the hitherto unknown or disregarded range offered by Britains, Starlux, Marx and Reamsa, or the assembly models made by Segom and Historex (although the cost of the latter was somewhat daunting). Alternatively, he could begin to collect flats, with the inherent difficulties in obtaining them, and the frustration and annoyance from the import duty and purchase tax charged by HM Customs. Or he could concentrate on the tiny war-game figures, and here indeed was a large field from which he could choose, and purchasing was simplicity itself. He could, however, if his income allowed, purchase from the specialist makers, and here the world was his oyster.

A by-product of the Statutory Regulation 1967 has rapidly shown itself in the feverish interest being taken in the now unobtainable hollow-casts. Auctioneers today find that a sale devoted exclusively to model soldiers is highly rewarding. The prices being realised for Britains' models is a revelation. At one sale in 1969 a box of ten Gloucestershire Regiment Infantry standing firing fetched £13, and eight Royal Marine Light Infantrymen (pigeon-chested version) the same price. A box of seven Scots Guards and Piper, and six 75th Gordon Highlanders with two pipers together realised £21. All these were oval base varieties. At a sale the following year Britains again predominated. Seven Montenegrins and eight Japanese together made £26. A horse-drawn pontoon wagon in the original box fetched £35, an advance on a similar lot of the previous year. Other makes are doing well also: a Heyde box of thirty-five 60mm Prussians went for £52 and, most extraordinary of all, Elastolin Nazis fetched £28.

It is the prices realised by models made by the master craftsmen that causes wonderment. A set of superb mounted and foot figures, ten in all, and all different, of the Battle of Hastings by the great Ping after Courtenay went for a mere £30; three versions of the Black Prince mounted and two other foot figures by Courtenay fetched £16; whilst fifty Courtenay knights averaged £3.15.0 each – about half the current price. However, auction sales are peculiar things, as anyone connected with them well knows, and no more can be drawn from some of the extravagant prices realised, but a number of dealers are emerging who are pricing old (and not so old) Britains at proportionate prices. We ourselves recently saw in a large London shop a collection of paint-battered specimens by Cherilea, Timpo and the like, including one or two of the 'Ivanhoe' knights, weaponless, at one pound each!

Collectors of model soldiers vary greatly in their tastes and in their habits. There are some to whom the hobby is a pleasant relaxation, to be pursued in its proper perspective to other interests. To others it is a passion that absorbs any consideration of time or effort. Some are able to express themselves intelligently in music or art or science or sport: others adhere rigidly to a specialisation that excludes all else.

Enthusiasm has at times led to covetousness, and within the last few years there have been one or two regrettable cases of actual theft in bulk. Happily, however, this is an exceptional manifestation of the collecting urge, and the average model-soldier collector is the soul of probity, exhibiting a warmth of enthusiasm which spans oceans and continents, a freemasonry of interest that knows no barrier of country or creed. The number of shops acting as agents for makers has greatly increased in Great Britain and the United States. In France one tends still to see the traditional displays of Mignot, Starlux, and Segom; only occasionally in a high-class book-shop is there a sprinkling of handmade models, whilst the foyers of most hotels display a case or two of Napoleonic troops. But in England, whilst there is still no central depot for model soldiers of all types, one can find Greenwoods in a North London suburb, Staddens galore, together with miscellaneous out of production hollow-casts in Piccadilly; the Sentry Box, Stadden, Ping and Courtenay in Burlington Arcade; Higgins in Yorkshire and Stadden, Greenwood, Hinton, Herald and Elastolin in Regent Street.

We ourselves were in one maker's own display shop recently, and it was difficult to move owing to the press of clients. A middle-aged city type was examining 54mm medieval models; a young man was delivering two dozen mounted Napoleonics which he had painted and mounted for the firm; another was purchasing a hundred war-game figures. The same animated scene will be witnessed at the numerous second-hand shops which have sprung up in various towns.

All this shows a healthy interest, but it is only part of the collecting scene. The results are seen in the houses of the collectors, and it is here that one realises the tremendous range and character of the art of model soldier making. It is with awe and delight that one examines the superb examples by des Fontaines, Stadden, and the like in the collection of Mr Stearns; the Courtenays of Mr Faulkner; the elegance of Brigadier Young's collection; the scope of Henry Harris and Mr Harrington; the steadfast purpose of Mr Richards and Mr Opie.

Other features not seen in shops are only to be found in the houses of collectors. Many a collector not entirely satisfied with a model will alter it, and some incredible results occur. A group in Stearns's collection, for instance, not his own work, but done for him, comprises two mounted early nineteenth-century combatants, the men being constructed from Historex parts, the horses converted from Segom. So skilfully has this been done, that unless one was informed one would assume that the group had been specially made by a skilled artist. Societies, with their stimulating competitions do much to sponsor ingenuity of this kind.

There are collectors all over the world who make their own models – some of them eventually becoming professionals. At society exhibitions and on collectors' shelves one sees these, and some (for example, those of Peter Wilcox) are really remarkable, both for their skill and their ingenuity. Even if the collector neither makes nor converts, he often embellishes his collection by the provision of suitable mini-dioramas, so that a group of related models gains a fresh lustre.

The actual number of models of all kinds to be found in collections in every part of the world is staggering, and we are constantly coming across ones that we have never seen before. One has only to look at the corpus of flats available currently – to say nothing of the millions which were issued prior to the Second World War. It is with a sense of wonderment that one hears of a collection of 80,000 in one house alone – a collection, which, incidentally, caused disaster to the house itself. Or to read of the cache, hurriedly buried underground at the approach of the German army in 1940, and unearthed after the Armistice by American troops. The tracking down of collections themselves is not an easy task. One would imagine that, given the names of the members of the various societies, this would merely be a matter of time. But there are

Many collectors are extremely skilled in making their own models. This British Grenadier of the 13th Foot, 1756, is 9 inches high, and made by Edward Saunders from a variety of materials. He is also interested in the making of 54mm models and 20mm figures for the war-game

many collectors who are not gregarious, and do not belong to a society. One hears of their possessions through a mutual friend. One can therefore only speak of an extremely limited number, and there must be literally thousands of assemblies of all types known only to a small circle of intimates. Jean Nicollier's book, for example, brings to our notice various collections in Switzerland of which we would not otherwise have known. It may be years before you discover that the shy man living in the next road, whom you pass every morning whilst the dog is taking you for a walk, has been a collector for years.

The devotion of some collectors to their hobby is truly remarkable. An example is the Australian collector who informs us: 'I am making a diorama of the Trooping the Colour, six feet by six feet, with Airfix 20mm models. There are 1,300 figures so far painted with eighty mounted conversions of Life Guards, Royal Horse Guards, the Queen, two Dukes and staff, from Airfix United States Cavalry. I started this eight years ago, and am still working on it.' These Australians are certainly tough. They fly thousands of miles with their models to a meeting lasting a few hours. Canadians do the same in the remoter parts of the North American continent.

And the beauty of the whole business is that there is no end to it.

Flats

J. R. Granville and Alastair Bantock,
Birmingham and Northampton, England

Happy is the collector of model soldiers who has a son (or a daughter) to share his interest. Elsewhere we will find examples of co-operation of this kind, but nowhere is it more marked than in the case of the Bantocks: J. R. Granville, the father, and Alastair, the son.

Granville is just on his seventieth year, and served in the Inns of Court Officers' Training Corps, and as a subaltern in the Queen's Own Cameron Highlanders in the First World War. He spent eighteen years as a Police superintendent in Ceylon between the wars, and then twenty-three years as a prison governor in the United Kingdom. Alastair, thirty-seven, served as a lieutenant in the Royal Artillery and the Surrey Yeomanry, RA, and is now a general medical practitioner in Northampton.

The first models Granville possessed, a present from his father some years prior to 1914, were shared with his two brothers. They were the typical Allgeyer productions, 30mm scale; the infantry, semi-flat, the cavalry provided with a spike to fit into the saddle. They comprised several hundreds from European armies, Indian horse, foot and elephant-drawn guns, Chinese archers, Arabs on camels, Japanese, cowboys and Indians.

By 1913, when Wells's *Little Wars* was published, Granville and his brothers were buying Britains' models, which they used for war-games with pellet-firing cannon, and later with dice. The Great War offered greater opportunities for expansion and Granville was able to bring back from France large quantities of Mignot's models. Transfer to Ceylon put a stop to collecting, but on his return to England in 1939 the collection was unearthed, and proved of interest to his young son Alastair and to his daughter. The Second World War then intervened.

In 1947, having joined the British Model Soldier Society, the two Bantocks discovered flats and were immediately attracted by the beauty of the tiny engraved figures, with their sense of movement, ease of storage, and enormous range of period and style, and the way that fine painting can bring them to life. They immediately disposed of their rounds and began to acquire the 30mm flat figures.

Attracted first by the Ancient World, they were faced with a large number of beautifully engraved models of peoples and races of which they knew little, thus stimulating a search for knowledge, resulting in the building of a reference library of books and illustrations. From then onwards it was the same story – a new period, more research, with the result that their joint collection now covers almost every period of history, with the exception of the American Civil War and the Franco-Prussian War.

From the beginning the Bantocks took opposing sides in a particular period. Thus Granville collected Assyrians, Persians, Carthaginians, Gauls and Britons, whilst Alastair concentrated on their opponents: Egyptians, Greeks, Macedonians, Romans, Germans and so on throughout the ages. In the Napoleonic Wars Alastair collected the French and their allies, and Granville the British, Spanish, Portuguese, Russians, Austrian and Prussian armies.

In the course of years they have built up a collection of single flats which have proved of great value to newcomers to the hobby who are ignorant of the range and variety of the medium. Potential collectors who are naturally chary of ordering blind from foreign manufacturers' lists of figures, printed as they are in French or German, can and do make use of the Bantock collection. It will be observed that several times in this book tribute is paid to the enthusiastic help given by them to newcomers to the hobby, and the writer himself can also vouch for their altruistic assistance on numerous occasions.

Their regular visits to Kulmbach have resulted in a world-wide acquaintance with other collectors, leading to reciprocal admiration.

They also specialise in the conversion of flats, an undertaking that would appear to be full of difficulties. For this they use a small electric soldering iron, changing heads, limbs and weapons, thus giving increased variety and creating new figures. They are equally skilled in altering figures in plaster moulds, and by engraving the actual mould, thus eliminating the need for soldering.

Nor do their tiny models remain in the cabinet, but are brought out to take an active part in the war-game.

Sgt Kenneth Charles Bastian, *Longthoughton, England*

Kenneth Bastian is in his middle thirties, and for over fifteen years was a Sergeant Radar Technician in the Royal Air Force (more recently a computer technician) and has been married for several years.

His chief original interest was in flats, which he began to collect when he joined the RAF, mainly to cut down the weight of baggage on postings, for, as we shall have occasion to see, servicemen like to take their collections with them on their enforced travels. One can so easily pack fifty flats into a small box, whereas fifty solids presents quite a problem. Bastian pays tribute to the assistance he received early in his collecting days from fellow collectors Staff-Sergeant Garrett-Taylor, the Bantocks, Archie Cass and Percy Connett. Among 54mm models, he is proud of his Stadden figures, numbering about two hundred and fifty, all painted by himself, and in the majority of cases converted from the original conception into an unusual or not so well-known uniform, for example a British Light Infantryman, 1815, into a *Verden Landwehr* of the same date. He also collects prints and books, and owns original water-colours by Shaffer, Scarf, Fosten, Stachurko, Redlin and Wacker.

His collection of flats falls into two parts, first the war-game armies: second, single figures and sets. The first section so far comprises 30mm flats of four distinct periods. The wars of Frederick the Great are represented by over 600 grenadiers, fusiliers, musketeers, dragoons, cuirassiers, hussars and artillery, based on the composition of the Prussian Army at Rosbach. The Battle of Vienna (1683) has armies of both contestants. Of Austrians, over three hundred and fifty figures (seven regiments of foot, two of dragoons, two of cuirassiers, and one of hussars, together with artillery, five fortress cannon, and five field guns); of Turks, two corps each of janissaries and of infantrymen, one of cavalry, with artillery train, one banner of Polish heavy and one of Polish light cavalry with artillery train, eight field and two siege guns: a total of five hundred flats. (Has he seen the diorama at Vienna?)

Of modern times he has collected a complete *Afrika Korps* (125th Panzer Regiment) of one hundred and twenty figures with four tanks and two self-propelled guns. Finally, loosely based on Homer, the Trojan War: one hundred and thirty models and seven chariots.

The 'single figures and sets' section stands at about 8,000–10,000 models, by Heinrichsen, Müller, Neckel, Ochel, Scholtz, Loy, Lecke, Cortum, Donath, Pohl, Gottstein, Tobinnus, Mittman (20mm) Sollner, Vollrath, Maier, and Winkelmüller and Mohr. He

embraces all periods, from the Greeks to the British Army of today, with the exception of the years 1816 to 1939. The sets include Scholtz's *Retreat from Moscow*, *Choral von Leuthen*, and *Ausfrach von Leuthen*; Neckel's *Ancient Egyptian Embalming* and *Ancient Egyptian Throne Room*; Müller's *Tannenberg*; Gottstein's *Battle of Hastings*; Cortum's *Alexander the Great*; Retter's *Rommel*: Maier's *Austerlitz* and *Burgundian Tourney*; Winkelmüller's *Napoleon at the Pyramids*, and a 10cm Horse Artillery Battery and KGL Artillery by Hinsch.

His interest in flats is such that he spent a fortnight with Aloys Ochel in an attempt to learn a little of the technique of the production of these fascinating little figures. More recently he has become fascinated by 20mm plastics with their possibilities of conversion.

Michael J. Creese, *Oldham, England*

Michael J. Creese is in his early thirties, married and a teacher of physics in a boys' grammar school. When he was about sixteen, after a visit with his father to Hamleys, he started to collect Britains which he repainted. A latent interest in Napoleon's army was nourished by the reading of A. G. McDonnell's *Napoleon and his Marshals*, and he soon turned to Gammage for the figures.

Later, at Manchester University, he met J. R. Granville Bantock, who introduced him to the fascinating world of flats. Creese did not immediately succumb to their charm however, comparing them unfavourably with the larger models, until he realised that for a few shillings it was possible to have whole squadrons of charging cavalry, each in a different position. Bantock suggested that he should get in touch with Rudolf Donath, who would send him lists and specimens, and his collection of flats began to materialise.

His collection falls naturally into two parts, one of 54mm models, the other of flats. The former consists mainly of French Napoleonic specimens, his aim being to cover every regiment in *La Grande Armée*. Adversaries of the French are represented, usually suffering defeat, and there is an occasional departure into other periods, notably the *Wehrmacht* of the 1939–45 era.

The largest portion of the collection is however, devoted to *zinnfiguren*, of which Creese estimates he must have some 5,000, the vast majority of which still

Above Medieval tournament. Flats painted by Michael Creese, forming part of his fine collection

Opposite Richard III and his supporters. Beautifully made models by Frederick Ping

An incident at Waterloo. Flats painted and assembled by Michael Creese

await painting. In 1961 he paid his first visit to Kulmbach, and was amazed and bewildered by the scope of the German flats. He was attracted by the idea of the diorama, but it was obvious that an ordinary dwelling house was too small to contain a model on the Royal United Service Museum scale, so he decided to concentrate on the more manageable size of eighteen inches by three inches and six inches in height, which would take an average of some thirty models. He has so far constructed dioramas representing the *Presentation of Captured Standards after Austerlitz*, *Ambush* (Spanish guerillas) and *Rommel with an 88mm gun*. At present he is painting figures for *Napoleon in Egypt* and *The Burning of the Standards in 1812*. In addition he has made some larger dioramas, including an open one without scenery specially to commemorate the 150th anniversary of Waterloo.

Amongst the flats the Napoleonic campaigns again predominate, but in this case all the combatants (British, French, Prussians, Russians, Würtembergers, Badeners and Spaniards) are represented. Among them is the remarkable *Retreat from Moscow* by Scholtz. As his collection grew it became obvious that he would have to limit the size of a particular regiment, otherwise he would be unable to store the accumulated boxes. An infantry battalion, therefore, consists of four companies, each of six men, one officer and a drummer or other appropriate musician. To these are added the headquarters, consisting of commanding officer, adjutant, standard, sergeant-major, two colour sergeants, and two pioneers, giving a grand total of forty. Similarly, cavalry regiments consist of two troops each of nine men, one officer and trumpet, company trumpet and standard.

He is more catholic in taste than might be supposed, and has representative sections devoted to many periods of history, beginning with the Greeks, Trojans, Macedonians, Romans and Gauls, the Middle Ages (including jousting knights), Frederick the Great and Wolfe, whilst the modern period includes Neckel's

Wehrmacht, together with Retter's tanks and vehicles, and the British and American armies.

He began painting his 54mm models in Reeves' Model Makers' colours, but soon turned to oils for his flats. The first results were extremely disappointing, but improvement came with practice and experience, and the amount of care he devotes to the painting is shown by his managing to complete on an average only four foot or two mounted flats per week. That the time and effort is well spent is shown by his success in exhibitions.

He has a large library, including plates by Rousselot and Knotel and Bucquoy cards, and keeps up to date with continental matters as he is a member not only of the British Society but also of the *Société des Collectioneurs des Figurines Historiques* and the *Deutsche Gesellschaft der Freunde und Sammler Kunsthistorischen Zinnfiguren.*

Dr Paul Martin, *Strasbourg, France*

The *Conservateur de La Musée Historique et la Musée Alsacienne de la Ville de Strasbourg* is in the happy position of being not only an ardent collector of model soldiers who has charge of a remarkable museum collection, but has ample opportunities of meeting fellow collectors from all over the world. His name is well known in the world of the model soldier as the author of a number of outstanding works on the subject and on military uniforms. The first to come to our notice was *Les Petits Soldats de Strasbourg*, published in 1950, an authoritative survey of a previously little known aspect. This was followed in 1960 by *Le Monde Merveilleux des Soldats de Plomb*, written in collaboration with Marcel Vaillant, which dealt with French and German models in lead and tin, whilst *zinnsoldaten* were treated exhaustively in *Der Standhafte zinnsoldat* (1962). His works on uniforms which have delighted collectors are *Le Costume Militaire* and *Der Bunte Rock.* His knowledge of the subject has brought him recognition from the *Société des Collectionneurs des Figurines Historiques*, of which he is an honorary member: he is a member of the committee of *Sabretache*, and Vice-President of the *Commission Internationale d'Histoire Militaire* (French section).

Martin was born in February 1901, married in 1931, and has a daughter and a son, Jean-Hubert, born in France in 1944, a collector in his own right, and Martin's future successor. At a very early age Paul was attracted towards military uniforms, and played with *les petits soldats de Strasbourg*, of which he has left a charming and nostalgic memory, and with the flats of Heinrichsen and Allgeyer, especially those of the armies of Frederick the Great and of Napoleon. Many of these he painted in conjunction with his friend Fritz Th. Schmitt.

In 1930 he began to move actively in the model soldier field, making contact with Paul Armont (Petrocochino) at Paris, Charles Lockwood in London, and Otto Gottstein in Leipzig. After having designed and painted pictures of banners, flags, and standards, costumes and uniforms for collectors and museums he made a series of designs for the *Tourney of the Golden Fleece*, 1450 (see *Le Monde Merveilleux* p. 42) and the *Porte-Bannières à cheval de Bourgoyne*, 1470 (ibid p. 39) which were adapted by Lucien Rousselot and engraved by Frank at Nuremberg, and 'edited' by Armont. He was also responsible to a large extent for inspiring such native artists as Rousselot, Keller and Armont, assisted by the house of Mignot, in starting a native school of creators of flats.

The basis of his collection is some 10,000 flats, both ancient and modern, for the most part painted by himself and his son. The bulk is composed of a very large number of the productions of Heinrichsen and of Allgeyer, dating between 1830 and 1890, in all their diversity, together with unique models by the lesser known makers, and others whose identity cannot be determined.

Needless to say, the collection is also rich in the

Above Spahis, *c* 1805. Cut-out paper figures, mounted on wooden blocks

Above Tiny semi-solid figures by Ammon, of Fürth, *c* 1900. The peg in the seat of the fallen rider may be clearly seen

designs of the Strasbourg school of makers of flats, of whom Bergmann is the best known.

Of course, one can say that the collection of the museum and the collection of its curator are inseparable, for without Martin the famous assembly might never have been achieved. So that in mentioning *Les Petits Soldats de Strasbourg* we link institution and collector together in an indissoluble union, for not only has he his own collection, but it is due to his efforts that the museum has over a thousand sheets of military subjects of all epochs and subjects, and near 200,000 figures already cut out and mounted, from 1790 to the present day.

His collection also includes solids and semi-solids of the Ammon type. Perhaps the most important is the famous polychrome grenadier of unknown origin (shown in the author's *Model Soldiers*, plate 22) that is the fore-runner of the modern master figure.

L'Idée Fixe

Peter David, *Montreal, Canada*

Canada, whilst possessing few model soldier craftsmen, and having widely separated sources of model-supply, has, nevertheless a rapidly growing circle of collectors. Among them is Peter David, of Montreal. His collection is in the main-stream of the model soldier world, comprising as it does specimens of the works of Lucotte, Mignot, McLoughlin, Lineol, Elastolin, Eriksson, Heyde and pirates of Heyde, and the special emphasis is on Heyde. Of these David possesses about seven hundred examples.

He has investigated the limitless possibilities of this prolific German firm as thoroughly as L. W. Richards. has tracked down the manufacturers of Britains, and has provided us with a complete list of the models he possesses, omitting those of which he has only heard or seen in illustrations, such as bivouacs or work parties. He points out, rightly, the great variety of positions of all types; sailors, for example, who were available marching, standing, kneeling and lying, with bugles and waving swords, whilst mounted figures could be holding lances, flags, rifles, swords, shields, spears, or bows, or looking through binoculars.

His collection comprises examples of various countries as follows:

Afghanistan mounted camel-drawn artillery. America (USA): Cavalry (Dress Blues, Blues and Stetson, peaked cap); infantry (New York 7th, Blues and Stetson, peaked cap and steel helmet); Confederate West Poïnt Cadets; Marines 1864–1917; Infantry 1775; Boston Policemen 1890; North American Indians. Arabs: cavalry, and on foot, with turban, burnous, and fez; and mounted on horse and on camel. Assyrians: infantry, cavalry. Austria: infantry and cavalry, 1812 and 1900. Carthaginians: Hannibal and elephants. China: Boxers on foot. Denmark: Guard infantry and cavalry; 1900 and 1930 infantry. France: Infantry and cavalry, 1815, 1870, 1914; Zouaves and Turcos, 1870. Germany: Infantry of Frederick the Great; infantry and guard infantry; Hussars, Uhlans, Garde du Corps, and artillery, 1870,

The German firm of Georg Heyde had the monopoly of the world market before the advent of William Britain. They made models in all sizes, of which these two are examples

A rare Camel Corps model by Georg Heyde

1900, 1914; Army nurses, General Staff mounted and on foot, Colonial Lancers, machine gunners, cyclists and motor-cyclists, 1900, 1914; pontoon train, 1890, Bands of the Garde du Corps, Guard Infantry, and Hussars, 1900; sailors, 1900. Great Britain: Life, Horse and Grenadier Guards, infantry (pith helmet); Indian Army foot and cavalry cyclists; Highlanders and Highlander Band 1900. Boer: infantry, 1900; Cox's Rifles, Camel Corps. Greeks: infantry and cavalry. Italy: Cuirassiers, Bersaglieri, 1900. Medieval: foot and cavalry, with banners. Masai: warriors with shields. Persians: infantry and cavalry (sixteenth century). Romans: infantry and cavalry; Victory March of Coriolanus, consisting of large and small chariots, bears, dogs, captured slaves, trumpeters, banners, horse and foot. Russia: Pavlovski Guard Regiment; Guard and line infantry (shako and fur cap); Cossack cavalry 1900. Spain: Conquistadores (sixteenth century); cavalry, 1900. Turkey: infantry 1900.

The sizes of the models range from less than 45mm to 45, 54, 65, 75 and 85mm, of which the 45mm are most frequently met with and the 85mm the most uncommon. Various types of horses were made: semi-round on base, almost flat, semi-round on base, almost three-dimensional, completely round on base, and free-standing, in all the above sizes, and at the halt, the trot, the gallop, and rearing. (David has investigated the alloys used, and has discovered that the heads are invariably of high tin content, from which the paint rarely flakes. A higher lead content – sometimes pure lead – invariably occurs in the torsos, the paint deteriorating. Swords and rifles are usually tin alloy, and, very rarely, pure lead.) As we ourselves have always observed, the quality of the modelling is superior in the larger figures, the anatomy of the smaller ones being at times quite grotesque.

He has discovered a number of figures which would normally be ascribed to Heyde, but which he feels may now in reality be the work of Haffner. It appears that he has been working on lines parallel to those of L. W. Richards, who has, however, arrived at different conclusions.

David not only collects, but makes his own models, for his own pleasure, in wood or metal. Over a number of years he has made an entire series of British, French, German and Russian armies. It began, as we so often find, when certain figures were unobtainable from commercial makers. The models are usually one of a kind, and unusual in that they are a type of semi-flat, that is, the reverse side is completely unmoulded. The author is proud to possess a really fine Russian cavalryman which David sent him. About 45mm high, the effect is of a completely round figure, and the impression of the icy Russian wind is admirably portrayed.

Further examples by Heyde. The difference in quality between the sizes will be noticed

Herbert Charles Faulkner, *London, England*

It often happens in the model-soldier world that a collector, beginning in a haphazard manner, becomes a specialist in one particular aspect. This is the case of Herbert Charles Faulkner, married, and by profession an accountant and company secretary.

He began collecting in 1958 in a modest way (beginning with Britains) as a relaxation from his professional studies. His lifelong interest has been the medieval period, including as it does the science of heraldry, and he is widely read in every aspect of the Middle Ages. It was inevitable, therefore, that he would be attracted by the models of Courtenay, and they became his main interest. They were, he ruefully admits, too expensive, and, in later years when production slowed down owing to the master's ill health, all too scarce for him to collect all that he would have wished.

However, Britains' 'Knights of Agincourt' – though commercial models, magnificently made – proved a welcome (and cheaper) addition, and he has them re-painted by a skilled craftsman friend.

From Courtenay it was but a short step to Ping, and he is particularly proud of his collection of models by this great man.

His original collection covered most periods and types of model since he tended to purchase anything that was particularly fine, but it is gradually being disposed of and replaced by medieval types.

His Courtenay collection consists of about eighty models, in practically every posture made. The mounted models number twenty-four, of which seventeen are English and Gascons and the remainder French. The English comprise such well-known personages as Henry V (twice), the Black Prince (with John de Sarnesfield, his squire, and Geoffrey Hamlyn, his armour bearer), Thomas, Earl of Warwick, Sir John Beauchamp with the Royal Standard, the Captal de Buch, the Earl of Suffolk, Sir Bartholomew Burghursh, Lord Braose, Sir Hugh Wrottesley, and Casimir, King of Poland. The French are John, King of France, Pierre de Chambley, the Duke of Brittany, Viscount de Beaumont, Sieur de Brosse, Bertrand de Guesclin, and John de Foix.

Of Courtenay's famous pairs, he has four: Sieur de Montagu and his son: Lord Roos and Sieur de Sancergues: Lord Roos and the Earl of Vendôme, and Sir Thomas Kingston and the Sieur de Rosay.

The foot-knights are again divided into two camps, there being twenty-one English and thirty-one French, among them being all the famous names, too numerous to mention, that are found in the pages of Froissart and of Monstrelet, together with a lone female, Isabel, Countess of Lancaster.

The Pings (forty-two in number) are an impressive collection, headed by the magnificent Richard III Court Scene, one of the most outstanding sets ever made. Each figure is a perfect likeness in miniature of one of the characters in the film version so admirably portrayed by a splendid cast that included Sir Lawrence Olivier, Sir Ralph Richardson, Sir John Gielgud, and Sir Alec Clunes. Here are the principal characters: Richard and his Queen, the Duchess of York, Buckingham, Derby, Lovell, Catesby, Ratcliffe, Norfolk, and Brackenbury, with standards and banners. The companion 'Battle' set is equally impressive in conception and execution, forming a violent contrast with the court scene, for whereas the characters in this are in civilian dress, here full armour and rich heraldic surcoats are worn – the King with banner, and squire with standard, Norfolk, Lovell, Catesby, Henry of Richmond, Brandon with banner, Rhys ap Thomas with standard, Stanley, Cheney and a man at arms. Other figures by Ping in Faulkner's collection are Henry V, Bruce, Richard I, and a number of knights, mounted archers and crossbowmen, and a diorama of Senlac. The hall-mark of all his models is quality.

Other medieval models in the collection include a large collection of Ping's conversions of 'Agincourt Knights', all painted with exact armorial bearings; a set by Greenwood and Ball in eighteen pieces of Magna Carta, and a number of Stadden's fine figures: the Black Prince, the Earl of Warwick, Sir Walter Woodland, John de Sarnesfield, Bassett, Bourbon and Percy.

His non-medieval models are now few in number, but choice: a few Staddens (Napoleonic, Frederick the Great, Julius Caesar, and others) a few by Gammage (including Greek warriors and a Dorian dancer) and some twenty-odd Greenwood and Ball 54mm; British, Indian and German armies of 1914 and 1945.

The Late Piero Nelli, *Rome, Italy*

Piero Nelli was born in 1926, and died in 1967. He took an active part in the Italian campaign against the Axis, an experience which stood him in good stead when, in 1953, he directed his first film, *The Lost Patrol*, the odyssey of a small group of the Sardinian Army during the first Italian War of Independence against Austria in 1849. Film making was his occupation, and in November 1964 he presented in London *The Biography of a Plane* during the International Festival of Industrial Film.

Nelli was at pains, however, to point out that he was not a militarist, and had no nostalgia for his military days. He believed that history is created every day by every man in his own life: the history of the past, is, perhaps, in these days, a subject only for the scholar. His model soldiers were to him a dream, a literary phantasy.

The collection was begun by his son Andrea who, out of his saved-up pocket money, eleven years ago presented his father with some of the ubiquitous Britains. Nelli retained his interest in the 54mm-type model, varying it occasionally with those of 45mm size, and he now and then ventured into the realm of the flat. The majority of the models are of the period 1850 to 1918, but sometimes he took in other eras.

Later he became more interested in the products of his native Italy than in those of foreign makers, hence a large section of his collection is a group of the models of the firm of Francesco and Luciano Antonini, the oldest Italian manufacturers of lead solids. The size is nearer 55 than 54mm, the quality – well, not exactly Stadden, nor Britains but, so claimed by Nelli and Antonini, more accurate than the latter. This group of about 280 models, with horse and mountain artillery and wagons, Service Corps and the Red Cross, includes all the units of the Royal Italian Army in 1900, together with King Umberto I and his staff. These models (which we had not previously seen) have a certain charm because of their naïvety, and what is lost in proportion is made up in colour. The riders, following the Continental tradition, are secured to the horses by a very large peg where they sit.

Nelli also collected models by Augusto Pranzetti of Sardinia and Ernesto Chiappa, of Turin. Both these Italians use a mixture of wood and papier-mâché. We illustrate a fine example of Pranzetti's work, a group of Italian Lancers of 1890, in summer battledress, evoking the atmosphere of Giovanni Fattori, the great Italian military painter. Pranzetti, who works only to

Italian Royal Lancers in summer battledress, 1880. Wood and paper models, 54mm in height, made by Pranzetti in 1964

order, has also made for Nelli a number of figures to represent an episode at the Battle of Custozza (1866) comprising gun and team, with mounted officer, infantrymen of the 49th Regiment of the Parma Brigade forming a square, together with the Staff and five charging *chevaux légers* of the 19th Regiment Guard.

Ernesto Chiappa specialises in the old Piedmontese Army, and typical of his work are a soldier of the Penalty Company, 1747; a soldier of the mutilated battalion 1744, and a superannuated officer 1800–14. Nelli's collection includes twenty models by Chiappa, illustrating Italian naval uniform from 1775 to 1918.

Finally, in Nelli's collection will be found a number of representative models from England, the United States, Spain and Russia, but his love was obviously for the products of his native land. The models are now at Padua.

P. Douglas Niekirk, *London, England*

Mr P. Douglas Niekirk has one consuming interest – the British Army. He does not make models, but collects the best, and only the best, in his particular line, which is the Waterloo campaign and 1914 Review Order. (Again fined down to dismounted officers.) His collection is not large, but what is lacking in quantity is amply supplied by quality.

He has models of all the British cavalry regiments and artillery at Waterloo, comprising twenty figures by Stadden; Gammage is making for him the thirty or so infantry officers. The largest unit is his sixty-odd collection of 1914 Review Order, consisting of RHA and cavalry (thirty pieces); Highland and Lowland Regiments, (five of each); Black Watch and Cameronians (in riding overalls – two); Scots Guards, Rifle Regiments (six); Ayr and City of London Yeomanry (two); and TA Queen's Westminsters. All these are by Greenwood and Ball. In addition, Greenwood made, as a special order, a London Scottish Officer in the present No. I Dress. Only a few of these were cast, and Niekirk has three of them in slightly different positions. Another collection consists of half-a-dozen Stadden Scottish Yeomanry of 1914.

All the models are in normal action (the Cameronian, for example, is putting on his gloves), there being none of the sword-waving or theatrical posturing that tends to destroy the realism of the figure by its exaggeration.

Niekirk also has a good collection of Britains' mounted British and Indian cavalry in mint condition, together with a number of sets of the Herald 'Eyes – Right' bands, but naturally his love is for his finer models, and his small collection is an excellent example of collecting specialised pieces along a restricted line.

James Opie, *Liss, England*

James Opie's earliest recollection of miniature soldiers is from his sixth year. Like many other collectors, Britains' products were his standby during his formative years, varied of course, by Hill and the many other lead figures that were obtainable after the Second World War. Gradually, however, he became acquainted with models in plastic, and decided to make them his prime consideration. With the gradual cessation in England of commercial lead figures, the makers began utilising the same moulds for production in plastic, and firms entirely giving up the manufacture of figures sold the moulds to other concerns, with the result that one can have a Cherilea figure in both lead and plastic, and a Johillco model made by Johillco in lead, and a Phoenix plastic figure made from a Johillco mould.

This appeared to Opie to open up a field for original research, and a second factor in his choice was the cheapness of the plastic model. As we have emphasised in other places (and have been taken to task by the purists for so doing) it is not easy for every collector to

The plastic 56mm figures made by Starlux compare favourably with others in this material. The medieval range (which includes delightful civilians) and the Romans are most colourful

afford the master products. It is the same in every branch of collecting. And as far as rarity goes, what could disappear as quickly from our view as some of the products of the minor firms of plastic manufacturers? So there enters the thrill of tracking down and capturing the unidentified, ephemeral model, seen once and never repeated.

Opie is enthusiastic in collecting the lead and the plastic version of the same figure, and attempts to complete sets rather than have the odd individual model. Wherever possible he preserves the original box – another fruitful source of research.

The main body of his collection consists of the leading British makers: Herald, Timpo, Crescent, Cherilea, etc – not a selection, but in most cases the complete range of publication. One striking feature of an assembly of this nature is the disparity between the best and the worst of the models. Opie, however, is not concerned with artistic merit: rather in the different styles and types of production. Hence he has an astonishing collection of models made in Hong Kong and also in Great Britain which are flagrant and atrocious piracies of the better (and the worse) makers. Needless to say, the majority of these are unmarked or masquerade under an artfully chosen *non-de-plume* (or should it be *nom-de-guerre?*). For our part they might well depart 'unwept, unhonoured and unsung', but, even so, they may be allowed a place in the model soldier scene, either as a warning to others, or as unconscious caricatures. Many of these curiosities are sold in polythene bags or large gaudy boxes which are amusing in themselves, and are to be found in the most unexpected places, such as chemists' shops and street markets, adding zest to the search.

Opie is not strong as yet in the makers of world-wide plastics, though this will doubtless come in time. He has, however, representative groups (mainly in this case of samples only) of such makers as Marx Miniatures, Guilbert, JIM, Clairet, Starlux (what magnificent models those Romans and medievals are!) and obscure Italian firms.

Besides plastics, he collects models in aluminium, and has a good selection of the products of Wendal and Quirrinal. A few selected Britains, and a Gammage model or two completes a 30,000-strong collection.

He studied history at Bristol University, which was naturally a great help in his collecting activities. In the large, rambling house in the country where he lives, he has ample room for expansion (an ever-pressing problem with many of us) and collecting is very much in the family, as his mother and father, Amelia and Peter Opie, are collectors of *juvenalia*, and are authors of a number of authoritative works on nursery rhymes. He works for W. H. Smith's central buying group.

Aluminium, a most intractable material, was popular in France and England for some years after the Second World War. Examples such as these, by Wendal of England and Quirrinal of France are now extremely rare

L. W. Richards, *Barking, England*

In most branches of scholarship there emerges an authority on either a person or a subject, one who by original research or perhaps intimate understanding of his chosen concern comes to be regarded as worthy of consultation. Examples readily spring to mind – Einstein on Mozart, Spitta on Bach, Lockwood Marsh on aeronautics, Dendy Marshall on railways, Betjeman on Victoriana, Wheeler on archaeology. To this gallery we add the name of L. W. Richards – and his subject? The productions of the firm of William Britain.

For years he has collected, viewed, dissected, assimilated, compared and recorded every figure ever made by this famous firm, whose models have formed the basis of so many collections. He has published a complete record of his findings in an admirable little book (*Old British Lead Soldiers*, 1969), and his researches, freely offered in altruistic style, have proved invaluable to collectors, as the present writer has reason to know.

One would think this was a sufficient achievement, but in addition Richards has made exhaustive researches into the history and productions of Britains' competitors, such as Hanks, T & B, Reka and Renvoize, a task that becomes more difficult as models gradually disappear from the market. As he is the first to admit, there are, understandably, still a number of models which have defeated even his most determined efforts at identification.

L. W. Richards was born in 1905, and had his first soldiers in 1913, although he took a keen interest before this in a collection owned by an elder brother; and regular Christmas and birthday presents of the familiar glossy red boxes began the collection. He has gone on collecting ever since, not with any regard to military

Every collector knows Britains' hollow-cast productions. They were made in several sizes and grades. The illustration shows a representative group of the 'B' range, 1896–1914

Hollow-casts by John Hill & Co (Johillco) Britains' closest rivals over a number of years

history, but with the all-embracing object of obtaining as many models as possible made in the past and present, a task impossible of achievement, but which has proved a target at which to aim. During his early days he was able to purchase figures by John Hill, Hanks, Reka and others, for a penny or so apiece, but their numbers were few and difficult to find.

By 1919 his collection had reached over four-hundred pieces, of which many were Britains' 'B' and 'W' series, which were sold at half the price of the normal size. Richards now regrets that at that time he was concerned only with the current issues, not realising that Britains in the period 1900–14 had replaced with other models the majority of figures they had introduced in the nineties. His main policy at the time being the collecting of regiments and battalions consisting of seven foot and an officer or four cavalry with an officer, he missed many single figures made by other manufacturers. Occasional variations were the purchase from large London stores of boxes of German Heydes and French Mignots in the days when twelve foot or six cavalry were available at six and eightpence the box.

At this time Richards kept a complete written record of his models. Each regiment had a separate ledger sheet, and each regiment had to have an officer. If one was not included in the box, a conversion was made. The regiments were grouped into brigades which were limited to one hundred for infantry and fifty for cavalry. As the numbers grew, more brigades were formed, and additional generals appointed. Many years later, through lack of time, he gave up listing his models. Instead, he determined to list all the boxes issued by Britains, who gave them running catalogue numbers, and at the same time to see or acquire the actual models listed under those numbers. This has constituted a long, patient and complicated problem, particularly as the models representing some of the regiments were changed three or four times.

The Second World War severely restricted his activities, but as soon as possible he resumed his search. A war kills many a model soldier firm but seems to prove a stimulus to new firms, and whilst the end of the first world conflagration saw the finish of such firms as Renvoize, Russell, Hanks, Turnbull, Abel and Fry (Reka lasting only a few years longer), new firms such as Crescent, Charbens, Kews, Richards and the commercial Courtenay came into being. All these, with the exception of Richards, resumed operations after the Hitler War, and were joined by a number of firms who are well known to us all.

Richards has also delved deep into the history of Georg Heyde and his imitators, and has come to the conclusion that many of the so-called Heydes are in reality by the house of Heinrich of Fürth. One collection that he examined consisted of the band of the Royal Horse Guards, six figures in jockey caps, the heads, riders, saddlecloths, saddles and stirrups all removable in the continental fashion, and in size equivalating to Britains'. These, and a collection of large size Kaffirs, were contained in two boxes, each bearing labels showing medals gained in 1875 and 1882, and the description *Figures Massives, extra fine composition: Zinn – Compositions – Figuren; superfine solid pewter figures*, together with a trade-mark of a knight with a banner and shield on an armoured horse, the letters GH above the horse's head. A visit to the Patent Office revealed that the makers were Johann Conrad and Johann Georg Heinrich trading as *Gebrüder* Heinrich of Fürth, 1895. Richards's collection now stands at about fourteen thousand models, and as he himself says, he gets the greatest pleasure and personal satisfaction from looking at his rows and rows of models, standing as they do on shelves in innumerable cabinets and cupboards, and recalling when and where he obtained such and such a figure. He is an extremely active member of the British Model Soldier Society, of which he has served his term as President, and rare indeed is the meeting or conference at which this large shy person is not present.

F. Glenn Thompson, *Dublin*, *Eire*

It is not unusual for a collector to specialise in one particular period of military history, or one special type of figure, but to concentrate all one's attention on one specific unit, embracing parallels in all countries, must surely be unique.

F. Glenn Thompson does just this, taking Guards Regiments as his theme, but the idea did not spring fully armed, like Jove from the head of Minerva. His collecting began as a child twenty-odd years ago with a set of Britains' charging Highlanders. From then on the collection grew along normal lines until it comprised several hundred Britains and a number of Authenticast models. It was shortly after leaving school that he learned of the existence of the British Model Soldier Society, and discovered the great world of the master craftsman. He determined to reorganise his collection, and to aim at quality. Specialisation in figures of Guards regiments and units of all countries and periods was begun, and has remained.

The size of his assembly is not great, but an amazing amount of research has been necessary for the completion of each model, whilst painting one figure alone (matt water-colour, oils for bearskins, horses, rifles, etc., and enamels for the shiny parts) often takes a week. Many of the figures are conversions of Britains, Gammage, and Eriksson, and the whole collection is

Above An Indian army officer by Gammage provided the basis for these conversions by Glenn Thompson into Guards officers. *Left to right:* Great Britain, Grenadier Guards; Holland, Guard Grenadiers; Denmark, Royal Life Guards

housed in a case with a background model of the Royal Palace of Amalienburg.

There are models of the Sva and Gota Lifeguards of Sweden at various periods, and the Life Dragoons of 1702, mostly by Eriksson, together with his fine casting of Gustav V. Denmark is represented by the Royal Lifeguards and the Garde Hussar Regiment, some of which are conversions from Gammage or Britains. For the Belgian member of the Royal Escort, Thompson employed a Britains Life Guard with a Gammage head. Holland has a Gammage officer of the Guard Gren-

Opposite Lancier, Chevaux-Légers Lanciers, 2e Régiment, G.I., 1811–14. At first sight a typical Berdou model but unique in that it is mounted on a spring

Garde Impériale
2e Chevau-légers lanciers
Lancier 1811-1814

Glen Thompson made two of these Royal Sva Lifeguards by conversion from existing models. *Top left :* Officer (Grenadier Guard) from a Britains' Guards officer in greatcoat, the head from a Gammage Napoleonic; Guardsman, from a Britains' ACW bugler with a Gammage head; *Bottom left :* Officer, *c* 1900 original by Eriksson

adier Regiment, a Britains conversion for a Jaeger of the Guard Regiment of Jaegers, and an officer of Princess Irene's Guard Fusilier Regiment. Other countries represented are Prussia (First Foot Guards and Giant Guards of 1729) Albania (Royal Guard) Greece (Evzones) Vatican City (Authenticast, Swiss Guard) Russia (Pavlovski Foot Guard) the Argentine (Horse Grenadiers) and Great Britain (Grenadier Guards from 1900 to 1955). These are Gammage and converted Britains, and added to these a Yeoman of the Guard, a dismounted Life Guard, and Her Majesty Queen Elizabeth II.

Thompson has a number of Eriksson's beautiful models, both 30 and 40mm, together with a selection of the figures he designed for Authenticast, still the best mass-produced lead models ever made. Completing the collection are contemporary commercial models from many countries, including Denmark, Greece and Portugal, which he collects as examples and therefore leaves as originally painted.

Unlike many collectors, he has other interests, including travel, motoring and dancing. Needless to say, his travels usually lead him to other countries where he is sure to be able to purchase model soldiers.

F. W. Wilson, *Colchester, England*

F. W. Wilson decided early in life his theme for collecting. Not only has he kept to this, but he has brought to it a rigid discipline and scrupulous perfection, organised on military lines.

Descended from a long line of professional soldiers and sailors, the son of a horse gunner who was a great authority on military history and heraldry, he inherited his father's large collection of military badges and books, much of his keenness on military matters, and not a little of his knowledge. Successively a scout, a cub master and scout master, and for over twenty years a Territorial in the Essex Regiment, visiting West Africa, Egypt, the Western Desert, Palestine, Trans-Jordan, Iraq and South Africa, and now an army civil servant, it is not surprising that apart from work on his collection the only other hobby for which he has the leisure or energy is the running of his Battalion Comrades' Association. Nor is army life remote from home, as he has a son who served in the Royal Engineers, a daughter in the WRAC (TA), his brother was twenty-one years in the Fleet Air Arm, and his wife is keenly interested in his hobby.

Wilson began to build warships and aircraft at the age of fourteen, and began collecting in earnest, gathering together a sufficient number of troops to man the ships and carry a very small punitive force. Up to 1939 he had about two thousand Britains and the like, but during the war the collection was packed away.

On demobilisation in 1945, he began again, and as Britains' products were virtually unobtainable, he experimented with plaster moulds, which, after two years or so, produced passable figures, and he now has about one hundred and seventy moulds which have produced seven hundred torsos and innumerable limbs.

He was never satisfied with the Indians produced commercially – they did not appear to conform to any particular 'class' type found in the Indian Army and, whilst serving with the 8th Indian Division in the

Part of F. W. Wilson's collection of naval craft, all of which he made himself

Middle East, he decided that this must be rectified. The 'establishment' was consequently reshaped on paper, and considerably enlarged and drawn up. This happened before Partition, which caused another upheaval, and he has only just completed the division into Indian and Pakistani groups – five hundred and two hundred respectively – of which he himself has produced some two hundred, mostly of kurta-clad Sepoys (Brahmin, Dogra, Jat, Khaimkhann, Mahratta, Pathan, Punjabi, Musulman, Rajput, Rangar, Sikh, and Tamil). The Indian–Pakistani units are represented by the actual class-composition of their respective regiment or corps, for instance, a sub-unit (section) of one Naik and seven Sepoys of the 2nd Battalion, 7th Rajputana Regiment contains Rajputs, Pathans and Punjabi

Wilson with part of his collection

Musulmans, representative of the class-companies of that battalion in 1941.

Wilson's collection as it stands consists of over six thousand pieces of 54mm size, made up of about ninety per cent of Britains (of which nearly half are conversions), the remaining six hundred being made by himself, the whole painted or repainted in oil enamel paint, which he prefers to matt finish, as he finds it handles and wears well, and is easy to clean. (No plastics, it will be noted.)

It would be tedious to list all the many sub-sections of the whole, so we will instead give the six main groups, with a little information about each. The first three groups are organised as a combined fighting force consisting of Headquarters Combined Operations and a Naval Task Force of eighteen vessels, organised as flotillas, and subdivisions, complete with ship's companies (three hundred and fifty) of Royal and Dominion Navies and the Royal Marines; a flight of five aircraft, Royal Marine Commandos and WRNS and QMRNNS. Waterline scale models of naval craft built to self-produced plans range from destroyers, to steam tugs and motor picquet boats, and a *Dido* Class cruiser is in course of production.

Next comes an Army Field Force, HQ (56), Cavalry Brigade (590) and two infantry brigades (2,400), regiment of artillery (4,300), engineers, postal unit, signal squadron (190) supply and transport, field ambulance, ordnance, workshop, provost company, cash office, veterinary section, field security, and WRAC. All these auxiliaries number over a thousand models. Completing this section is a composite Air Squadron of Royal and Dominion Air Forces comprising all units. The squadron possesses twelve aircraft, armoured cars, self-propelled and anti-aircraft guns, rifle sections, service police with dogs, WRAF and PMRAFNS.

In addition, Wilson has assembled a large group of ceremonial and non-field-force troops, comprising a carriage procession of the Royal Family, Royal suite and Prime Minister, bodyguards, with mounted entourage of Sea Lords, members of the Councils, ADCs, equerries, outriders, two divisions of the Sovereign's Escort, with mounted band and trumpets of the Household Cavalry. There are also colour parties of the Navy, Marines, Air Force and all the Dominions. Searchlights, Bofors guns, sound locators and heightfinder are additional features of this section.

The next section is devoted to the foreign contingent of three hundred models, representing forty-eight different states with their national colours, and finally a small historical group of thirty figures, each representing a battle honour of his own regiment from 1742 to 1945, consisting of models by Gammage, Britains and his own castings. Included in the whole collection are over eleven hundred musicians, forming forty-one distinct bands.

Finally, there is a terrific range of guns and vehicles, all made by Wilson himself, including fourteen guns, twenty 'A' vehicles, forty-one 'B' vehicles, one 'C' vehicle (crawler caterpillar fitted with bulldozer), and twenty animal transport vehicles, including two bullock tongas.

Wilson is a perfectionist, attending to the smallest detail. His military bands for instance, are instrumented to Kneller Hall scale, and the transport platoons carry miniature ammunition (boxed and loose), petrol, oils and lubricants in cans, drums and kegs, blankets in bundles of ten, bread and groceries and Indian supplies by the sack, box, or keg.

In Wilson's collection you will find no array of magnificent models, no concentration on prime pieces by the master makers, but a solid, workmanlike assembly of modest pieces, unusual in that it forms a perfect, rounded whole.

David and Yvonne Winter, *England*

If you were to visit the Museum of the Durham Light Infantry and the Durham Arts Centre, you might well see a display of model soldiers labelled 'presented by David and Yvonne Winter'. The two young collectors have a number of things in common. They were both in the Royal Air Force; they were always posted together; they agree in their preference for one period of history; they are equally skilled in painting their models, and they have always been fascinated by things miniature. It was not, however, until late 1959 that either of them started anything constructive in the way of model soldiers.

The first awakening of interest began when David was still at school. and became acquainted with the masterpieces in Hummel's window and, years later, it was there that their collecting really began. Not, however, by the purchase of a Stadden or a Ping, but by David's conviction that he could paint models to a comparable standard. The purchase of a Herald American Civil War officer followed and the result of the repainting exceeded expectations.

The next few months were spent in repainting the models they already possessed, and after careful observation Yvonne decided to try her hand, and the results were such that they thereafter worked as a team.

They cannot give any particular reason for interest in the American Civil War, which has remained their favourite field for collecting, but there is a suggestion in the back of their minds that the film *Gone with the Wind* may have been at least partly responsible. Married in 1960, they joined the British Model Soldier Society, and concentrated on model figures to the exclusion of all other activities. Their interest in the Civil War led to an invitation to display their models at a Liverpool Museum exhibition entitled *Merseyside and the Civil War.*

A posting to Cyprus created problems. It was decided to take their collection with them, but the amount of painting they were able to do was somewhat reduced, owing to the climate during the summer. But they still continued their activities, and an intensive campaign produced a number of contacts with commercial and private makers, resulting in the acquisition of a new flood of figures. Their original aim was to build up a collection of single figures to represent all the uniforms of the chosen war. They have so far gathered together about one hundred and seventy-five models, but they have information about uniforms in excess of this. Finding that some figures were unobtainable, they took to commissioning special unpainted models, hence the presence in their collection of works by Saunders, Greer and Ping.

Recent concentration has been on small groups

This 54mm model of Robert E. Lee was made by Norman Cooke

rather than individual figures, and, owing to the conditions of service life prohibiting dioramas, they have adopted the American way of an unenclosed stand of a small group, complete with accessories they themselves make. Despite temptations they have remained remarkably faithful to the 54mm American Civil War figure, although at one time they had ideas about a 'single figure by every maker' collection.

The Winters came to see us shortly after their return from Cyprus, bringing their collection with them. The models were still in the boxes in which they had travelled through Europe, and we derived as much pleasure from watching their reactions as one lid after another was removed as they did in seeing once more the models over which they had spent so many hours of painstaking labour. The expected makers (Hinton, Gammage, Imrie, Murray, Stadden, Scruby and Bussler) were much in evidence, together with models by Jackson, Green, Custer 'Little Round Top', Scheid, Trucraft, Fabre, K-S Miniatures, and Cox. Commissioned models include a group of fifteen by Saunders, seven by Greer, one by Cooke, and a lone Ping.

Yvonne left the RAF when her husband was sent to the remotest part of the North. Subsequently he was posted to Brunssum and transport of the six different artillery teams and the other miscellaneous dioramas proved too great a headache for them. Sadly, reluctantly, they disposed of the specialist collection which they had so enthusiastically assembled, but each model is still in good and appreciative hands.

Lyle Thoburn, *Gates Mills, Ohio, USA*

Lyle Thoburn was born in 1906 in Erie, Pa, and dates his interest in military matters from during the Great War, when in Montclair, NJ, he saw many United States and foreign uniforms. He began collecting in the days when such a hobby was regarded as a peculiarity, and is gratified to see that the interest is now so widespread. He began with paper soldiers, soon, however, changing to lead – the inevitable Mignots and Britains. Part of his present collection consists of these and many other commercial makers, which, together with his more important models, consists of about fifteen thousand items.

The other section comprises master models by Imrie, Baldet, Berdou, Courtenay and Stadden. His service during the wars explains his main interest. He served eight years in Troop A, 107th Cavalry, Ohio National

Guard (also known as the Black Horse Troop, the First City Troop of Cleveland, and the First Cleveland Cavalry at various periods) ending as first lieutenant. In the Second World War he saw action in the South Pacific, the Philippines, Okinawa and Japan with the Fifth Air Force (Service Command) 1942–6, and retired as lieutenant-colonel. A graduate of Princeton University, he has been in private business all his life.

The cavalry years influenced his collecting leanings, so that for a number of years he has concentrated on the history of cavalry, that of the Napoleonic Army and, in particular, that of the United States, with emphasis on his own unit. He has found that the best way to achieve his purpose is to commission the best makers, and to

An unusual collaboration between a collector and two makers. Lyle Thoburn did the research and the designs, and commissioned the models from Berdou and Imrie-Risley. Berdou made the horses and the complete model *bottom right* of the Trooper, Troop A, First Regiment Ohio Volunteer Company, Spanish-American War, 1898. The other riders were made by Imrie *top* Troop A 107th Cavalry, Ohio National Guard, 1929; *bottom left* Major, 1st Squadron, Ohio Cavalry, Mexican Border Service, 1916

this end he does the research and indicates the design, passes this to Knotel, who makes water-colour drawings, and in turn passes them on to the selected modeller. In this way he has built up an enviable assembly of mounted and dismounted models. Many of these have been made for him by Stadden, Baldet, Imrie and Berdou, whilst the last has been influenced even to make figures of United States cavalrymen, a thing he at first said he would never do!

Thoburn works to a set plan – five figures of each unit consisting of trooper, officer carrying standard, trumpeter, drummer, and general officer. In a number of cases the horses have been made by Berdou, and the riders by Imrie. The solution of the support of the hooves of the moving horses as used by Berdou in some of these models must be unique. Quite charming and obviously to Berdou's taste are his models of the Ohio National Guard, 1909, and the First City Troop, Cleveland, Ohio, 1877–81, with the strong French costume influence.

Stadden again, is represented by commissioned work, this time a number of models depicting the Battle of Princeton, a battleground over which Thoburn walked as a student, and from Harry G. Barker, Jnr, comes a

Berdou, Imrie-Risley, and Thoburn again. Units of Troop A, 107th Cavalry, Ohio National Guard, 1937–40

The characteristic Berdou flowing support is shown in this Trooper, 1st City Troop, Cleveland, Ohio, 1877

remarkable Troop A, 107th Cavalry Drill team, Hussar Dress uniforms of 1936.

Marcel Baldet has made Thoburn a number of dismounted figures, all of his special unit, and he has supplemented these with some that he has purchased from other collectors. Amongst others acquired in the same way are a few early Berdous, and a number of equestrian models by B. Vanot of Paris, a student of Lelièpvre. These are well up to the standard set by his better known compatriots.

Although he himself does not say so, his special pride and joy must be his Berdou collection, eighty-five or so, the majority specially made for him by the master. In the French figures he has concentrated on trying to produce four or five models typical of one cavalry regiment, primarily of the Imperial Guard, First Empire. Usually there are a trooper, a bugler, an officer carrying the standard, a kettledrummer (if applicable to the regiment) and in some cases a general officer closely connected with the regiment. All the figures are mounted, the horses standing, walking, trotting or cantering. Napoleon, naturally, is represented, at the entry into Berlin in 1806, together with Marshals Ney, Murat, and Poniatowski, and Generals Lepic, Beauharnais, Comte d'Ornand, Colbert, Pully, and Nansouty and Roustan.

The United States models, numbering nineteen, range from a trooper, Light Horse of the City of Philadelphia, 1775, through a Colonel Second Light Dragoons, 1812, to a First Lieutenant, Troop A, 107th Cavalry, 1940. In addition to these there are a number of horses only. In some of his models in more active motion Berdou has introduced as a support for the hooves a most remarkable metal curve, almost like a wave. No other maker has used this idea and, amazingly, it does not appear out of place, although highly artificial. One model, indeed, goes so far as to have a central stand of flexible metal which allows horse and rider to vibrate. With anyone other than Berdou the result would have been disastrous.

Lyle Thoburn commissioned these splendid Berdou models, he himself supplying the historical information necessary for accuracy. *Top:* Bugler, 1st City Troop A, Ohio National Guard, 1887; *Centre:* Trooper, 1st City Troop, Cleveland, Ohio, 1881; *Bottom:* Stable Sergeant, Troop A, Ohio National Guard, 1909

Means to an End

An Austrian Group

There is a small group of Austrian enthusiasts who use their collections expressly for the creation of vast dioramas, and they and their collections are so constituted that they are interlinked one with the other. Their work will be recognised by visitors to various Austrian museums, where some examples of their dioramas have been on show from time to time.

One of the group is Ludwig Gartner, a pharmacist and chemist born in Vienna in 1900. As a boy he busied himself with toy soldiers, and was encouraged by an elder brother who on every possible occasion presented him with little dioramas of flats, with houses and trees made by himself.

During the First World War there was a huge exhibition of flats, mostly by Heinrichsen, in Vienna, arranged by Hofrat Dr Werner, who possessed over thirty thousand models. Young Gartner saw this, and also the first big dioramas in 1924 which figured the 'modern' manufacturers of Ochel and Scheibert. Gartner began collecting seriously between 1930 and 1933, when he was able to see the first of the giant dioramas constructed by Colonel Willy Teuber-Weckersdorff, the 'father of the Austrian Collectors'. In this *Battle of Aspern*, 1809, thirty thousand models were used in an area of forty-eight square metres, whilst in the diorama of Prince Eugen crossing the Danube in 1717 a proportionate number were used.

Gartner began to emulate these creations, and in 1939 began a siege of Vienna, three metres square. A year later he emerged in public as a collector and dioramist with the *Battle of Hoechsterr*, 1704, which was shown at Niessner's shop in Vienna. This exhibition had important consequences for Gartner, as it was here that he met a fellow enthusiast, Roger de Riedmatten, with whom he was henceforth to collaborate. They began work immediately, and in Gartner's flat they constructed *The Battle of Peterwardein.*

The Second World War interrupted their work, and it was not until 1954 that they could get together again. Meanwhile Gartner had been forging ahead on his own, and in 1954 he showed *The Battle of Zenta*. The two collectors joined forces again with *Wagram*, five thousand models, sixteen square metres. The model was transferred to Wagram, then to the Military Academy at Weiner Neustadt, then dismantled, the flats returning to their owners for further use. Meanwhile, Gartner and de Riedmatten agreed on a plan of campaign for a series of dioramas depicting the history of tactics. Each would collect certain specified periods, so that each collection was complete in itself, and they would then fit these sections together when required. So far only parts of this vast scheme have been realised.

In 1959 an exhibition in honour of the highly popular Archduke Johann was planned to be held in Vienna. In charge of this was the well-known international figure Dr Erich Kröner-Grimm, known for his enthusiasm for anything in the model-soldier line. The three collectors got together, and decided to build for the exhibition a diorama of the Battle of Sacile, 1809, the Archduke Johann's greatest military success. This sixteen-square-metre model, comprising five thousand flats, was transferred after the exhibition to the Military Academy.

In the following year the Austrian Collectors' Society held an exhibition in Vienna, and a new version of Zenta, created by Gartner and de Riedmatten, received

Battle on the White Hill, near Prague, 1620. Five thousand flats, size 20 and 30mm, were used in this diorama composed by Kröner, Gartner, and Diener. A portion only is shown, that of the action in the centre

such acclamation that museums and institutions began to take an interest in dioramas. A year later a new version of Prince Eugen's crossing in 1717 was made by Gartner and Kröner. Now in the Donau Museum, it occupies twenty-four square metres, and incorporates four thousand five hundred flats and approximately one hundred boats.

At the *Heeresmuseum* there is a terrific representation of the siege of Vienna by the Turks in 1658. It was constructed by the full team of three, assisted by Frau Gartner, took two years to construct and employs three thousand flats and one hundred cannon, and the saps and trenches made by the Turks are admirably shown. In 1964 Gartner, Kröner and Dr Erich Diener co-operated in the *Battle near Prague*, 1620, using five thousand models in an area of sixteen square metres. In this diorama the terrain and placing of the figures was directed by Kröner, whilst Gartner was in charge of the right wing of the Imperialists. Gartner and Kröner also co-operated in a *Battle of Leipzig*, 1813, which was exhibited in *One Hundred and Fifty Years Vienna Congress* in Wiener Hofburg.

All the men concerned in these gigantic enterprises are still in the prime of life, and there seems to be no limit to what they may achieve. What amazes us is how the time is found to embark on these constructions, let alone carry them through to their conclusion. From our own knowledge of Dr Kröner's activities, let alone of the others, of whom we cannot speak personally, it seems little short of a miracle.

Dr Kröner was born in Vienna ten years later than Gartner, and his boyhood also was blessed with toy soldiers, chiefly the little wooden figures, carriages and such like, produced in the Sudetenland. His contact with more conventional models was at the age of six, when he, like Krauhs, was given a number of Wollner figures, which he used, together with self-made armoured cars, ships, forts and the like in a destructive war-game.

Entering the sixth form at the grammar school made such pursuits untimely and his interest switched to the historical novels of Karl May, Verne, Dumas and Dickens. Study for a profession left no time for model soldiers. Then, in 1938, while on a visit to Berlin, Kröner chanced upon a shop featuring Ochel flats, and, after long hesitation, he purchased a model of Francis I. This soon led to other purchases which he began to paint. He regrets that at this time he was not able to contact either the collectors in Berlin or the renowned Scholtz.

Seven years' army service and absence from Vienna followed, but on his return he was able to get in touch with the Wiener Sammlerkunde, the precursors of '1683', and more important, a meeting followed with the aged K. A. Wilke, the great historical painter. A lasting friendship developed, resulting in the transfer to Kröner of the interest that the old man had in the Thirty Years' War. The collecting of models of this period offered several practical advantages: the number of combatants was such that dioramas of normal proportion could be attempted; uniforms as such were non-existent, so that, provided the feathers of hats were painted red, blue, green, or white, and the standards, officers, and drummers distinguishable, each model could be made to serve as either Imperial, Swede or Frenchman. Kröner was able to build up his collection with many ordinary foot and mounted figures and a huge collection of contemporary standards, drummers, pipes and officers, as a guide to the different regiments of the various combatants. This collection was augmented by the better part of Wilke's after his death, and by the purchase of part of the Slonecky collection.

Kröner is proud to recall that Wilke considered that he and Slonecky were the best pupils he had ever had,

A chess-set composed of Eriksson's models

both of them carrying on Wilke's tradition of effective painting of light and shade to give the flats the proper effect when used in dioramas.

Some years later Kröner took an executive post in the *Gesellschaft 1683*, and began to edit *Sammlernachrichten*, fostering international interchange with other countries to such a degree that today half the members are from outside Austria. He is now Managing President of the society. His list of the types of the Thirty Years' War is a great help to all who specialise in that period, and anyone who is fortunate enough to receive regularly the large orange envelope containing *1683* and who is able to read German will vouch for the excellence of the production. Dr Kröner is an international figure who has done much for the co-operation of collectors all over Europe, and we ourselves had the privilege a few years ago of first introducing him to the British Model Soldier Society where he made a typically witty speech, and later entertained him in our own home, where he endeared himself to our wife and daughter by his courteous manners, and evident enjoyment of what to him must have appeared a very simple meal.

Major H. E. D. Harris, *Frimley Green, England*

Our first meeting with Henry Harris was through his connection with Malleable Mouldings and his consequent knowledge of the intricacies of the history of Comet, Authenticast, Wennberg and Winkler. This he placed freely at our disposal, and some years later we were able to reciprocate by helping him with his own book *Model Soldiers*. He himself is vastly amused at being chosen as the sole representative of Great Britain in Baldet's *Soldats et Figurines de Plomb* where a group of Malleable Mouldings bears the caption *ensemble d'un amateur anglais*.

Harris, indeed, sometimes takes an amused view of model soldiers and model soldier collectors. One discovers this in the illustrations to his book – the cat in the Aldershot Barracks scene (p. 95) and the characters in *The Officer Goes Home* (p. 102) for example and, resulting from his profound knowledge, he injects sly humour into many of his groupings. Conversation with him is stimulating, and every now and then one learns of some minute, hitherto unknown detail of dress or equipment or armament that comes from personal knowledge or observation. His humour bubbles over, and every now and then comes a sly but kindly dig at the 'lords of the Society', as he calls the hierarchy of collecting circles, in many of whom he finds a pomposity which leaves itself open to a little gentle prodding. Mankind, and collectors in particular, he finds, as did Walter de la Mare, 'too mortal solemn and shallow'. He can shoot at his target, but never in spite – his knowledge of humanity and his tolerant and far-reaching outlook remove any suggestion of bitterness or malice from his criticism. But he does not suffer fools gladly.

Although he modestly calls himself a student, he is in fact a most knowledgeable writer and lecturer on military history and traditions. His collection of some four or five thousand models has been deliberately built up over the last twenty years to act as a three-dimensional visual medium for historical pursuits. It is divided into a number of sections: the main collection is British and Indian Army, 1890–1916, with certain minor overlappings to include particular items, for example Royal Coronation figures, 1953, and a naval section; then there are Irish soldiers, Irish regiments in the British Army, the Irish Brigade in France (the 'Wild Geese'), Irish soldiers in the United States Forces, the modern Irish Army (that is, post-1922), the Republic of Ireland unit with the United Nations; Papal figures consisting of Popes of the twentieth century, Swiss and Palatine Guards, Papal gendarmeri, colours, bands, etc; and the unusual and authentic, amongst them Sedentary Gunners of Lille, Mounted Band of the Mexican Spy Company, Belgian dog-

Major Henry Harris, well-known collector and lecturer on army matters, with part of his large collection

drawn machine-guns, Evzones, Irish Papal Zouaves, Indian State troops.

The nucleus of the collection was three to four hundred toy soldiers which had survived his boyhood. His father was a regular soldier, and on leave from France in 1916 he brought him a selection of toy soldiers, followed at regular intervals by the familiar Britains' red boxes. These were all installed in the Harris's quarters in Beaumont Barracks at Aldershot.

On occasional visits to London young Harris was struck by seeing that his toy soldiers were a very different thing from the high quality models just appearing, and those in the Royal United Service Institution museum another thing again. Any thought of collecting, however, was dispelled by the outbreak of the Second World War and Harris was now engaged with reality.

While waiting for D-Day his unit was detailed to take part in a 'Salute the Soldier' function, and he was appointed as liaison officer to a local authority. After a lot of brain-racking, Harris diffidently suggested his models. The idea was immediately seized upon, and the long-deposited collection hauled out of storage. He recollects its sorry appearance – but the exhibition was a success.

After the war Major Harris turned to the study of military history as a serious interest, and it occurred to him that model soldiers would be a good medium for illustrations. He looked over what he called his 'rabble in arms' very critically with a view to their forming a nucleus for a serious collection. He joined the British society, where he observed the fine models made by the specialists and the private makers (the latter, then as now, offering their conceptions for sale at the meetings). He was lured into Hummels and Hamleys with disastrous results to his pocket. After a couple of years of this type of buying he had a fine but haphazard collection, lacking in homogeneity. The search for a central theme led him to consult the makers, specifying regiment, period, dress, rank and to some extent the attitude and position of the figure required. But apart from the heavy financial outlay necessary, he soon realised that a collection based on his own ideas would have to be created mainly by his own efforts.

At this time he was considering a complete 'Order of Battle', that is a complete list of the regimental cadres, HQ, staffs, corps and services, types and postures of the officers and men, vehicles, equipment and accessories. He worked out the plan with a kindred spirit, Roy Dilley, and found that the total would be some fifty-five hundred pieces. A rough estimate of cost made him realise that the scheme could only be achieved by his becoming a 'converter' on a big scale.

Down at Deal, Fred Winkler, an erratic genius in advance of his time, evolved a method of casting short runs of lead figures in rubber moulds from masters made by Holger Eriksson. These required centrifugal casting, and he used an old hand-operated gramophone. Harris served a short apprenticeship with him by winding up the machine and regulating the speed. Indeed, this short experience gave him thoughts of casting for himself, but he abandoned this in favour of converting.

His methods have changed from the early gropings of inexperience to the practical skill of the expert, and the varieties he achieves are quite remarkable. Each of twenty or so mounted khaki figures in every group are, for example, so altered from their originals, that the position of every head varies slightly, so does the posture of the rider, one slewing round to speak to his neighbour, one leaning forward, one adjusting his stirrup leathers and so on. Major Harris has made a profound study of horses, and is scrupulous in his use of the correct type of mount used by the various arms of the services. He achieves this by removing a rider from a steed that is inappropriate and substituting a more suitable rider cut from another horse.

Most of the commercial makes are used, particularly those of Britains, Timpo, Cherilea and Charbens. Many are bulk purchased, unpainted castings direct from the makers, so that he always has a large stock of torsos, heads, legs, weapons, arms, gun parts and spare wheels. He also makes extensive use of the best type of plastic model, especially those made by Herald, Starlux, Malleable Mouldings, and Mokarex.

His conversion programme has been given a fillip by the many exhibitions he has mounted for various purposes, including such events as the Edinburgh Festival Tattoo of 1961, and annually at Aldershot.

Part of Major Harris's collection on public display. He makes the architectural models himself

With the help of his wife and several assistants, he stages an imposing display, aided by the fine architectural backgrounds he himself constructs. These form a dual purpose – display and storage, for the lid of the model of Horse Guards Parade, for example, lifts off and provides space for the storage of the boxes of models inside. Careful packing and scrupulous accuracy of storage are essential for the saving of time, and his storage charts reminded us of the purser's cargo allotments that our brother used to bring home when on leave from the merchant service, before the war.

He has two permanent displays, one at the National Army Museum, the other at the Irish Army Military College at the Curragh, County Kildare, each of which is changed every year or so. The models are also used to illustrate his lectures. Some of the unusual types that he delights to include in his exhibitions are cavalrymen dismounted, infantry on mounted duties, regimental signal sections, escort troops to generals commanding, bagpipe band to the Royal Navy, regimental bands with 'jingling johnny' and glockenspiel, mobile pigeon loft (horse), of the Great War, and an early aeroplane being transported by a horse-drawn wagon. Furthermore, he specialises in vehicles of all kinds, and many beautiful models of his own construction are displayed in cabinets in his house. He is a stickler for accuracy, and has an impressive collection of documentation.

Apart from the set-scheme and exhibition figures, Harris has a collection of 'cabinet' models, which include many by Gammage (outstanding are the Coronation figures) a number of the rare Treforest Mouldings and examples of the Belgian firm MIM, naturally a number of Malleable Mouldings and Authenticast, original Erikssons and a few early Staddens (he finds the more recent ones out of scale with the rest of his collection). An interesting recent purchase is a set of over three hundred plastic models made for the Belgian coffee firm Café Storme, which illustrate Belgian history from the cave-man to the present day.

He has worked out an unusual and satisfactory method of making small dioramas. He uses old television cabinets which are emptied of their electronic apparatus. We were particularly impressed by the *Prayer before Battle*, the satirical *Russian Steamroller*, the group of French officers (1914–18) and the *Army Forge*.

Harris feels that many collectors live in a vacuum of their own creating, and believes in a more liberal approach, with the interchange of ideas and of models. He himself built up a circle of friends who willingly assist whichever of their fellows needs help in the painting or the conversion of models. This, he feels, is the true essence of collecting.

Major F. B. Thornborough, *Bexley, Australia*

An amusing situation arises when a collector of model soldiers admits that their acquisition is a means to an end. That, however, is the confession of Major Thornborough, and his admission proves (if proof were needed) how diverse the model soldier world is.

Frank Braithwaite Thornborough was born in 1914, and is married with two sons, one born in 1947, the other in 1949. By profession he is Commonwealth Stock Control Manager of Woolworths Ltd, Australia. He saw pre-war service as a lieutenant with the First Medium Brigade, Royal Australian Artillery, and in 1940 joined the Australian Imperial Forces. Successively Troop Commander, Intelligence Officer RA, Staff Captain RA and DAAG, he saw service in the Middle East, Ceylon, New Guinea and New Britain. After the war he was Battery Commander, 23rd Heavy Regiment RAA. He is a member of the Society for Army Historical Research, the Guild of Military Antiquarians, the Military Historical Society of Australia and the British Model Soldier Society, and it is the first three that give the clue to his interest – military history and, in particular, the study of military uniform, and he uses the model soldier to record his researches.

He has a collection of more than five hundred 54mm models of which over four hundred are by Stadden, the remainder being made up of Hinton, Gammage, Imrie and Almiral. In addition, he has over four hundred Stadden 30mm models, and he does all his own painting, preferring enamels.

He does not restrict his researches to any one country or period, but the history of the British army is his main interest, and the Royal Artillery in particular. The idea of using model soldiers as part of his study began when he started retouching some Britains for his sons. From this he hit on the idea of trying to interest them in his hobby by enlisting their help in converting their toy soldiers into a representation of each of the regiments of the British army in pre-1914 full dress. They proved so interested that eventually they ended up with not only a figure of each regiment in this dress, but also a figure of each regiment in 1954.

All these figures have long been disposed of to other

Opposite Mounted troops of the Indian Army, 1910–22, made by Winkler, in the collection of Major Harris

collectors, but from this humble beginning evolved the idea of using specialist figures to record the study of the growth of uniform design. Both John and Peter are skilled model painters and help considerably in the building of the collection, and Mrs Thornborough acts as art director, and is as proud as any of them at what has been achieved.

The Stadden models offer him the greatest scope for his studies, and it is only where no Stadden figure is available that he fills the gap with Gammage or Hinton. Imrie and Almiral give him additional interest in uniforms of the United States and Spain, as does Wootten; he has several of the latter's historic Australian characters.

He groups his figures into small tableaux, which he finds adds interest to the collection (it also conserves space). Variety is brought to the display by the interspersion of action groups formed by 30mm Stadden and Hinton models.

His collection begins with a late Paleolithic hunter and his mate (Gammage) and ends at 1953 with a group of nineteen Staddens and Britains. Egypt is represented by sixteen Gammage models including the magnificent chariot, Greece by Stadden and Hinton, Assyria by Hinton, Rome (including portrait models of Julius Caesar, Hadrian and Marcus Aurelius) by Gammage, Hinton and Stadden. A small medieval group consists of Gammage, Stadden, Hinton (30mm) Herald and Elastolin (it is surprising that Courtenay and Ping, who have no rivals in this field, are omitted). A single Spanish Conquistador is by Almiral, the English Civil War by Stadden, Gammage and 30mm Hintons. Stadden, Imrie and Hinton provide troops for the Marlborough campaigns, the Seven Years' War (including Prussians, and Canadians with an Indian guide), Austria, 1762; France, 1770–5, and the American War of Independence by Stadden (54 and 30mm) and Gammage. The American Revolution section includes British, Hessian and Loyalist troops.

The Napoleonic Wars have provided Thornborough with plenty of scope, and this period forms a large portion of his collection, overwhelmingly dominated by Stadden models in two sizes. Here the French are represented as strongly as the British.

Stadden First World War models in the process of being painted by Major Thornborough

Major Thornborough arranges many of his models as mini-dioramas. The photograph shows a portion of his large collection

New Worlds to Conquer

Peter Blum, *New York*

Peter J. Blum has one of the most outstanding collections in the United States. In 1951, whilst in the United States Air Force serving with the Office of the Secretary of Defense making film documentaries, he began collecting Greenwood and Ball and Stadden models, and at the same time commissioning figures from Imrie. At first he specialised in the Napoleonic wars and any piece that was outstanding in any period. Now, however, he has turned exclusively to the American War of Independence.

His collection in terms of bulk is small, some three hundred figures in all. But each model is of the finest possible quality, and made to order by the artist most suitable for the job. Much of the information necessary

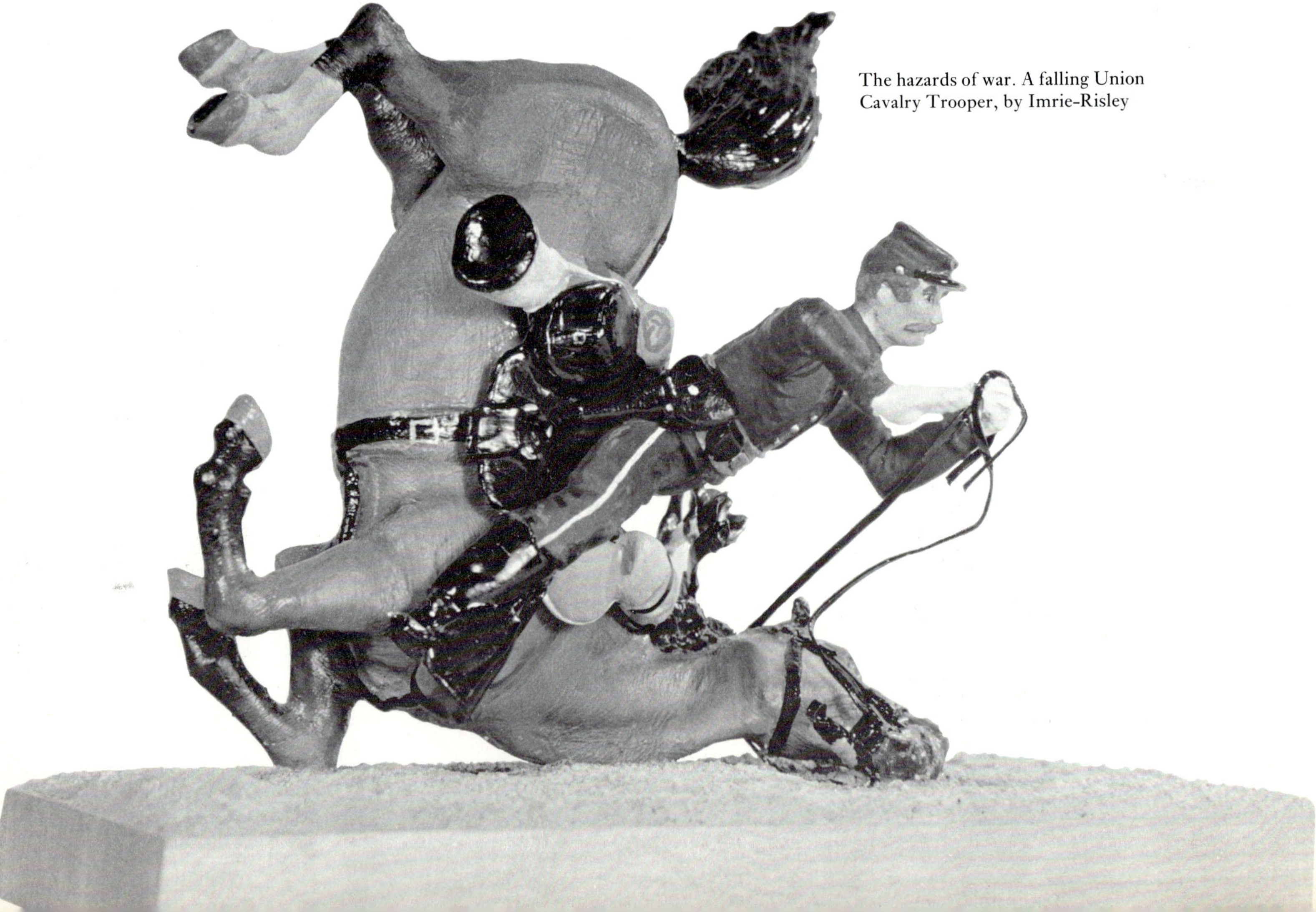

The hazards of war. A falling Union Cavalry Trooper, by Imrie-Risley

for the authenticity of the model is supplied by Blum himself. He also collects military weapons and equipment, and attempts to provide examples of the arms used during the Revolutionary War to accompany the figures. He considers his collection of books the most important of the interests he has in military history, and to him the actual models are the culmination of military research.

Much of his time away from the CBS Newsfilm work is spent in correspondence with collectors and historians all over the world – in fact he enjoys this even more than the actual acquisition of models. As is well known, he wrote the text of *Military Miniatures*, that delightful little pocket-book, and also the introduction to the American edition of Baldet's *Soldats et Figurines de Plomb*, and is a frequent contributor to model soldier journals. His latest venture and, one imagines, a culminating point in his career, is the setting-up of a shop handling all types of militia.

How is it possible to describe a collection with such a wealth of material? Few of us are fortunate enough to possess models by such eminent makers as des Fontaines, Baldet, Lelièpvre. Blum has them not in single specimens, but in numbers. His des Fontaines, for instance, are a collector's dream – the purposeful Duguay-Trouin and Montcalm, the dignified, splendid Washington and Lafayette, the fine officer of the Regiment Agenois. His Staddens also, are lovely specimens of their kind, including the near perfect models of Prince Eugene de Beauharnais and Baron Colbert, together with Napoleon, Wellington and their staffs, Scottish troops and Scottish and French standards.

He is fortunate in possessing the four-inch-high Champlain and a number of other models of the same size by Imrie. In standard size he has the magnificent American Revolution gun-team and a number of American Civil War models by the same maker.

Whatever the period, and whoever the maker, one can be assured that the resultant model is of the finest, and Peter Blum must indeed be proud of his collection. One can illustrate only a few of his models, but photographs of others are available in other publications, and it may be that one day he may delight the model-soldier world by publishing a review of his own collection.

Duguay-Trouin, a 54mm solid lead model full of character by des Fontaines

Mr John Hanington, *Wimbledon, England*

One of the most recent entrants into the world of model soldier collecting, and one of the most enthusiastic and all-embracing in his interests is John Hanington, a large, genial, kind-hearted man. He is by profession a surgeon and obstetrician, leading, as one may suppose, a fairly hectic life, with a proportion of night work and long hours. The calm necessary for his work is reflected in his bearing and in the quiet enjoyment with which he moves from case to case of soldiers, deriving equal enjoyment from a single, simple commonplace model and from a rare piece, and sharing that pleasure with others. His wife (who is a doctor) and his two sons take an equal interest in the collection (and in the comfort of their guests).

He has been collecting for the last twelve years or so, and began, it is gratifying to us to know, through reading our *Model Soldiers*, as a relaxation from his normal activities. It opened, he says, a new world. Previously he had collected water-colour drawings, but found the market prices increasing beyond his means. The model soldier provided an outlet for his collecting interests at a reasonable outlay, and apparently unlimited horizons. His collection is a constant joy to him, and he gets from it all that he could wish for in the way of a hobby. He, like Cornelius Frazer, acknowledges the pleasure he has derived from contact with the Scottish Model Soldier Group, under Commander Hamilton, and is a member of the British and several foreign societies.

He estimates that he has approximately twenty-eight thousand models, all collected during the last few years. He is omnivorous, and every possible aspect is represented. He is busily engaged in mounting his models on bases, titled on the front: a terrific but rewarding task with which he is always behind. He has tried his hand at painting and converting, and obtains great pleasure in making small dioramas, but sensibly refuses to repaint old models.

Most of all he treasures the large sets issued by the 'hard core' of the model soldier trade, Heyde and Mignot. These complete assemblies are, as will be readily understood, becoming by their nature difficult to obtain, so that it is a pleasure and an experience to find a complete Heyde field ambulance of three hundred pieces, the magnificent 1912 Delhi Durbar by the same maker, the 1905 Coronation set, several First World War groups with guard dogs, wiring parties and signallers, a Frederick the Great Coronation set, and four thousand miscellaneous models by the same manufacturer.

He has over a thousand Lucotte models, including a complete set of Napoleon's staff, and a number of Mignot rarities, including transport. One collection of which he is particularly proud is a set of six-inch French 1870 infantry in *carton comprimé* – a material not often met with. He has ten thousand Britains, ancient and more modern, including a set of their transport, together with the rare Barrage Balloon and Cierva Autogyro. The transitory competitors of the period are well represented, as well as an abundance of the later trade manufacturers both in lead and plastic, together with the latest Herald and Elastolin productions. Less often seen, and again in large sets, are the pre-war Elastolin composition figures, mainly German army types, complete with pontoons, inflatable dinghies, signalling gear, searchlights, etc. Alongside these Continentals are their imitators – Lineol, Durso, Fabrique Belge, and other manufacturers whose productions are scarce.

Flats are also very much in evidence (over ten thousand of them) and modern works figure prominently – Stadden, Greenwood, Hinton, Gammage and the like, and he is especially keen on the models of Marrion.

The last two years have been spent in completing extensive dioramas of the surgical aspects of the battle of Waterloo. These were primarily for a lecture on this subject at the British Model Soldier Society Waterloo

Right The remarkable Lucotte collection owned by Mr Hanington

LUCOTTE
THE THREE COMPONENTS OF THE MOUNTED FIGURE
LUCOTTE
Grenadiers of the Guard
LUCOTTE
CARABINIER
LUCOTTE
LUCOTTE
Regt. d'Etrangers – Regt. d'Isembourg Ie
LUCOTTE
Trumpeter, Empress Dragoons
THE LUCOTTE 'BEE' TRADE MARK
LUCOTTE

Convention, but have since been lent to the Wellcome Medical Museum. The display consists of four cabinets showing the main British hospital at Mont St Jean farm, the surgery at Hougoumont, the main French Hospital at le Caillou, and a collection showing the various surgeons and ambulances used. He is hoping to have a complete collection of models through various campaigns.

His collection is most beautifully housed in what was once a conservatory, and here, in very tall glass wall cases, stand the rows and rows of models, crowned by military headgear and flanked with weapons and drums, and one wall is completely glazed to form a cabinet for early uniforms. Hanington is constantly purchasing fresh models, and it may well be that he has added considerably to his collection since this was written. One may be sure, however, that whatever he acquires gives him much pleasure, which in turn is transmitted to his many collector guests.

Shamus O. D. Wade, *Dublin*, *Eire*

Collectors of model soldiers consist of two classes: those whose collections grow inevitably and without apparent urgency, and those who, having purchased their first models, are stricken by a consuming fire and amass an imposing array in the briefest possible time.

Shamus Wade undoubtedly belongs to the latter category. As a child he acquired the odd commercial figure or so and later forgot them. Then, one day, on impulse, he bought some Herald's Trojans, and, he says, 'stuck them on the mantelpiece'. These were immediately followed by Britains' 'Knights of Agincourt'. So it began, and today he has a most catholic collection, consisting of examples of practically all known makers, and many figures whose manufacturer remains unknown.

It is difficult to find a single theme that runs through the collection. What, for instance, can one find in common between Skinner's Horse and Bashkirs of the Russian army of 1812, or between the King's Royal Irish Hussars and Osceola, Chief of the Seminoles? Wade thinks that what they have in common is the ideal of the soldier as a 'bold warrior' rather than the 'uniformed sheep' – the soldier who has deliberately chosen the profession of arms, rather than the uniformly dressed conscript. That is why so few Napoleonic figures are to be found in his cabinets.

Following the first tentative purchases, he began buying Britains in quantity – and he now even has a vicar, a station master and a milkmaid. He concedes that his collection is not as fine as that of L. W. Richards, but he does possess some models that Richards has not been able to find. The Britains section includes such rarities as the CIV wagon, the South Australian Lancers in two different uniforms, the early bolted-on-arm 12th Lancers and Scots Greys, the small size Royal Horse Artillery in both review order and Boer War khaki, the specially made RASC water cart, and the Barrage Balloon unit. Perhaps the most impressive item is the White Camel Corps – the biggest box Britains ever issued. Wade knows of only two other sets.

Britains' cavalry and infantry include a large contingent of British troops including the 'Soldiers to Shoot' (see *Model Soldiers*, page 128) and troops of the Empire: foreign countries represented include such exotic forces as Abyssinians, Togolanders, Mexicans, Venezuelans and Uruguayans.

Wade also has a fine collection of Heyde pieces. One of the most extraordinary items of this most prolific of commercial makers is the Royal Engineers Flying Wing of 1908, consisting of a horse-drawn balloon control wagon complete with riders and operators, with a globular balloon attached to moorings. The personnel consists of twenty-three foot figures in scarlet and eighteen in tropical kit, including haulers on the ropes, whistle blowers, telescope-peerers, and bicycle riders. There is also a tent and an airship. This set he bought at auction, two other collectors standing down from the

Opposite Shamus Wade with part of his collection. The Polish Winged Lancer can be seen on the third shelf down from the top

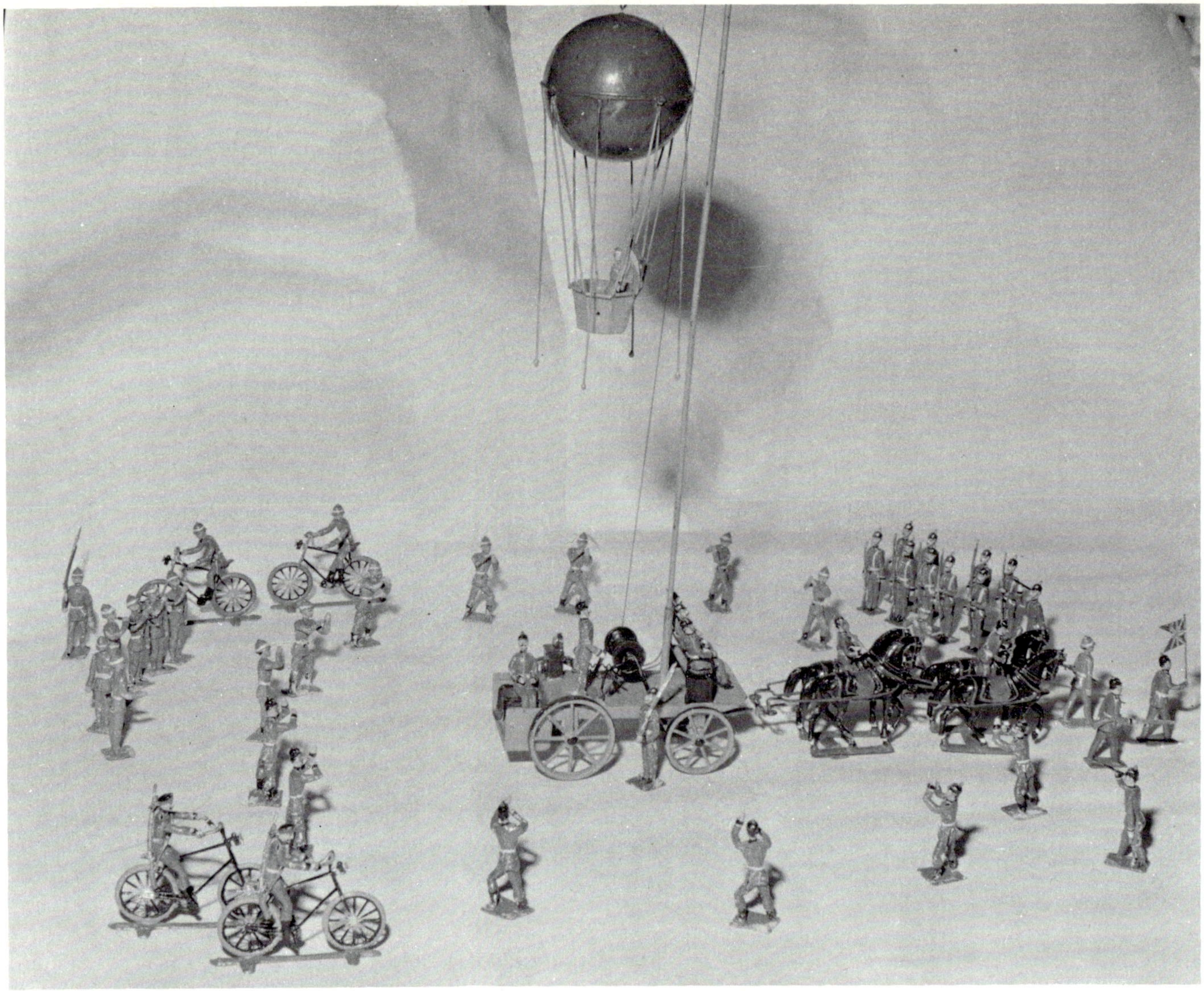

Heyde Royal Engineers Balloon Section, Boer War

bidding. Many of Heyde's figures have often appeared to us to be clumsy and ill-proportioned but there is no denying the ingenuity and detail that have gone into the conception of such an assembly. Perhaps more attractive to our mind is the remarkable elephant gun (possibly part of the Delhi Durbar set). This consists of two elephants and mahouts, a gun and limber, with

Heyde's remarkable elephant gun team

two gunners sitting thereon, and four out-riders on camels. Certainly the elephants must be the finest ever made. L. W. Richards rightly calls it 'one of the wonders of the model soldier world'. Akin to this is the group of the Nizam of Hyderabad's Camel Lancers: ten troopers, a bugler and two officers. Two Bedouin with removable headgear ride the most successful model of a camel at full gallop that we have ever seen.

Other Heyde items include the Boer War RHA gun-team; a British military cyclist; Kitchener (in two different uniforms); Lord Roberts; a representative from a Cherry-Picker mounted band; a Zeppelin pilot and crew; Saxons and Normans; two soldiers whose swords may be withdrawn from their scabbards, and a dead Lancer.

Commercial makers are further represented by figures by Armitage, Carman, Fylde, Fry, Hanks, Lincoln Logs, Lucotte, Malleable Mouldings, Niblett, Reka, Renvoize, Taylor and Barrett, Wendall, W. Courtenay and the usual array of the more recent makers. Among these are the works of the unknowns – some having the charm of the primitives, as for instance sailors in straw hats that have the appearance of carved wood; a Rifle Brigade figure so realistic that he might spring into action at any moment, and an Indian clinging to the flanks of his pony and firing at the same time.

Some years ago Brigadier J. F. Benoy collaborated with L. Groves to produce a very large number of tiny figures illustrating the British Army of the Peninsular War. Wade bought the entire collection of over two thousand figures but was later reluctantly compelled to dispose of a number of them. He did, however, retain a representative block, including infantry, cavalry, horse and foot artillery, bands, mules and wagons and the Duke of Wellington and a Spanish priest. He has arranged these in two ways: first a background of dark mountains seen through mist and cloud, across which crawls an endless stream of guns, mules and wagons and, in contrast, a village square, gay with officers, bands, standards and brightly dressed troops. The effect is really outstanding.

Nor does he despise plastics, which he feels are just as important as lead models. He has written often and characteristically in defence of their cheapness and suitability for conversion. Indeed, as we ourselves have said elsewhere, when the plastic is designed by a master, as in the case of a Selwyn-Smith (Herald) or a Stadden (Cavendish) the result transcends the material.

'Connoisseur' figures are represented by fine models by Gammage, Hinton and Stadden, and include thirty-two Gammage and Stadden Indian Army models, a magnificent Polish Winged Lancer (Stadden) and a Private of the Regiment Edward Dillon, a French émigré regiment (Irish-Catholic in origin) in the service of the British, 1800–10 (Hinton). But of all the specialist makers, Ping is the favourite. One of the reasons is that a Ping figure is never duplicated.

Wade commissioned Ping to make for him the 'World's Twelve Greatest Generals', Wade stipulating which figures he desired. His choice is an interesting one: Genghis Khan, Spartacus, Alexander the Great, King Arthur (the Romano-Celt, Arturius Ambrosianus, not the Malory-Tennyson travesty), Alfred the Great, Julius Caesar, Lord Napier of Magdala, the Duke of Marlborough, Osceola, Kutusov, Chaka, and Hannibal. Wade has given us his reasons, but they are too lengthy to quote. Suffice it to say that Ping was an admirable choice to immortalise them, and they are magnificent conceptions. Wade has others by Ping also including a Toussaint l'Ouverture, Colonel Skinner, Michael Collins, Saladin, Khublai Khan, an Assyrian archer, a Greek hoplite, a Stewart clansman, and a Persian Immortal. Perhaps the most interesting one, from a purely personal point of view, is the figure of Field-Marshal Wade, of whom it is said 'he is a man whom one can trust with anything except a woman'. Here he is shown in hot pursuit of a young lady!

Finally, Wade has tried his hand at conversion and has some quite interesting results to show. More recently he is creating his own models, and has become one of the leading dealers in second-hand ones. An advertising campaign copywriter by profession, his wife comes from Trinidad, and is a barrister-at-law, and early in married life he worried about her being a 'model soldier widow'. (There are 'widows' in other spheres, such as cricket, golf and fishing.) But he soon realised that his fears were groundless, and that she was becoming just as keen as he was over the collecting of model soldiers. His only regret is that he once missed a complete set in the original box of the large-size Heyde mounted dignitaries at the Coronation of Edward VII, including the Kaiser, European monarchs, and Indian Princes. Perhaps it will turn up again.

The late C. Ashton McDonnell,
Devon, Pennsylvania, USA

Charles Ashton McDonnell, whose death in 1967 was a sad blow to the model soldier world, was a landscape engineer, married and with two sons. His collection (still, happily kept in being by his sons) numbers approximately twenty thousand models comprising single specimens, groups, and large and small dioramas, and embracing the period from the Roman Empire to the present day. Especial interests of his were the American Revolution, ordnance, tanks and artillery.

His mother actually started his collection for him, and perpetuated it for many years, while he was still a youngster. She recognized his interest in history, especially military, and encouraged it by gifts of miniature soldiers. He recalled vividly the day when a box of Heyde Romans, complete with chariots, war elephants, and so on was placed in his hands, but unfortunately many of the models were too good for a small lad of seven, and many casualties resulted. Then father stepped in, and lessons were given in the welfare

US Marines landing at Iwo Jima.
Diorama containing mainly Authenticast models.
Assembled and arranged by Terry McDonnell.

and preservation of model soldiers; a lesson that was never forgotten.

The collection grew in size and scope as, with the ending of the First World War, he was able to purchase Britains, Mignot, Lucotte, Warren and others, and the interest continued into college days, when other more exciting interests intervened, and the models were packed away. Even so, periodic inspections were made, and always the interest remained, however much it was veiled by other matters.

After the Second World War, his young sons became actively interested in military subjects, and the collection again became a living thing. History repeated itself, with grandmother, mother and father all participating in the hobby. The collection constantly expanded, and now embraces many rare pieces; over a thousand specimens by Heyde (of which a large number are in complete sets), besides Courtenay, Greenwood and Ball, Stadden, Imrie, Gammage, Britains, Authenticast, Mignot, Lucotte, Bussler, Baldet, fifty by Harle, and over a hundred each by Métayer and Vertunni. There are many very fine conversions, and a great number were painted by McDonnell himself.

When the Miniature Figure Collectors of America was formed McDonnell became a charter-member and the second President, and when the Company of Military Historians was born he was again a charter-member, and for some years a governor.

One of the things that distinguishes the McDonnell Collection from so many others of equal scope is the use to which he has put many of the models. Elsewhere we

Lee and Jackson before Chancellorsville by Imrie-Risley

have noted co-operation by wives, sons and daughters in the hobby – here is a striking example of the assistance rendered by two sons. Over the years, they and their father created striking dioramas, converted figures, painted castings, and constructed back- and foregrounds. The result is a striking collection, marrying fine figures to splendid settings. The emphasis is on American history, especially the period of the Revolutionary War. *George Washington at Valley Forge* and *General von Steuben drilling the frozen troops* (models by Imrie, Stadden, Scheid and Bussler, together with plastics and conversions) were assembled and arranged by Terry McDonnell, who also constructed *US Marines landing at Iwo Jima* (Authenticast and conversions) in collaboration with his brother Chick. An important group of incidents at the Battle of Brandywine was created by Ashton: Proctor's Battalion; British Dragoon Line Infantry; General Wayne's Pennsylvanians, and *Von Rall's Hessians meeting Wayne's Pennsylvanians* (all the models in these by Imrie and Stadden); an extremely realistic *Continental Army defeating Von Rall at Trenton*

(Bussler, Stadden, Jones, Scheid, Authenticast, and conversions and originals by Ashton); and *General Knox hauling the guns from Fort Ticonderoga to Boston in 1775* (Scheid, Gammage, Stadden, Heyde conversions – sleds and oxen by Ashton) completes the Revolutionary period, whilst during the *Old French War* the *Ambush of Braddock* is alive with screaming Indians (Stadden, Imrie, plastics and conversions).

Turning to the Civil War, we have a selection of events at Gettysburg – Southern troops in action, the Federal Army moving up, and the Northern Army attacking (all by Bussler). Interspersed with these are an *Attack on a French Foreign Legion Fort*, a *Caesar in Egypt* (arranged by Chick, figures by Stadden and Gammage) and a medieval battle scene. Clever use has been made of coloured reproductions of battle-pieces as backgrounds for the models, especially striking being Stadden's *Guarding the Colours*, *Spotsylvania* (by Terry); and *Lee and Jackson before Chancellorsville* (by Imrie).

Brigadier Peter Young, *Tewkesbury, England*

It was Ping who suggested that we would find a visit to Brigadier Young rewarding. He was then living at Yately, and we accordingly arranged to meet at Camberley, Ping coming from Kingston via Staines, ourselves from Farnham via Aldershot. When we arrived we found Ping already sitting in the front seat of a small car with a very large Brigadier, overlooked from the back by a monstrous Alsatian dog. The dog proved gentle, and a hair-raising journey across the derelict Blackbushe Aerodrome, enlivened by the witty remarks of the Brigadier, brought us to Yately. Here, as we went from room to room, it became increasingly clear that this was no ordinary collection. We have seen many of larger proportions and of greater variety and, obversely, smaller and with the accent on a very restricted range. Two things were immediately apparent. The first was the impression of an unusually intelligent mind directing the display of massed groups of models, of which we shall have more to say. Secondly, the quality of the figures, apparent at the first glance, was confirmed on a more careful inspection.

Brigadier Young is a military historian and author of note. He can remember his first gift of soldiers at the age of four, and has collected off and on ever since. Whenever he becomes bored with any of the figures in his collection, or finds that they no longer seem to have the perfection that he demands, he disposes of them. His interests include the English Civil War, the mid-eighteenth century, and the Napoleonic Wars, although he admits to becoming surfeited by the endless stream of models of this era being made by all the best makers. The Middle Ages and the Ancient World are represented, but not strongly, together with a few examples of the 1870 period.

Prince Rupert. A magnificent model by des Fontaines. (Formerly in Brigadier Young's collection, now owned by Philip O. Stearns)

His favourite makers are des Fontaines, Stadden, Surén, Ping, Métayer and the commercial models of 'Palx' (Alexandre). The test he applies to all his models is a sense of period and the realism of the action. These qualities are admirably displayed in his collection.

One of the most endearing things about his groups is the presence of civilians. Believing that soldiers do not live in a vacuum, he collects *figurines historiques* besides military models, and therefore he pays as much attention to the non-combatant as to the military arm. That is why one finds *cantinières*, for instance, in a group of the 1870s, beautiful women with Royalists of the English Civil War, females in distress in a Ping medieval village skirmish, the Countess Rimsky-Korsakov at the court of Napoleon III, Gammage's Egyptian dancers being watched by Roman soldiers – indeed there are two diorama settings, one of the interior of a French theatre in the mid-seventeenth century with no military interest at all, the other of a square in Paris where Prince Rupert and a few other cavaliers are the only military types.

His dioramas are most ingeniously contrived, built as they are on the shelves of glazed bookcases and corner cupboards, and using the three- to four-foot frontage and two-foot height to great advantage. The first that took our eye was an exquisite setting of the court of Napoleon I, crowded with the Emperor and his staff and their ladies (all by Stadden). Yellow silk curtains with golden braid and swags represent a huge tent, on the walls of which are emblems of the Empire, miniature maps and trophies of arms. Another imposing display is a battle during the American War of Independence, seemingly hundreds of British being engaged in the taking of a large and battered Colonial-Georgian mansion, defended by as many Americans, nearly all the models again by Stadden, and present in remarkable variety. We have said elsewhere that in our opinion Stadden's American Revolutionary War figures are his best, and this massing of examples confirmed our opinion.

We knew 'Palx' models only from the illustrations in Baldet's book, and it was most interesting actually to see them in numbers. Young says he used to buy them on the left bank of the Seine, and they cover almost the entire range of civilian types of mid-seventeenth-century Paris. Slightly larger than the average size, they are admirable for town scenes and serve equally well for English settings. We have no equivalent in this country. The interesting thing is that Baldet labels them as by Alexandre and yet both he and the other learned members of the *Société des Figurines Historiques* say they know nothing of 'Palx', nor do they link them with Alexandre. So often, in the history of model soldiers, one finds these little mysteries cropping up.

Young has grouped his 'Palxes' admirably in a bustling, lively display set in a square in Paris, where the models fit naturally into a background of appropriate architecture, and with their sober fustian form an admirable foil to the more flamboyant figures of Prince Rupert and his sister. The theatre scene already mentioned is equally exciting. Here the open galleries are full of the richer merchants, watching a play by Scarron or Molière taking place on the stage to the left, with swashbuckling gallants and more sober merchants or civil servants. Interspersed with the 'Palx' figures are others by master makers, all fitting naturally into place.

The medieval skirmish by Ping is gradually being assembled and, of course, has not yet received a setting, and there are others in preparation.

We have reserved our description of the most outstanding achievements to the last. One is an amazing evocation by des Fontaines of the eighteenth century. The setting is of a piazza on the edge of a Venetian canal. The flagstones are bathed in moonlight, and contrast strongly with the shadowed facade of a canal-side palace in the background, and the dark shapes of buildings, one to the left, a palace, the other, to the right, a church. In the middle of the scene the actors are full in the moonlight – a desperate encounter between two skilled swordsmen, a swooning woman, and, in the shadows, a manservant and a priest. Young calls this a scene from Casanova, but it might equally well portray Act One of Mozart's *Don Giovanni*. Here is the evil Giovanni, the enraged Commandant, the weeping Donna Anna, and Leporello. The setting is Venice, not Spain, but that matters little.

The second impressive diorama is the large living-room of the house of a Royalist during the English Civil War. Probably everyone is familiar with the picture *When did you last see your Father?* – this is a much more subtle interpretation. Here is a group of stern Ironsides, one slouching arrogantly in a richly upholstered armchair, flanked by a standing Puritan, implacable eyes shadowed by a steeple hat. Facing them with outward calm is the resolute figure of a Royalist lady, around her a restless skirmish of Cromwellian troopers roughly handling her attendants. The first thing that is obvious is the quality of the models. The Napoleonic Staddens are all of the very best (as are those of the American War scene) and the troops in the background of this diorama are obviously of the same quality, each hand-picked by Young himself, preferably of the first casting, and of the finest painting. But the most breathtaking models are those by Josianne des Fontaines. We have no hesitation in saying that they are among the most beautiful models we have ever seen. Built up of successive solderings in the Ping method, they are the interpretations of her art based on information supplied by Young. A slow worker, the result justifies the time taken. Elegance is the key-note, as in the dashing Rupert and the sensuous Don Giovanni, but there is at the same time an implacable sternness in the Cromwellian figures. The male figures are probably unique of their kind, and their female counterparts certainly so. Brigadier Young has a number of these, including a truly beautiful Countess Rimsky-Korsakov, Prince Rupert's sister, and the women in the civil war scene. The delicacy of the faces and the hands is quite remarkable, the dresses beautifully managed, no detail is overlooked, and the way the lace is handled is superb. The overall elegance is quite exceptional.

The lovely settings, with their perfect scale and detail, are the work of Brigadier Young's son-in-law, François Caron Delion, who brings a typically Gallic touch of elegance to his work. The theatre diorama in particular is most satisfying.

Besides the set pieces there are a number of models by other makers, such as Métayer, Lucotte and the like and, upstairs in a huge war-game room, a large collection of 30mm models. Here is the full range of Stadden's remarkable Napoleonic creations, and all that Surén has so far produced. Those that are not painted by the makers are finished by J. Johnson, as Young himself finds the work too exacting. The war-game army is equally distinctive. Based on the mid-eighteenth century, the models are by Stadden and Surén, with a large quantity specially made by Saunders and Charles Stuart Grant. Not only is the artillery arm prominent, with all the necessary equipment, but the huge table is laid out with a French chateau and forts made with the most remarkable accuracy by William Holmes, who is also responsible for a large collection of model ships and assault craft. The forts have their gun emplacements, and such is Young's humour that one finds a Surén Roman Consul and Duke of Cumberland on pedestals, simulating stone statues! Another nice touch is an octagonal village gaol which has a roof that lifts off, disclosing the inhabitants.

Brigadier Young's collection may not be the largest we have seen, but it is certainly one of the most exciting, and it is probable that he has by now added more Pings in appropriate settings. Since writing this review we have learnt that Brigadier Young's Palx have been disposed of, and that his des Fontaines now form part of Mr Philip O. Stearns's imposing collection. The Brigadier's dynamic personality is such that by the time this is published he may well have completely changed his collection.

Miscellany

Eugene and Wilma Custer, *Jamaica, New York, USA*

The Custer collection is an example of a love of the model figure that began in early days, lay dormant, and then received fresh impetus in later years.

Eugene Custer's mother, a High School French teacher, took him with her to France on several sabbaticals. Naturally, like any boy in Paris, *Au Plat d'Etain* acted like a magnet, and the first Mignot sets were purchased. Britains, naturally, proved the second attraction, but (germ of later collecting) the Greenwoods and Courtenays, which at that time (in the early 1930s) were beginning to appear in American stores, were the unattainable longings. Even as early as this he began to create and cast his own models.

Eugene and Wilma Custer with part of their beautifully displayed collection

Married to Wilma, he left his Britains and his Mignots with his mother, but, little by little, in the way these things do happen (we ourselves have gone through this phase) the little figures began to appear in the new Custer home in the transparent guise of decoration. We have met many collectors' wives who with difficulty bear with their husbands' hobbies, patronising, sarcastic, hopeless, resigned. A number are faintly interested, pleased to help or admire, without ever themselves developing any marked enthusiasm. Occasionally we have met one who is equally enthusiastic, and possibly has the collector's instinct herself. One good friend of ours collects New Hall pottery, her husband specialising in prehistoric and early historic finds. They house their respective collections in separate cases, and harmony reigns.

Wilma Custer is one of those who actively shares her husband's interests, and she could see that these Britains and Mignots creeping apologetically back meant that upon Eugene the divine frenzy had once more descended. A teacher herself, with an abiding love of history, she could visualise an extension of her own knowledge, and, a housewife, she knew that nothing was a better promoter of social relaxation when entertaining than a collection of objects to be examined, admired, talked about, or even joked about. It was she who introduced into their home the first Greenwood and the first Courtenay, and later, the first Stadden.

Few of the original purchases remain on the shelves today, but at least one of each set is carefully packed

Battery on Little Round Top Models and diorama made by Eugene Custer

away. Many of the others have long since been converted.

Early in their marriage (after 1945) Eugene again took up modelling and casting, this time in earnest. Those were the days when few good figures, particularly of American subjects, were available. As a machinist and tool-and-die-maker he had special advantages. Over ten or twelve years he painstakingly turned out about fifteen finely-detailed figures, as well as a Civil War cannon. These were sold commercially for a time, but the amount of work put into them did not warrant the continuance of this practice. Moreover, the advance of a certain Charles C. Stadden was filling the gap in the American military miniature stores.

Our reaction is to feel a distinct loss at the knowledge that no more Custer figures are available.

Some of the most effective figures that he made are a Captain, US Marine Corps (*c* 1812) (the legs perhaps a little clumsy); a Major, New Jersey Blues, 1776; a Hessian and a British Grenadier (American War of Independence); a drummer, Captain Mullen's Company of Continental Marines, 1779; a private in the New York 7th Regiment, and one in Troy (NY) Citizen's Corps (our favourite); a rifleman of Richmond Light Infantry Blues (their favourite); and a most impressive little diorama, in the American manner, of a battery at Little Round Top during the Civil War. It is particularly striking as photographed against an enlarged coloured illustration of the period. The painting of all the figures was done by Wilma who, starting from scratch, reached a high proficiency. Not all the figures were so successful, however, as is inevitable,

Richmond Light Infantry, American War of Independence. Model by Eugene Custer

and we feel that they would like to forget a certain Gordon Highlander, whose head is impossibly sunk into his shoulders.

The Custer collection consists of presentation figures, the preferences being for the fine quality products of Courtenay, Ping, Greenwood, des Fontaines, Stadden, Stock, Murray and Imrie-Risley. Of these the finest have been obtained in recent years. Particularly striking is the *Chasseur à cheval de la Garde Impériale*, 1808, the superb Prince Eugene de Beauharnais, and the Napoleon at Eylau, 1807, all by Josianne des Fontaines, and exhibiting to the full the exceptional skill and artistry of this remarkable artist.

Another part of the collection consists of plastics by Marx, Revell, Lineol, Mokarex, and repaintings and conversions. All these figures are carefully worked on and touched up to make as fine a piece as research and handwork can make it. Many of them (including the finer ones) are purchased unpainted, and the humble plastic becomes a collector's piece under their skilful hands.

Of recent years they have been busy giving appropriate mountings to their models – a small but telling detail so often absent in many collections. For instance, a *sans culotte* stands on cobblestones, a Grecian lady on a tiled floor, a British Colonial on flagstones, a French Court trumpeter on an inlaid wood floor. This having been done, the models are placed on a double row of six-inch shelves on top of two-shelf bookcases, bringing the figures to near eye level. They are protected by sliding glass doors; glass domes or square covers house set-pieces, and beautiful use is made of hanging cabinets, with picture frame fronts and mirror backs.

The Custers have no other hobby.

Cornelius Frazer, *Amsterdam, Holland*

One of the finest collections among reference libraries of uniform and costume, in the form of books, prints, albums, postcards and cigarette cards, numbering in the region of thirty-five thousand items, is to be seen in a modest house in the northern suburbs of Amsterdam.

It is owned by Cornelius Frazer, a Dutchman of Scottish ancestry, whose four charming daughters all

Opposite A magnificently colourful model by Berdou of a *Timbalier*, *Garde Impériale*, *Grenadiers à cheval*

bear English names, and it is to Frazer that Dutch collectors refer for information of details of uniforms or correct colours.

Frazer was born in 1911, and between 1918 and 1923 began, as a young boy, buying paper sheets of small size, each containing eight or ten footsoldiers or four mounted men in two rows. All the armies of the world were represented, and the soldiers all wore full-colour uniforms of red, blue, green etc, and all for the price of less than a penny a sheet! These figures were cut out carefully by young Frazer (capturing the joys so well described by Paul Martin in his *Les Petits Soldats de Strasbourg*). These were, of course for playing with, but later Frazer began to preserve the figures and the intact sheets. In Amsterdam he discovered an antiquarian bookshop, where he found old Épinal and other sheets in enormous quantities, and, in his own words, he 'bought and bought, also duplicates'. Exchange of these with the two or three collectors there were in Holland then, and with contacts abroad, swelled his collection, so that today it is one of the most impressive in the world. He reckons that his complete sheets must number about fifteen hundred. They include English, Dutch, Belgian, Spanish, Italian, German, Austrian, French, and Portuguese, together with about one thousand five hundred cut-out soldiers, painted by Frazer himself, mounted on blocks, and with suitable backgrounds for exhibitions.

Cornelius Frazer often places his models on display. Here he is seen assisted by his wife whilst preparing for an 'English Week' exhibition in Amsterdam

The oldest sheets date from 1811, and the newest are the latest contemporary ones from Spain. Many are in colour, and those in line he has coloured in a contemporary style; although, as we will discover, he collects other types of model soldiers, the sheets are his principal interest, rousing a sense of nostalgia for the time when there was, as he says, 'no Meccano, miniature railways, camping, sport, dancing, radio, television and the Beatles.' All this, we suspect, is said with tongue in cheek, for in reality Mr and Mrs Frazer and their four daughters are the friendliest and jolliest people.

It would be impossible to give a full list of the sheets in Frazer's collection, and a résumé must suffice. A careful study of his manuscript catalogue discloses that Italy heads the list, with 'Stella' represented on two hundred and ten sheets and 'Stella Maria' on one hundred and ninety-eight, followed by Burkhardt with one hundred and sixty-one, and Péllerin with one hundred and eleven. Whereas the Italian publishers' sheets deal with Italian armies only, Burkhardt's extend over the other European nations, together with the United States, China, Korea, Russia, and British India, whilst those issued by Péllerin include also China, the Boer War, Montenegro and again the United States. Others represented are Neu Rappin, Wentzen, Schultz, JSM Kuhn, Gangel, Alou, Nancy, Oliver et Delhaert, Silbermann, Jacobsen, Meger, Staar, Breepols, Hujos of Barcelona, Epinal, Kavoteide, Bellerhog, Eneret, Vincent, PC (Lisbon), Carval, Mariel Vange, Marchi, Images Neurin, Didion, and Stuttgarter Bilderboger.

Among this galaxy it is interesting to note that Hujos, Péllerin and Delhaert all issued sheets dealing with the Boer War, Gangel one of the Vatican troops, and Schultz one of Neapolitans. Countries usually overlooked are represented here; Hungary, Arabia, Korea, Switzerland, Finland, and the armies of Sardinia and Piedmont.

Second in his collection comes his assembly of some five thousand flats, all self-painted, and many of non-military subjects. Flats are favourites with the Dutch, and so he has ample opportunity for exchange. His sets include Stone Age man, prehistoric animals, a rococo ball, the Court of Philip II, an Assyrian slave-market, building the Sphinx, Friedrich Wilhelm von Preusse, and medieval scenes. From these he constructs dioramas, of which his most impressive is perhaps *Napoleon in Amsterdam*.

His interest in the third section of his collection began, he says, after reading Bob Bard's book and our own *Model Soldiers*. He began to appreciate the works of the best of the makers of solids and hollow-casts, because, he says, they are easier to see and have as much detail as the flats, and offer great opportunities for conversion. History now repeated itself. He had once found a horde of paper-sheets, now he was fortunate in finding a large collection of Britains and Heydes; much battered, but, because of this, very cheap. These he repainted and converted, and they, together with his large and varying quality plastic figures, form part of his three thousand-strong collection of round models, many of which now appear as Dutch military bands. In recent years his interests have become more catholic and he is especially interested in the fine models made by Alymer of Spain, of which he has nearly a hundred, together with a number of large boxes containing alternative heads, headgear and equipment.

His interest is in the old colourful uniforms, the full dress of today, and in military bands, and he can mount a tattoo of more than five hundred foot and mounted 54mm figures. Finally, kits made by Segom, Airfix, Aurora, and other makers round off his collection. He is treasurer of the Dutch Society, and acknowledges his indebtedness to the information from Commander Hamilton and the Scottish Model Soldier Group.

As an accountant, he has to work with accuracy and detail, and he brings these virtues to the arrangement and classification of his models, his printed sheets, his volumes of illustrations, his postcard albums, and his row upon row of books.

Frazer's wife and daughters take an active part in his interests, assisting in cutting out, painting and mounting the paper figures, and arranging them for exhibitions. When they visited us at Farnham it was a joy to see the enthusiasm with which they joined in the conversation, and the interest displayed in our own models was by no means confined to Cornelius. We ourselves know that on our periodic business visits to Amsterdam we always endeavour to make the journey under the River Y to the 'model-house' in Havikslaan, and to the Frazer welcome. We always depart enriched by the humanity of the household and with a number of 'doubles' in our briefcase.

Michael V. Hitrovo, *Ambler, USA*

Much of the pleasure of collecting model soldiers results from the contacts one forms, either in person or by correspondence, with fellow collectors in all parts of the world. We ourselves have been most fortunate in having formed friendships with enthusiasts in Holland, Spain, France, Sweden, Switzerland, Italy, Austria, Germany, Canada and the United States, to say nothing of those in our own country. It may be only a brief note or a postcard offering help. Sometimes contact comes in the form of a long letter, giving advice or recommendation. Occasionally there is an actual meeting, when over a 'high tea' in the garden ideas have been exchanged.

The first freely volunteered assistance from a complete stranger to be experienced by us was from Michael Hitrovo. To a newcomer in the field, groping vaguely towards an understanding of the vast and intricate detail of which this new world was composed, his altruistic friendliness was indeed a blessing. Since those early days of authorship, some fifteen years ago, correspondence has been free and frank, often with the interchange of models (much more on his part than on ours) and he has never been anything but helpful; often, indeed, when in poor health or burdened with more important affairs. If, therefore, this notice appears of disproportionate length, it will, we are certain, be excused by the reader, as an expression of sincere admiration and gratitude, and as an example of the true cameraderie which can exist between collectors.

Michael V. Hitrovo comes from an old family of Russian untitled nobility, tracing their ancestry to the end of the thirteenth century. Military service was a family tradition, broken only by his father (a jurist) and his uncle (a civil engineer). Despite this the tradition lingered, and military playthings were the toys of his childhood, his favourites being Heinrichsen flats. As he grew up he added to them, until in 1919, when he lost both his parents during the Russian Revolution, he also lost his collection. Survival was difficult during the chaotic aftermath of the revolution, but in 1921, at the age of nineteen, he managed to escape to Poland, making the fifty-mile journey on foot. He was accepted

Michael V. Hitrovo inspecting a model at an American exhibition

into the Russian *Real-Gymnasium* in Czechoslovakia where he continued his interrupted education. In 1924 he graduated with honours, spent over a year at the Prague Polytechnic and then, with the aid of friends, emigrated to the United States to continue his studies at Antioch College in Ohio. He obtained his BA degree in 1934. At that time jobs were scarce, and he eventually found himself in social work, living in Philadelphia. In 1941 he left for Chicago to take up academic work leading to an MA degree. He achieved this and returned to Philadelphia in 1944. However, in 1953 he changed to engineering draughtsmanship, and is still continuing this pursuit.

During his early student days all recollections of his collection had lain dormant, although his interest in history, (which had begun at an early age) was active. But about Christmas 1939 he saw some Britains in a large store, and fell!

Gradually he met other kindred souls who possessed Mignots, Vertunnis and Courtenays, but his salary was small, and he now had a wife to support. So he began recasting Britains and tried his hand at conversion. He learned the hard way and is, even today, quite pleased with the recollection of his early plaster moulds. Naturally, his interest lay in Russian Army types, and he managed to create a collection of the Russo-Turkish War period and the Russian Imperial Guards of 1910–14. Connections with the Philadelphia Collectors' Group (later the Miniature Figure Collectors' Society of Pennsylvania) and the discovery of J. Edward Jones's (Moulded Miniatures) American and Revolutionary War figures followed, together with further experiments in casting; this time of Aztecs, Toltecs, Mayas and ancient Egyptians, the creations helped and inspired by study at the University of Chicago Oriental Institute Museum and the Chicago Institute of Fine Arts. At this time, as seems inevitable, the Napoleonic period began to exert its fascination, and French and Russians of 1812 made their appearance.

Whilst in Chicago he discovered through Jones the flats of Ochel, and later got in touch with Gottstein, with whom a friendship began until the latter's death.

By the end of the war he had a fairly representative Napoleonic collection, and specimens of Vertunni, Mignot and Courtenay. As new makers came into the market their products were added, especially those of the American Revolution and a few Civil War figures, although this conflict has never been a favourite with him. Gradually sets and units changed to single figures, such as models by Gammage, Murray, Imrie, Stadden, Métayer, Ballada and Greenwood and, with the richer variety of figures available, home-casting ceased.

Among his favourite models are an Imrie French *voltigeur*; a Marlborough-period British sergeant and a French Marshal by Stadden; a Roman General and a Mohawk, also by Stadden, but specially painted by William Fenerin of San Francisco; Queen Victoria, Henry VIII, Elizabeth the Queen Mother and Queen Elizabeth II, all by Ping; King George V and Queen Mary by Courtenay; and a group of Vertunni's portrait figures (see *Model Soldiers* plate 53).

His collection is enriched by gifts from friends – some of whom are collectors who make a limited

Napoleon, his family and his staff. Models by Vertunni which are now very rare

number of figures for their own pleasure and to give away. Such a friend is William Greer, from whom Hitrovo has a number of models of which he is especially fond, including a medieval bombard group, the shield of which can be raised or lowered by means of a rope. A conversion by Greer, of which the original was a Britains marching figure, is of an Inca priest prepared to capture the flame from the Sun; others are of the Biblical Gideon and a fine mounted Danish Guards Hussar, the original of which is in the Officers' Mess of the Regiment. Mrs Helen West's models fascinate him, too, and he possesses several of these, including Eric the Red, Sigurd the Crusader, Boris Godunov and Joan of Arc. Figures by other makers include Custer's Marine Officer 1812, a Saunders French *voltigeur*, a Duke Stock Etruscan and an Alan Clayton conversion group of the present English Royal pair.

Carthaginian War Elephants. 30mm flats by Gottstein and Beckel

To complete this section of standard size rounds, mention must be made of a group of figures showing the uniforms of the Russian White Army, made by Hitrovo after original research and presented by him to the Museum of the White Russian movement, and a group of twelve men and an officer of the Duke of Cumberland's Sharpshooters, 1793, which was awarded a prize at one of the exhibitions of the British Model Soldier Society.

Hitrovo's preoccupation with history, both military and social, has led him to construct a number of dioramas, all the figures of his own casting: a party in the house of a rich Egyptian of the Eighteenth Dynasty, a stone-age camp, a religious procession of the Aztecs, Egyptian peasants, planting and ploughing, and a Russian street scene (*c* 1900). But now all his time is devoted to his flats, of which he has a very large collection, many of which (especially those issued by Hafer) he makes into dioramas. There is hardly a set by a contemporary that he does not possess (provided, that is, that it falls within his special periods of interest). He is above all especially interested in the 'Alt Aarau' flats. He has a complete set of a promenade in the park, a large market scene, Biedermaier period, and a Swiss farm, complete with chalets. Heinrichsen and Allgeyer he has in plenty and a set of very rare flats depicting American Civil War officers (see *Model Soldiers* plate 73). Flats, he says, are so suitable for diorama making and the care and time spent on painting and shading them is rewarding.

Another side of his collection is his display of single examples of different commercial makers, both in lead and plastic, many still unidentified, but made as representative of maker's marks as possible. The identification of early Britains and their pirates and competitors is a simple one he says, compared with the attempt to classify the flats of different makers and sizes.

Finally, he has a large collection of paper soldiers, many in uncut sheets, and consisting primarily of Péllerin and Nancy publications, some dating back to the French First Empire, in some cases in reprint side by side with the originals. The collection also includes a number of rare sheets issued by McLaughlin (1900–20).

Hitrovo's tastes, like his collection, are varied. He likes Russell Flint water-colours and Russian military painters, but has no time for 'pop art'; he enjoys classical and lighter music and the bagpipes, but deplores the modern idiom; has an abiding love of opera; avidly collects postage stamps, books, and cigarette cards, especially those of military interest. His reading ranges from Herodotus, Thucydides and Homer to historical novels, also history, archaeology and anthropology.

He belongs to model soldier societies in America, Great Britain, Germany, Austria and Switzerland and keeps himself up to date with the activities of other bodies. Correspondence has always been heavy and of latter years ill health has caused him to curtail many of his activities.

We end with a quotation from one of his letters which, in our opinion, sums up the man:

> If I can be of some help to a collector, be he a member of our Society or not, and especially to younger or newer collectors, I am satisfied. If, in addition, a friendship is formed, that is an extra blessing and a bonus.

J. G. Garratt, *Farnham, England*

John G. Garratt was born in Wallasey in 1914, just at the outbreak of the Great War. His earliest recollection of model soldiers is of receiving them as gifts from an uncle who was killed towards the end of the war. The gift he remembers most clearly comprised a field ambulance with its khaki-clad attendants. His family had been connected for generations in some form or other with shipping and he grew up in the atmosphere of the great port of Liverpool. He was not however influenced by it, his thoughts turning to art, and if things had gone smoothly he would have pursued a career as an architect. However, this was not to be and after some vicissitudes he became an antiquarian bookseller's assistant and is now chief bibliographer for a firm specialising in the buying and selling of rare Americana.

To go back to formative years; whilst a boy in Liverpool he developed a liking for the Middle Ages, which still remains, but at the same time he had the average boy's interest in Britains' and Hill's products. Together with a close friend, he built up quite a considerable array of the usual Highlanders, naval detachments, lancers and guardsmen in their familiar glazed red boxes. At the age of sixteen, when the family left Liverpool for Brighton, these boxes were given away and the phase of interest seemed completely obliterated in the newly-found world of outdoor sketching. No spark was lit even when a collection of Heyde Romans with chariots came his way but he now remembers with regret the casting out of what must have been a Courtenay knight.

Drawing and writing (on architecture, local history and the like) and the absorbing interest of his bibliographical studies occupied him fully until the war when, having passed Grade III, he spent six hours, by mistake, with the Royal Army Pay Corps at Sidcup. The error was soon rectified; the army decided that he would have made the world's worst soldier (a sort of Corporal Schweik) and he was left in peace for another eighteen months. Then the Air Ministry decided they could use him and he spent the next four years at a maintenance unit in Gloucester.

On demobilisation, and now married, he decided to resume bookselling and returned to Brighton. Painting and drawing still occupied much of his leisure and the acquisition of a house with a long garden introduced him to a new art. So it was not until some years later

Above The author completing the painting of a collection of Schweitzer flats

that he casually observed in the window of a toyshop a collection of mounted medieval figures which so appealed to him and his interest in the possibilities of heraldic painting that he decided to buy half a dozen. These turned out to be Timpo's 'King Arthur' series and, having painted them in authentic colours, he was so pleased with them that he eagerly sought fresh models. These inevitably came along and by the time Britains' 'Knights of Agincourt' made their appearance the collection had grown.

A meeting with L. H. Cox and Captain Jewson followed, opening up an entirely new world. Research is part of a bookseller's business and, having 'ghosted' one work on eighteenth-century water-colour painting, written another on drawing and compiled the history of a local village, the urge made itself felt to discover more about model soldiers. The collectors whom he met seemed extremely vague in their knowledge of dates of issue or even of ascription of maker and he likewise found little help forthcoming from more official sources. A visit to the Public Library and research in the British Museum revealed the paucity of the literature on the subject. Then came a letter from the collector for whom he had acted as 'ghost'. In effect it said that the writer had been asked to do an article on model soldiers for a projected encyclopaedia of antiques to be published in several volumes. He was too old, and would Garratt do it? In despair Garratt turned to his wife. 'You can do it,' she said, and he did. He now realises the blunders he perpetrated but later, when a further commission for an article appeared in a famous magazine for connoisseurs, he was able to cover the subject with greater authority.

The idea then occurred to his wife that a full-scale book was a necessity. Again he demurred, lacking the courage to face so big a task, and again his spouse proved the solid rock, ever encouraging, putting up with the litter of half-painted models, manuscript and reference books, the visits of enthusiasts and photographers. Nothing however would have been achieved

Opposite These two exquisite set pieces, an eighteenth century duel, *above*, and 54mm Cromwellians and Royalists, *below*, are perfect examples of the work of Josianne des Fontaines

Three Boer War models, 54mm by Marrion

without the altruistic help of collectors and manufacturers all over the world.

Garratt's collection is not a large one. His interest lies mainly in the Middle Ages and he has examples of troops of this period from many different countries and makers. Apart from the many examples of commercial type, there are representative models by Gammage, a dozen or so foot and mounted Courtenays, some of Hinton's medievals, two beautiful Pings (one a gift, one a commission), a Crimean War officer by Hinton, a Stadden Zouave, two Romans and a magnificent Russian of 1812 by Murray, a few South African War troopers by Marrion, a whole group by Kaufmann, some delightful tiny models by Niblett and Higgins (including a bravura 54mm Pepys by the latter), various models by Alcocer, David, Surén, Wooten, Cooke, Broman, Jackson and Cliffe Arquette, a Historex, an example by Arnholm, a most lovely collection of Erikssons, some painted by the master himself, a Series 77 and four lovely models by Brunoe. Nearly all these fine figures were gifts from the makers.

There are some unusual models in the collection, such as a number by Café Storme, a group of medieval figures by Mokarex, but cast in lead, and a complete set of Reamsa's 'El Cid', given him by George Erik. He has two fine little models made by Charles Sweet, sent to him from America, some beautifully painted 'tinies' from Peter Gilder, a number of Suréns, and a collection of Dickinsons.

He has no regrets for his lack of interest in the Napoleonic period and has no leaning towards regimental dress. The idea of large masses of any particular regiment has never appealed and he has not a single example of modern troops by Britains or Heyde.

The other part of the collection is the assembly of flats. Here again the Middle Ages predominates and he has managed to acquire a representative selection by most of the various well-known and not-so-well-known makers. There is a large series by Ochel, some by Neckel, a magnificent group by Gottstein-Blum (given him by Michael V. Hitrovo), a host of original Heinrichsens (including a tournament), Rössner's most interesting conceptions and a fine series of charging knights by Scholtz (again a gift, this time from the maker). Many of these were used and converted where necessary in a diorama of the Battle of Lewes (now in Anne of Cleves House, Lewes) but sufficient remain to make one day a large diorama of a typical battle of the thirteenth- to fifteenth-century period. There is also a large group of original Heinrichsen Greeks, Romans and Carthaginians, Egyptians (including some fine chariots), a handful of Saxons, Vikings and the like; then, after the Middle Ages, *Landsknechts*, Elizabethans, Thirty Years' War, Seven Years' War,

Marlborough, a few Napoleonics and some later periods, mainly of Swedish manufacture, and above all a very rare Høy.

Allied to these is the civilian section, including solids, plastics and flats. The flats embrace ancient times, the Middle Ages (with a market scene by Heinrichsen), Rössner's delightful nobility and peasants, Chinese by Müller and a few of the English Sovereign series by Carbago. He also has a few of the large flats, notably one of Frederick the Great by Schweitzer after Hilpert, Washington (equestrian) by Rössner, a *Landsknecht* by Scholtz-Lecke, medieval warriors by Lorenz, a lovely set of tournament knights by Schweizter, a marching infantryman of about 1800 by an unknown German maker and Rössner's beautiful Persian Hunting and Fairytale sets, for the painting of which he consulted coloured reproductions of the manuscript Poems of Nizami, on which they are based. Other sets of which he is very fond are Hafer's Nefertiti, Egyptian fowling and the medieval hawking scene from *Les Très Riches Heures du Duc de Berry*.

Civilians in the round include many from ancient times, one of Hahn's rare plaster troubadours, pirates,

Above A very rare Danish flat by Høy. The lion is missing from the top of the King's helmet. In the possession of the Copenhagen Museum, who recast a few models from the original mould for presentation purposes only

Left It is refreshing to find that some makers will produce models with no military connection. This fine bullfighting figure is one of a series of portraits designed by G. Erik, once of Wimbledon, South London, for Reamsa

Above A Minoan bull-jumper. A flat by Hafer

a lovely large pair of eighteenth-century rococo figures from Italy, the delightful horse-riding 'Herald' models and a fine collection of Merten's 40mm medieval ladies and children. One most amusing figure is a six-inch caricature of Don Quixote, the head and limbs of which shake when touched, which the author's daughter brought back from New York.

Many of the models still remain unpainted as Garratt finds that his other activities – which include drawing, bibliographical research, listening to classical music, gardening, church-work and Sunday School teaching, to say nothing of gathering material for books on model soldiers and correspondence all over the world – leave him little time for this.

As will be seen, he is not, unlike so many collectors of model soldiers, completely absorbed in the technical details of his chosen field and is rarely seen at those gatherings where the talk is of shabracques, the differences of the various facings of the troops of the eighteenth century, the military composition of bodies of men, the working out of war-games and the like. He prefers to work quietly in the background, assimilating information and forming his own judgements of the respective qualities of various makers, varied by an occasional visit to Hamleys, Hummels and Tradition, or a day with a congenial maker or collector, such as Frederick Ping, Henry Harris, Cornelius Frazer or Eric Kroner-Grimm, who have a wide range of intelligent interests.

Norman F. Judd, *Killiney, Co Dublin, Eire*

Norman F. Judd is a retired fellmonger, a company director, a borough councillor, a Peace Commissioner and a model soldier collector. His chief interest is in the welfare of the people of the villages of Killiney and Dalkey and he admits that if it were not for the attention and care of his ever sympathetic wife, his collection would not be kept as clean, dusted and cared for as it is at present.

It is many years since he began to take an interest in the model soldier, as a sidelight of military history, and it has remained an absorbing pastime ever since. His range is wide and he collects models of all nations, makers, materials and periods. One might say that he and his wife live in a military setting for their house, standing on a wind-swept hill and built in 1870 as a replica of a French chateau, could also serve as a medieval towered and crenellated castle.

Judd's activities in the model soldier world have progressed sporadically, long periods of inactivity alternating with a flurry of buying. Indeed, about 1953, his interest was actually flagging but was revived by his discovery of the British Model Soldier Society.

Opposite A vivid reconstruction by Ashton McDonnell of the Ambush of Braddock. Models by Stadden and Imrie, and conversions by the collector

Norman F. Judd

Through becoming a member he discovered the excellence of Gammage and the wonder of Courtenay. His regret is that he purchased no more than thirty-six of the latter at a time when they were reasonably priced compared with today.

His collection is perhaps most remarkable for the examples on a large scale of two firms of widely differing materials and styles. Some years ago he discovered Segom, a well-known Paris firm who issue slightly odd-shaped plastic figures which the purchaser assembles and paints. This resulted in his collection of models of the Irish Brigade in the service of France in 1770, famous as the 'Wild Geese'. Of the Regiment of Dillon he has forty men and four standards, and other regiments include Clare-Berwick and Walshe. His other collection was due to his most extraordinary acquisition by purchase by weight (15cwt!) of a vast number of Eriksson's castings direct from the Galta Eireann factory when the ill-fated Authenticast movement was forced to close down. Of the lesser-known ranges there are: modern Swedish troops in tricorne hats, Brazilian Jaegers, 1870, Spanish falangists in red berets, Papal Guards in fatigue uniforms, Austrians and Danes of the Seven Years' War, Senegalese, Moroccan and Algerian infantry of before 1914, Maginot Line troops, West Africans, Sepoys, Philippine Infantry, Cromwellian pikemen, Brazilian Indians, and Siberian Guards of 1904.

As we have already indicated, Gammage stands high in his estimation, and he naturally includes the Egyptian slave-girls and the Shardanu bodyguard. Other models of ancient times are Nebuchadnezzar and Rameses II, both by Mignot. Stadden is another favourite of Judd's, and many of his Napoleonic range are present. Nor does he scorn plastics, and here one can compare the pre-war Elastolin (Washington crossing the Delaware) with the later change in style and material (mounted Huns).

Perhaps the most exciting portion, however, is the small collection which we can only suppose are by Métayer, which Judd picked up at auction some years ago. Each is on its individual stand, with a brass plate bearing the legend pinned on.

We are indebted to Shamus O. Wade for some of the information given above.

Examples of the purposeful infantryman. Models by Eriksson, produced by Authenticast

J. H. Bevan Rees, *Northampton, England*

Bevan Rees constructing an Egyptian temple as a setting for some of his models

To many collectors, the actual making of models is difficult. Even if they have abundant artistry and a knowledge of uniform or costume, the technical processes involved may well prove unsurmountable as both the making of a mould and the casting of the resultant figure need time and a suitable environment. Some have the necessary skill and patience to paint bought castings but are clumsy when it comes to moulding or carving an original figure. The question has often been asked: 'Why bother to make your own when there are so many types available?' A reasonable enough argument. One answer is that there are yet many examples of many periods and countries which are not readily available, even with the avalanche pouring out from commercial maker and specialist alike. Another factor to be taken into serious consideration is expense. If the war-gamer contemplates the employment of dozens of models, the multiple cost of even these 20mm figures, the cheapest in the model soldier range, can be considerable: and it is quite easy to see that a battle scene of twenty or so Courtenay knights or a square of Gammage or Stadden Waterloo British can cost a considerable sum.

Apart from this there is the achievement angle – the fulfilment of the co-ordination of research, experience, artistry and craftsmanship which results in the creation of a model which is the brain-child of its maker.

That is why there are, in the legions of collectors of model soldiers, a large number who, whilst prizing the creations of others, also create their own. The professional is still bound to a certain extent by the question of possible demand – the amateur (using the word in the true sense) can divest himself of this consideration.

But those whose inclination is not for the actual making and casting of models but who are capable of creating something different by building on an existing figure, are also legion and, judging from some of the examples that we have seen, can claim to be artists in their own right.

J. H. Bevan Rees is such a one. By profession a chartered municipal engineer employed in local government and married but having no children, he has seen twenty-one years service in the Territorial Army, Corps of the Royal Engineers.

As was inevitable, Britains' products were his earliest purchases and even at this stage of his development he arranged his models in simple diorama form. It was in 1931, however, that he really began collecting in earnest. From his earliest days he had been fired by knightly chivalry as recounted by Froissart (and who can resist the trumpet-blast of that pageant of the Middle Ages?) and his fascination with the period

Ancient Egyptians, each a variation of one standard Britains' model

found fulfilment in the advent of Courtenay. Britains' Tournament Set also increased his scope.

In course of time, as an ever-increasing number and variety of products became available, his interests widened and the collection now embraces a varied range of military and civilian types of many periods. It numbers some three and a half thousand models of which about two thousand are Britains or conversions thereof, together with ancillaries such as artillery, transport and vehicles of many periods. The total collection includes many figures by Gammage, Hinton and Stadden and the usual miscellany acquired and kept for various reasons. All are 54mm models in metal.

Rees's main interests have now been fined down to four: the Ancient World, with special emphasis on the Old and New Testament times and the civilisations of the Bible; the seventeenth century and the English Civil War; Royal Engineers and Royal Artillery, together with their historical predecessors; and civilian costume. He is at the moment concentrating almost exclusively on the Ancient World, which to him is just as fascinating as the Middle Ages once were, as well as the Royal Engineers.

A high proportion of the figures have been produced by conversion from standard commercial castings and the whole of the process is done by soldering; no extraneous materials such as plasticene, plastic wood, barbola, toothpaste tubes or similar expedients being permitted. When completed every figure must be homogenous and capable of being handled and resisting reasonable wear and tear. Rees has done very little casting as he finds that conversion has more than fulfilled his requirements. Indeed, at times the fascination of conversion has brought painting to a standstill. The well-known and delightful herald from Britains' Tournament Set for instance has formed the basis of thirty or so different and varied medieval figures, whilst the running Zulu by the same maker has been the model for creating over sixty Old Testament, Egyptian, Canaanite, Hebrew and similar figures. The set of Britains' 'Eastern Peoples' has also formed an admirable starting point for the creation of other Biblical types.

Many conversions are less extreme, consisting merely of varying the attitudes without altering either type or period, as when a walking figure is brought to a halt, or a standing or running figure is changed to a kneeling position. Virtually all his Hebrews are conversions of Britains' models, as are many of the Egyptians which, however, are supplemented by Gammage and Courtenay. Of the Romans, many are again by Courtenay and Gammage, with Hinton (he finds Stadden's scale incompatible with the others), whilst the Assyrians are by Hinton and Courtenay.

All these figures of the Ancient World are being slowly incorporated into dioramas which, when completed, will be photographed for use in religious instruction. Rees constructs his own dioramas from the original design to the making of buildings, trees, tents, carts, cooking utensils and the like. Apart from these, he has made a number of dioramas including *Prelude to Battle* (an English Civil War group) and a RE mine lifting party.

Rees first came into contact with Courtenay's models in 1931, when he saw them in Morrell's (now Hummel's) in Burlington Arcade. They were one of the first serious attempts by an English artist to create and market historical figures worthy of being described as 'collectors' pieces' and at that time were what we today would regard as fantastically cheap.

Of the ancient models made by Courtenay, Rees has the beautiful Nefertiti, the Pharaoh Seti I, Cleopatra and a slave-girl with long-handled fan, a Phoenician officer and two variations of a foot-soldier; an Assyrian and a Babylonian spearman; an infantryman with a long siege shield; and a bowman, a trumpeter and a standard bearer (which is a variation of the foot-soldier). Two Roman gladiators, one with a sword, the other a retiarius, were withdrawn early, but not so the marching legionary. There is a gap until there comes a series of Vikings and then the pace increases through the eleventh to thirteenth centuries (Knight of St John and Knight Templar, Richard I and Crusaders) until the later Middle Ages are reached and here we cannot do more than ask the reader to turn to the notice on Courtenay or to Hummel's Catalogue. Certainly Rees has a most impressive collection of early figures in all styles – foot knights (some with detachable helmets) mounted combatants, longbow men, men-at-arms, esquires, double figures in combat, personalities in different heraldic bearings and a long range of important personages including Edward I, Joan of Arc

Royal Engineers lifting mines. Conversions from Timpo hollow-casts (Rees collection)

with three of her captains, Edward III (two figures) and several of the Black Prince, his wife and court ladies.

Later history is represented by Henry VIII and his Queens, Wolsey, Queen Elizabeth, Drake, Raleigh, Mary, Queen of Scots, Lady Jane Grey and headsman, Charles I and II (in two versions), Nell Gwynne, musketeer, pikeman and officer of the Regiment of Footguards, ending with monarchs of our own era.

His Royal Engineer figures are all conversions from Britains, Timpo and others and are intended to depict every activity. For detail he makes use of official photographs, training manuals and the like.

Allan Robinson-Sager, *Toronto, Canada*

Mr Robinson-Sager is a typical example of the slow evolution from acquisitor to collector. As a boy he played with Britains' models incessantly but upon his family's departure for Australia, the collection became detached from the rest of the luggage and was never seen again. It was not until years later that the advent of Britains' 'Knights of Agincourt' and the Herald 'Wars of the Roses' rekindled the latent fire.

The medieval period held sway in the form of dioramas for some years, until the acquisition of an Imrie Napoleonic group of gunners with a cannon caused a change of heart. With what he can now only regard as utter folly, the Agincourt Knights were consigned to the flames of the furnace.

Soon after this he left Australia, determined to devote some part of his time and activities to the searching out of fine models and making the acquaintance of collectors. In this he was greatly helped by an amiable American dealer with the evocative name of Lewis Evans. (One versed in Anglo-American history will know that an eighteenth-century Lewis Evans is revered as a great writer on geographical and cartographical matters whose works command very high prices.) Evans, a staunch Anglophile, was agent for the emergent Stadden, Gammage and Hinton (then Hinton-Hunt) and Robinson-Sager spent much time

Heinrichsen flats, 20–60mm, and semi-solids, together with original boxes (Robinson-Sager collection)

and money in his store adding to his collection of models and building up a fine reference library of Napoleonic uniform material.

This led to the gradual acquisition of a separate collection of commercial figures by Mignot, Heyde and Britains, together with reference books on the period. These he regards as the most significant of all the toy soldier makers because they reflect the fashion and public taste of their time and have a more lasting influence that that of the others of more specialised talents.

Flats, too, began to interest him, especially those of Heinrichsen, and others between 1840 and 1900. In addition to these he has a very large collection of fine quality moderns, including the extraordinary Scholtz's *Retreat from Moscow*.

Arriving in Canada he attended his first Society meeting equipped with a large diorama composed of Stadden 30mm figures. These proved of great interest to members who had not realised the possibilities of these delightful little models. Joining the tiny Staddens now is a veritable swarm of Surén's fine models in the same size. Allied to this, although not of the same quality, is a very large collection of the early Grove and Benoy figures, which he was fortunate to buy in bulk from Shamus Wade.

The evidence would tend to show that his main interest is in solids and hollow-casts, but Robinson-Sager is insistent that, for the connoisseur, the engraved 20mm Continental flat is the last word for its accuracy of engraving, its animation and its historical significance. Furthermore, its capability for display, either singly or with others in diorama form, its size, and its capacity for storage are not to be ignored.

Robinson-Sager's occupation as an art director in advertising gives him a solid basis for experimenting in painting, which he lavishes on his flats. He also favours an artistic setting for these, considering that the result justifies the amount of time spent on bringing out to the full the qualities inherent in these little figures.

Early models by Heyde in the original box

Charles A. Sweet, *Bristol, Conn, USA*

Charles A. Sweet is one of those individuals who get through their ordinary work and then proceed to employ their leisure in an astonishing variety of ways. He is a banker and is naturally attracted to professional activities including the past presidency of the Suburban Bankers' Association, a Directorship of the Bristol Chamber of Commerce, membership of the Bristol Real Estate Boards and a committee membership of the Connecticut Bankers' Association. Allied to these one can list Past President of the Bristol Rotary Club, Director of Superior Electric Company of Bristol, Trustee of the School of Banking, Williams College, and Commissioner of the Bristol Board of Education.

Charles A. Sweet in his workshop

His activities outside his calling lead him to such different things as his Congregational Church committee, cubmaster, hunting, fishing and 'Play by Play' radio sports announcing. At his college he played football and baseball and wrestled with both his subjects and his colleagues. During the Second World War he was a lieutenant in the United States Navy.

Married to a woman who herself has many interests, has been on the staff of the Peabody Museum and been concerned in several African archaeological expeditions, and having three sons, Sweet's full, rounded, eclectic life is completed (or, perhaps, they would all say, revolves round) his embracing love of the model soldier.

He has thousands of models of all sizes and periods, many of which he has made himself. The first figures he can remember owning were a set of First World War soldiers. The basis of his collection is formed by the commercial models that he acquired from time to time. He has a thousand odd Britains including the horse-drawn vehicles and gun-teams so popular between the wars (but not, however, the pontoon train, which he would dearly love to acquire); sets of all of Mignot's ancients, medievals, and some of their Napoleonics; some models by Figur, a tremendous number by Heyde and Spenkuch, painted and unpainted, including a number of chariots and the usual accumulation of figures by lesser-known and unknown firms, including a number of Austrians of the 1890s, and Spaniards by the same maker.

Gradually, he began to realise that authenticity was the one thing worth striving for, and with this ideal before him he began to collect the works of the masters. He now owns a magnificent array of about one hundred and fifty Courtenay knights, including twenty mounted. These he keeps in a large glass case, in simulated battle, and they prove a constant delight to one with an abiding love of history. Parallelling these is a collection of twenty of Ping's individual creations and, going further back in history, Gammage's 'Ancients'. A selection of American makers is an obvious part of his collection and comprises figures by Imrie, Murray and Bussler.

One of the largest sections is devoted to the work of Stadden. Of the 54mm size he has several hundreds, including many painted by himself. Equally prized are his Stadden miniatures, over a hundred of the original 30mm range, among which are five dioramas, a set of Gordon Highlanders, Waterloo era, pikemen and musketeers and, above all, a horse grenadier of the late 1600s. Particularly rare are his hundred one-inch figures, British, Prussians, French, Dutch and Spanish which were withdrawn from the Stadden range after a short time and are much prized by collectors. Again

The war-game table as set up by Sweet

in this size he has a group of Cromwellian pikemen which are even more rare, and the only ones in their scale that he has ever heard of (similar models, however, made by Niblet and Higgins are in existence).

As we have remarked elsewhere, collecting the smaller size figures has become a very favourite and rewarding occupation. Besides his Staddens, Sweet has a large collection of 20 and 30mm productions by other makers, including a complete group of various European powers of the 1890s by Scruby, a tremendous group by SAE and a Napoleonic army consisting of models by Greenwood and Gammage.

Not content with this, Sweet makes his own models, of which he has produced thousands, all beautifully painted and serving a dual purpose – for war-games and for display. He works in the 30mm size and has completed armies of the medieval and American Revolutionary War periods. He begins with a wooden prototype. After casting, filing and buffing, the figure is painted, often with the assistance of his sons, and as often as not incorporated in a diorama. A mounted knight he sent us shows that he uses the continental method of pinning the detachable rider to the saddle.

Sweet is a member of the Miniature Figure Collectors of America, the British Model Soldier Society and the Company of Military Collectors and Historians.

The War-gamers

We have noticed that an increasing number of collectors specialise in the 'miniature' figure, that is, one not exceeding 30–40mm. The majority seem to prefer to acquire them for use in the war-game (which is spreading rapidly in popularity), rather than for exhibition in a glass case. A word or two on the history of the war-game would seem appropriate, although we have no intention of discussing its actual rules.

The royal Dauphins were given model soldiers not exclusively as playthings but with a purpose. The automata made by Hautch were used to educate the Prince in army manoeuvres and the use of automata in various forms such as trellis tongs (an example by Captain Riviere is well illustrated in Harris's *Model Soldiers*, p. 42) continued into the nineteenth century, an outstanding example being Captain Wathen's little equestrians on springs. Blocks printed with figures were also in use but all these types were designed for use by a single person and it is the *Kriegspiel* as shown in Germany in 1824 and perhaps earlier that is the forerunner of the present war-game. The idea was developed by the Polish General Mieroslawski and the Prussian Major Kuntz. Heinrichsen also wrote a pamphlet on the subject, as did Tschischwitz in 1862.

The war-game, primarily designed for army personnel, was introduced to a larger audience by Lloyd Osbourne's notes on the interest displayed in it by Robert Louis Stevenson and to an even wider public by the publication of H. G. Wells's *Floorgames* in 1911.

The first germ of the idea is in the pamphlet *The Great Wargame for Young and Old* published in 1908, which Wells wrote for Britains, and in his *The New Machiavelli* (1911). He followed this by *Little Wars* in 1912–13: it had an immediate success, although his method of subjecting his models to actual physical injury by artillery is now looked upon with disfavour.

The advent of the enlightened collector, bent on preserving and not destroying the toys of the past and the present, sounded the death-knell of the Stevenson-Wells era and the dice and the measuring rule rook the place of the spring-breach-loader gun. No longer are little wars conducted piecemeal with improvisation of rules and models of all shapes and sizes; they are now scientific and computerised and can be conducted over the telephone, perhaps extending over weeks. With the newer scientific approach the need for models of a set size arose. There is some doubt as to whether a manufacturer made the first 'miniature' figures as an experiment or with this aim in view, or whether there was sufficient interest among collectors for them to persuade the makers to renounce the 54mm model. Be that as it may, the Spanish firm of Alymer claims that it was the first to introduce the smaller model. Grove and Benoy made a series fitting into copper stands early in the 1940s but they are now rarely met with. The makers whose 20–30mm models appear in most present-day collections are Stadden, Greenwood, Gammage, Hinton – all established makers of larger models and, more recently, Dickinson (who is now also turning his hand to 54mm figures) and Surén.

The models of the ill-starred firm of Swedish African Engineers, which had a remarkable vogue around the 1959–60 period, have proved most successful, being useful if not elegant, the clumsy casting spoiling the beauty of the Eriksson designs, and occasionally one comes across a few Skybird examples. Starlux make some excellent larger figures, as do Mertens (Berliner Miniatur-Plastiken) and Elastolin,

Above Drawings by G. Embleton which Charles Stadden converted inio 30mm models

and Eriksson's own masterly models are well known; but on the whole, the war-gamers prefer the smallest sizes. Prominent among American suppliers are Thomas and Scruby, whilst the plastics of Airfix have proved a godsend by reason of their variety of pose and cheapness of price.

The setting up of the figures and the arrangement of the landscape unit must take so long that one wonders what time can be left for the actual battle. Some war-gamers, having arranged their terrain, leave it as it is for their various engagements; others, more exacting or ambitious, plan a fresh landscape in keeping with each and every battle. Some, again, do not bother overmuch. Joseph Morschauser, for example, uses a few miniature trees set in an area covered with dark green paper, which thus represents a wood, a few tiny houses set on some grey, brown, or yellow paper is a town, a few slabs of wood with rounded corners are low hills. Charles Grant is another believer in sim-

Right Destruction in the Nursery. The old method of playing the war-game. From *The Graphic*, 1877

plicity. His terrain is composed of houses, trees and the like made by him and his son; hills are represented by one-inch contours of soft board. These are used in preference to elaborately arranged scenery, because they find that this elaboration tends to localise the action. Another factor they find important is the cleanliness of simplicity, very necessary for a permanent set up, enabling the game to be continued indefinitely.

Peter Gilder, by contrast, believes that beautifully painted models need an appropriate setting. He is especially skilful in making naturalistic terrains and employs many types of house of the period appropriate to the campaign in progress. His collection, comprising over three thousand Stadden, Gammage and Hinton models, all of the Napoleonic period, is delightfully painted and serves not only its primary purpose but at the same time is a delight to the eye. Jack Scruby is another advocate of the scenic setting. He has a twelve-foot by six-foot telescoping war-game table, on which are placed period houses roads, hills, trees, fences and all the other things necessary for realism. He enjoys setting up as much of the actual battle as possible and feels that he is thus involved from the beginning. Also of this way of thinking is Charles A. Sweet, Junior, who uses available model buildings appropriate to the battle. He tries to represent the actual placing of the accessories as accurately as possible, referring to contemporary engravings for the information, as in his *Battle of Guildford Court House*.

Charles Reaveley is fortunate enough to possess a complete room which he can use for his hobby, so that his war-game table (eight by five feet, extending to ten feet) is a permanency. His main interest is in the late nineteenth century which, in his opinion, gives the most easily integrated war-game. The figures, several thousand of them, are of 20 and 25mm scale and cover the Napoleonic period, the American Civil War, the Franco-Prussian War, the Northwest Frontier campaigns and the Second World War. A large percentage are of his own design and casting, which he learned some years ago from Lieutenant-Colonel J. R. Nicholson, together with specimens by Hinton, Scruby, Thomas, Skybird and prewar Dinky. He originally collected 54mm models, until introduced to the war-game by the late Captain Sachs, and he brings to his smaller figures the same care and attention that he lavished on the larger ones, maintaining a high standard of painting.

The above note on Reavely introduces another aspect of the war-game, that is, the type and number of models employed by devotees. Morschauser uses whatever is at hand at a given moment. He has used (and still does on occasion) Britains' 54mm figures, 30mm models by Scruby, Stadden, Eriksson, 22mm Airfix and 20mm Greenwood. The numbers depend on the game and the size of the table. A company of infantry can be one tray containing three figures, a dozen such trays, or a single tray containing a lone figure. Each tray is marked to correspond to a roster sheet which lists the strength of the particular unit it represents. The strength can vary. The figures are never removed from the trays, the casualties being marked off the roster sheet beside the name of the unit. When the strength of the unit reaches zero the whole tray is removed. He has fought battles with as few as forty and as many as three thousand pieces.

Charles Sweet's armies are mainly 30mm models with emphasis on the Middle Ages and the American Revolution. Of these two distinct periods ninety per cent are of his own design and casting. He has in addition an army of the 1890 period, including the overseas empires of the various European powers, composed of Scruby's products, and a complete Napoleonic army in 20mm mostly by Greenwood and Gammage, completed by his own originals and conversions. He paints all his models in such a manner that they may be used for exhibition and competition and completes them with a full complement of musicians and colours.

The battles fought by the Grants are between exactly similar armies, numbering some thousand foot

War-game figures by Greenwood in a realistic setting

and two hundred and fifty cavalry, with about ten guns per side, plus engineers, pontoons and the like. The models are all 30mm plastic, representing two armies of the mid-eighteenth century, say between Fontenoy and the end of the wars of Frederick the Great. Both armies are more or less fictitious, one being composed of an amalgam of the central European nations, the other predominantly French. With these armies individual battles are fought – some imaginary, others as near a reconstruction of an actual encounter as can be realised on the table. Tactical problems are evolved, and a continuous campaign is maintained. The latter is worked out on maps made by Charles Grant and a campaign may go on for months, with innumerable engagements ranging from the pitched battle to the head-on collision of skirmishing cavalry (which he says is much more difficult to resolve). Whilst we were visiting Brigadier Young we were interrupted by a telephone conversation between him and Grant, at the end of which it appeared that the latter had been annihilated!

Young uses an immense table, with merely a sketchy semblance of naturalism, consisting of a few grouped trees, some gravel and one or two most beautifully made fortresses. The battles he fights are mainly of the eighteenth century and he uses 30mm models by Surén, Saunders and Stadden and pirated Erikssons in plastic. The overall impression is that the miniature army is magnificent, irrespective of its purpose.

Young's methods of play are admirably set out in his book *Charge!*

Donald Featherstone, the enthusiastic propagandist of the war-game, uses a table of eight by five feet, surrounded by a six-inch raised wall of painted scenery which is changed to suit the particular terrain. The natural features are simulated by squares of hardboard, either sixteen or twenty-four inches on a side, upon which are built hills, sunken roads and so on. His armies consist of 30mm models by SAE (also plastic piracies of the same firm), Stadden (although these are rather large) and Scruby, and his own castings from original masters and from conversions of commercial figures. He also has two complete Napoleonic period armies of Hinton and Gammage and two armies of Airfix American Civil War figures. An offshoot is a small force of English archers and men-at-arms of the Crécy period in flats.

There are undoubtedly many collectors who use flats for the war-game. One of these is Sergeant Bastian who has assembled several distinct armies of these tiny, finely engraved models from the Continent. Nor must we omit the Bantocks. Their Napoleonic armies are each organised in divisions of between two hundred and forty and three hundred and fifty infantry, with supporting cavalry and artillery, according to the different nations, in an endeavour to keep as near as possible to the type of organisation in use at the time. The average infantry regiment consists of four companies of one officer, one sergeant, one drummer and ten men, plus Battalion Headquarters. A cavalry squadron is made up of two troops of one officer, one sergeant, one trumpeter and eight troopers, plus Squadron Headquarters. The men who distinguish themselves are all named and a record kept of their services and those of their regiments. Where possible many of the names used are those of actual men who served in the regiment in the original period. The places of those killed are filled by promotion or appointment. The record of the regiment is used to determine its morale, which may be an important factor in deciding the course of the next engagement.

They use a set of triple map boards (six inches to the mile) of the 'Interchangeable War Game' designed and supplied by Captain S. Sharpe (Retired) late 3rd Middlesex Rifle Volunteers, together with painted type metal blocks to represent the units. This was handed down to Granville by his father and must date from about 1890. Each player has an identical number of boards on which he moves his own force and there is a third set for an umpire. This enables the action to be fought without always seeing the enemy's dispositions, and emphasises the importance of reconnaissance, concealment and surprise. It is not until the opposing forces actually make contact that the actual ground is constructed and the flat figures make their appearance to resolve the action. Where necessary they draw their own actual scale maps – of particular relevance in modern war-games, where concealment is of such importance. They have built up large opposing forces for the two World Wars but find the complications of armaments make modern warfare very involved; they prefer the wars of the ancient world or of the Napoleonic era.

The Young Enthusiasts

Timothy Head, *Scarborough*, *England*

Many a young collector-to-be has gazed spellbound at the array of models in Hummel's window in Burlington Arcade: Niblett, Courtenay, blazoned and armoured; versatile Ping; Scottish clansmen, knights, kings and queens; full-dress uniform by Greenwood; presentation Sentry Box, Napoleonic Staddens under a huge magnifying glass. And at Tradition in Piccadilly the whole stock of Stadden *en masse*. Magnificent, but not for them.

The casual reader, glancing at some of the plates in the present volume, may feel the same. Here, he might well say, are the world's collectors, here are the world's finest makers. But should it always be caviare? Is there bread to eat, or must we always have cake? The impression might well be formed that the model soldier world consists only of masterpieces for the rich man, to be purchased regularly by the shelf-full.

If that were so, what hope for the beginner, limited in experience and probably in cash? (There is always the tendency to fight shy of the humbler, easily purchased items, but we who have been collecting for maybe only a few years know how quickly they become unobtainable.) It is with the young beginner in mind (but more as an excuse to express thanks for an entirely unsophisticated and charming letter of appreciation for our previous book) that we write this section on Timothy Head (and two others) in the hope that it will encourage others of their age.

When we first corresponded with him he was at St Peter's School, York, his home being at Scarborough. He is not very good at sport, he says, but enjoys boating, and belonged to the school rowing club, which performed on the River Ouse. He is interested in drama, directing rather than acting, and wrote a play for the Scarborough Drama Festival. He has also made a film, helped by a few friends.

He was given his first soldiers at the age of six. He remembers them well – twelve bandsmen, pre-war Britains, with moveable arms. Whenever possible his father took him to Bridlington, where there was a shop which dealt in commercial models. Later, a visit to London led to the fascination of Hummels and one or two fine models were purchased; no more, because of the expense. His ideal was to be able to afford Staddens, Courtenays, Pings, and a mounted Nibletts.

At present his collection consists mainly of hollow-casts and plastics, with a preponderance of Britains, amounting in all to nearly six hundred models, the most costly being two by Gammage (a Napoleonic infantryman and a hoplite). The models Timothy particularly likes are the set of Cherilea Vikings, Herald's Trojans, Reynold's lead Vikings (no longer obtainable), Timpo's 'Arthurian knights' and the Quentin Durward set, Britain's 'Knights of Agincourt', Herald's 'Wars of the Roses', Starlux knights, Herald's 'American Civil War', and their 'Eyes Right' series, Timpo's 'Waterloo' and 'French Foreign Legion', Cherilea's 'Black Prince', a Heyde marine (40mm) a Johillco Arab, an Elastolin Confederate, a French aluminium figure, and last, but certainly not least, three small Eriksson horsemen. Some of these he has repainted himself, but generally speaking can allow little time for this pursuit.

In 1958 he visted Paris, and was fascinated by the collection of models at *Les Invalides*. He is alert to the model soldier world, as he has already discovered the Marston Moor diorama, transferred from the disbanded Royal United Service Institution to York Museum.

He likes his home town and makes the most of the beach and the country when at home. He paints, and exhibits at the local art society. At the moment he is reading Fine Arts at Newcastle University, hoping one day to make a career in some branch of this. He looks forward to the day when he will be earning enough money to allow him to add more frequently to his collection of models.

Gregory Kurdian, *Wichita*, *Kansas*, *USA*

A perennial surprise to the author of a reference book is the number of letters he receives. Some are laudatory, a few merely offer criticism, a few sound criticism, many request help or advice or assistance. They come from such far-separated places as New Zealand and Wichita. One intriguing specimen came from the latter. From the enthusiasm of the phrasing it was clear that the writer was young. Correspondence followed, and it transpired that Gregory Kurdian was indeed young. What was surprising was that whilst still at school he had formed a model-soldier society consisting of three members – surely an example of young enthusiasm.

Timothy Head with a few of his models

What is more, his letters were headed 'Kurdian Enterprises', and it was later discovered that he dealt (also while at school) in ancient weapons and firearms.

The next time we heard of him he was in Italy on a study course, and a present of a number of models by Italian makers showed that he had not lost interest in his hobby. His most recent letter is headed 'Kurdian Travel Agency', and he admits that most of his time is occupied by this. Only occasionally now is he able to devote time to his models, although, on the other hand, he has the opportunity of purchasing foreign productions from time to time, during his periodic visits to Europe.

At first his collection was, as would be expected, a miscellaneous one made of figures that he chanced upon, together with a liking for war-games in general. Since his return from Europe he has concentrated on very specific lines, and now collects Russian and German Imperial, Napoleonic and United States troops, and above all, everything to do with Italy, especially the Italian army from the First World War to the present day. He feels there is little accurate information available regarding this period, and would like to feel that his studies will have some permanent value for other collectors. To assist himself in these studies, he collects as many actual uniforms and head-dresses as he can, and these in turn aid him in his conversion of models of other periods into those of Italian interest. He finds that figures of the Napoleonic period and French troops of the Great War are the most useful for this purpose. He has a very large collection of books and prints, and weapons of all descriptions.

He has joined a number of societies including those of America, France, Germany, Italy and Great Britain, and all in all the name of Gregory Kurdian may yet be one to conjure with.

Wolfgang Weiss, *Brunswick, Germany*

The third of the trio is Wolfgang Weiss, who was born in 1941, and is studying chemistry at Brunswick. His interest in history began when at grammar school, where he was fortunate enough to have a teacher who brought to his subject immense enthusiasm. Weiss was fascinated by the idea of man's fight for freedom throughout the ages, especially the inner strength given to the Greeks in their struggle against the Persians.

He began collecting reproductions of ancient Hellenic life and, at the same time, was introduced by another boy to toy soldiers, with which they played the rough war-game. This led him to search the toy shops, and he was successful in finding flats of Greek hoplites. From then onwards, all his pocket money went on flats, and he began to visit collections and exhibitions.

He was able to observe the excellence of the painting of professionals, and, having learned the art of water-colour (or perhaps gouache) at school, he decided to paint his models in this medium. The result was such that he began to be noticed by other collectors, and from them he received advice and encouragement. He has been to every conference held at Plassenburg Castle, Kulmbach, since 1957, and his ideas have blossomed in the genial atmosphere created by the collectors and makers who gather there annually. In fact one collector was so enthusiastic that he gave young Weiss three complete sets of models on the understanding that he confine his collection to figures of ancient times.

At one of the first meetings he had the good fortune to meet J. R. Granville Bantock, who invited him to England to see him and his collection. Weiss acknowledges how much he is in his debt. He had already experimented in the making of silhouette figures out of sheet tin, and Bantock taught him to solder and make fresh figures out of several pieces of different figures with plaster moulds.

Weiss's aim is to draw and engrave and produce his own models when he has completed his present studies.

As has been shown, his main interest is in the way of life of ancient civilisations centred round the Mediterranean, and his collection comprises some two to three thousand standard size flats and some cut out of tin. Although the assembly is more or less a 'type' collection, he has also made a number of dioramas of the ancient world, and at an exhibition in 1964 he showed dioramas of ancient Egypt, a Greek market place, Nero fiddling while Rome burned, and others, painted flats for other exhibitors, and had on show some of his own cutouts. We are very impressed with his own 6cm cut-out of Don Quixote and Sancho Panza riding into the Andalusian sunset in search of knightly adventure.

Don Quixote and Sancho Panza. 6cm flats, made and painted by W. Weiss, the scenery by E. Thiel

Makers and manufacturers mentioned in the text

ABEL and FRY *London* (*c* 1910–14) Manufacturer of poor quality 50mm hollow-casts

AIRFIX *London* Contemporary manufacturers of plastic kits, and 20 and 54mm plastics. Designed by J. Niblett

ALCOCER *Barcelona* Contemporary manufacturer of 54mm solids

ALLGEYER *Fürth* (before 1800–96) Manufacturer of flats (mainly 30mm) semi-solids and solids. Principal competitor of Heinrichsen. Successively Johann Christian, Johann Friedrich, Konrad

ALMIRALL *Barcelona* Contemporary manufacturer of high quality 54mm solids; the foot soldiers are rather attenuated, and the horses not particularly successful. Currently designing *The Canadian Collectors' Series* for R. Payen, a dealer, of Iberville, Canada, the first models being Wolfe and Montcalm (mounted)

ALYMER (Angel Comes Placencia) *Burjasot, Valencia* (*c* 1928 on) Manufacturer of 20mm models. Claims to be the first to introduce these. Can at times be obtained in England but very expensive

AMERICAN METAL FIGURES (W. H. Long) *Bay City, Michigan* (*c* 1949–56) Manufacturer of poor quality 54mm solids

AMERICAN SOLDIER COMPANY *Glendale, N.Y.* (*c* 1904) Manufacturer of 54mm hollow-casts

AMMON *Nuremberg* (1794–1921) Manufacturer of flats and semi-solids, of various sizes. Successively Johann Wolfgang, Christoph, Christian

ANHOLM (R. F.) *Copenhagen* Contemporary private maker of 54mm solids

ANTONINI (Francesco and Luciano, 'Figir') *Rome* (1927 on) Manufacturers of 55mm solids, the riders detachable

ARMITAGE *London* (*c* 1930) Short-lived firm of manufacturers of poor quality 54mm hollow-casts

ARQUETTE (Cliff) *Idaho* Contemporary maker of large, carved wood figures, dressed in natural materials. Strong element of caricature. American Civil War personalities. Replicas in 54mm in lead made under his direction by Thomas

ARTHUR (H. J.) *London* Contemporary maker of large, carved and painted wood figures, very attenuated and elongated. American Revolutionary War; American Civil War; British Army from 1650

AUTHENTICAST *USA-Eire* 54mm solids designed by Eriksson and others for COMET. Original in design and well cast

BALLADA (Michael) *Paris* Contemporary maker of fine quality 54mm solids. Of recent years working only to commission

BANNER-MODEL *Copenhagen* (1948) 50mm solids

BAPTISTE (E.) *Paris* Contemporary maker who works under the name of André Hubert. Avowed purpose: to produce a limited number of models for his own pleasure or to give away, or to sell to any who wish to buy. Solids, 54mm in the traditional French method

BARCLAY *USA* (*c* 1914) Manufacturer of inferior quality 54 and 60mm hollow-casts

BARKER (Harry G. Jnr) American private maker

BECK (Franz) Contemporary German maker of flats

BERGMANN *Strasbourg* (1800–1904) Manufacturer of large flats. Successively Antoine-Joseph, Charles Theodore, Charles

BERNE (Maurice) *Paris* (*c* 1935–?) Manufacturer of solids, aluminium, papier-mâché

BITTARD (Jacques) *Paris* Contemporary maker of fine quality 54mm solids. Collaborator with Pepin in creation of flats

BOUTET (Reg) *Granada Hills, California* Contemporary maker of 54mm solids of fine quality. Limited range of personality figures. Trade name CAMEO

BRIGADIER-STATUETTE (Carl Alexander) *Copenhagen* (*c* 1954) 45mm solids

BRITAINS (William Ltd.) *London* (1893 on) Most famous of all manufacturers of model soldiers. Invented the 'hollow-cast'. Mainly standard 54mm size. In 1954 incorporated Herald Miniatures (plastic). Lead models now for export only

BULL *London* (1877) Advertised a number of gun-metal models 'made at different times during the last seventy years'. None has so far been identified

BUSSLER (Dr K. G.) *Wollaston, Mass.* (Before 1948 on) Maker of 30 and 54mm solids

CAFÉ STORME *Mouscron* Contemporary coffee importers who include plastic models in the tins of their product. An incredible collection of figures depicting every period of Belgian history, both military and civil. Horses sometimes out of scale. (Produced by R. Gillet of Paris)

CARMAN (W. Y.) *London* (fl. 1938–45) Maker of 54mm solids. Combined with O. Gottstein and Dr L. Barnes to produce CARBAGO flats, the first to be produced in England

CASANELLAS (Baldomero, La Guerra) *Barcelona* (1896 on) Present owner: J. Capell Coixet. 40mm solids, more recently plastic

CAVENDISH MINIATURES LTD. (M. Martin) *London* Contemporary manufacturer of small range of excellent 54mm plastics designed by Stadden

CHARBENS & CO LTD. *London* (*c* 1920 on) Manufacturers of lesser quality 54mm and smaller hollow-casts and plastics

CHERBAND *Paris* (*c* 1900–50) Manufacturer of solids

CHERILEA PRODUCTS *Blackpool* (1948) Prolific manufacturers of inferior quality hollow-casts and later of plastics. Exception in quality: the 'Baronial Series' (Black Prince; Marlborough)

CLAIRET *Paris* Contemporary manufacturer of small range of 54mm plastics

COMET METAL PRODUCTS *New York* (1938 on) Manufacturers of 35mm semi-flats; 35–40mm semi-solids; 54mm solids. Most famous products AUTHENTICAST models produced in Eire 1947–50

CONLEY (F.) *Visilia, California* Contemporary maker of 54mm solids. At one time associated with Scruby

COURTENAY (W.) *London* (*c* 1935–50) Manufacturer of hollow-casts of no significance

COX (L.) Contemporary American maker of 30 and 54mm solids

CRESCENT TOY CO LTD. *Tottenham and Cwmcarn* (1922 on) Manufacturer of hollow-casts and plastics, varying quality

DELEAU (Mademoiselle E.) *Paris* Contemporary maker of 54mm solids of fine quality

DENECKE *Brunswick* (Before 1820–1916) Manufacturer of flats. Eventually bought over by Rieche, 1916

DICKINSON (Neville) *Southampton* Contemporary maker of 20mm solids, with, more recently, 54mm. Scales vary, some horses far too large. Previously known as ALBERKEN (R. Gould and P. Gilder)

DORAN (E.) *London* A manufacturer of not particularly good 50mm solids of the medieval period who enjoyed a brief partnership with R. Courtenay at the beginning of the latter's career. Some two-figure groups occasionally seen in second-hand shops

DORFLER (Hans) *Fürth* (*c* 1890–1945) Manufacturer of semi-solids and solids

DU BOIS *Hanover* (1830–*c* 1890) Flats of fine quality. A set of Romans sold at auction in London in 1969. Successively J. E. Ernst

ELASTOLIN FABRIKATEN (O.&M. Hauser) *Neustadt* (*c* 1930 on) Most prolific manufacturer of plaster composition (up to 1939) and plastic (from 1945) models. Pre-war large models, clumsy, with wire armatures and thick bases. Complete sets now rare and command high prices. Later models 8cm, with duplicates in 35mm. High degree of detail and colour, riders detachable. Siege weapons and artillery also

FABRE (Christian L.) *Upper Derby, Pa.* Contemporary private maker who occasionally will sell a model. Main interests German Army 1939–45, Napoleonic cuirassiers and modern French Army, including standard bearers. Is experimenting with 6½-inch solids

FIGUR *Ablon, S. et O.* Contemporary manufacturer of 30mm semi-solids. Designed by Commandant Borie

FRANK (Ludwig) *Nuremberg* (1890–1957) An engraver of flats of great eminence

FRY (A. Ltd) *London* (1914–18) Manufacturers of poor quality hollow-casts in imitation of Britains

GOTTSCHALK (J. Wilhelm) *Nuremberg-Fürth* (1768–1843) Flats, various sizes. Principal engraver F. Eggiman.

GOTTSTEIN (Otto) *Leipzig-London* (d. 1952) A designer of flats of international repute. Associated with a number of short-lived concerns. Prime mover in the creation of the dioramas formerly at the RUSI Museum

GREER (William E.) American collector who makes 54mm solids or helps others in their design

GROVE (L.) and BENOY (Brigadier) *Birmingham* (1945) Makers of 30mm models fitting into stands

GUILBERT *Paris* Contemporary manufacturer of 54mm plastics

HAFER (Wolfgang) *Cassel* Contemporary maker of flats

HAFFNER (Johann) *Fürth-Nuremberg* (1838–98) Manufacturer of flats, semi-flats, semi-solids, solids. Fine quality productions. Successively Johann, Johann, United Toy Factories (Fortner & Haffner, *c* 1880), Johann Stadtler

HAHN (Herbert) *Vienna* (*d.* 1957) Part-time maker of 40–50mm plaster figures and architectural models. Hardly known outside his native country

HAMES (Leon) *Lambermont, Belgium* Contemporary maker, using modelling plaster to construct his 15–16 cm-high figures. When painted equivalent to finest porcelain. Specimens to be found in the collections of the Princes de Liège and Princesse Paola

HANKS BROTHERS & CO *London* (*c* 1900–*c* 1914) Poor quality hollow-casts; slightly larger than Britains

HARLE (William & Dorothy) *Washington* Contemporary private makers of 54mm solids

HASELBACH (J. C.) *Berlin* (*c* 1848–*c* 1900) Manufacturer of flats

HERALD MINIATURES LTD. *London* (*c* 1951 on) Finest quality 54mm plastics. Firm started by M. Zang and R. Selwyn-Smith. Subsequently absorbed by Britains Ltd. In 1958 introduced the revolutionary 'Swoppets' range

HEINRICH (K. & J.) *Fürth* (19th–20th century) Semi-solids and solids

HEINRICHSEN *Nuremberg* (1839–1945) Largest manufacturer of flats. Successively Ernst, Wilhelm, Ernst Wilhelm, Johannes: widow of last still alive and will do restricted business with favoured clients

HEYDE (Georg) *Dresden* (*c* 1870–1944) Prolific manufacturer of semi-solids and solids of varying sizes and quality

HILL (John & Co, JOHILLCO) *London* (*c* 1900 on) Prolific manufacturer of hollow-casts. Plastics introduced 1956

HILPERT FAMILY *Coburg-Nuremberg* (*c* 1720–1822) Manufacturers of flats of varied sizes; first to make portrait-models. Tremendous influence on subsequent designers. Successively Andreas, Johann Gottfried, Johann Georg, Johann Wolfgang. Moulds purchased *c* 1805 by J-H. Stahl. Later still by A. Haring

HISTOREX (R. Gillet) *Paris* Contemporary manufacturers of finest quality 56mm plastic models in kit form. Designed by Leliëpvre and very expensive. Concentration so far on Napoleonic troops

HØY *Copenhagen* (*fl.* 1848–50) Maker of flats of whom little is known

INDUSTRIA SOPRAMMOBILI ARTISTICI *Turin* (1954 on) Manufacturers of solids. Standard size and slightly larger. Wide range. Riders detachable

JACKSON (C. d'O. Pilkington) *Edinburgh* Wooden statuettes

JACKSON (Samuel C. 'Jane') Contemporary Canadian maker of 54mm solids

JIM *Paris* Contemporary manufacturer of 54mm good-quality plastics

KEWS *London* (*c* 1930–40) Manufacturer of hollow-casts of little merit and less significance

K-S MINIATURES (Donald K. Steiner and Peter Kramer) *Alexandria*, *Va.* Contemporary makers of 40mm solids. Specialists in Mexican War, Civil War navy, etc. Makers of dioramas. Models may be seen at Navy Museum, Washington

LECKE (Hans) *Hanover* Contemporary engraver of flats of the greatest eminence.

LINCOLN LOGS (J. L. Wright) *Chicago* (*c* 1910–43) Manufacturer of 54mm metal alloy figures

LINEOL *Dresden* Contemporary manufacturers of plaster composition figures similar to early models by ELASTOLIN

LORENZ (Johannes Gottlob) *Fürth* (1800–*c* 1850) Flats, various sizes. Some moulds now owned by Anton Caspari of Hof

LUCOTTE (F.) *Paris* French manufacturer of outstanding solid models. Some doubts exist as to the exact date of the firm's foundation, but Mignot say that they commenced work '*avant la Revolution*'. Characteristic trademark of Imperial Bee flanked by L. and C. Most known models date from about 1870. Taken over by Cuperly, Blondel and Gerbeau in 1825, and later by Mignot.

MCLOUGHLIN BROTHERS *New York* (*c* 1900–12) Manufacturers of paper sheets and 54mm hollow-casts

MADLENER (Ludwig) *Munich* The doyen of modern designers of flats. Has had a profound influence on the growth of the art

MAIER (Sixtus, father and son) *Nuremberg* With Frank the most celebrated engravers of modern German flats, whose skilful craftsmanship has done much to raise the art to its present high level

MALLEABLE MOULDINGS *Deal* (1947–50) An early venture in plastic material, with arms and heads affixed to torso. Many designed by Henry Harris. Directed by F. Winkler and sponsored by COMET

MARRION (R. J.) *London* Contemporary private maker of 54mm solids who sells occasionally or gives away. Great characterisation of models, mainly British Army 1870–1900. Moulds made in silicone rubber by R. Gould, models carved from blank castings and accoutrements soldered on

MARX MINIATURES (Louis Marks & Co) *New York* Contemporary manufacturers of plastics in vast numbers and differing sizes, all issued in self-colour only. The best are excellent

MERTEN (Berliner Miniatur Plastiken) *Berlin* Contemporary manufacturers of 20, 40–60mm plastics, of hard variety, riders detachable. Large range of subjects, many figures in each set. Some unusual ranges, such as medieval hawking

METALART MINIATURE CO (J. Edward Jones and Ella L. Hume, later MOULDED MINIATURES *Chicago* (*c* 1929–60) Manufacturers of 54mm hollow-casts

MIGNOT (CBG) *Paris* French manufacturers of solids, still in business and probably the oldest firm in the world still functioning. The initials stand for Cuperley, Blondel and Gerbeau, an amalgamation which absorbed Lucotte and was in turn taken over in 1875 by Mignot. Small range of flats designed by Armand, Rousselot and others, the Napoleonic range exceptional, the Joan of Arc figures most disappointing

MILITARY MINIATURES *New York* (*c* 1948–50) Designed by John Scheid. Manufacturers of 54mm good quality solids

MIM (E. Steinbach) *Belgium* (*c* 1935–48) Manufacturer of solids of good quality

MINIFIGURE COMPANY *Tucson, Ariz.* (*c* 1961) Manufacturer of 54mm solids

MOKAREX *Paris* Contemporary plastic models issued in tins of coffee. Standard size, or slightly larger, self-coloured only. Wide and unusual range, many civilians being represented

MOULDED MINIATURES (J. Edward Jones) *Chicago* (*c* 1929–60) Manufacturer of 54mm hollow-casts

NECKEL (F. C.) *Stuttgart* Well-known contemporary distributor of flats

NIBLETT (John) *Sidcup* Contemporary maker of solids and designer of plastics. One of our first purchases was a miraculous 20mm mounted knight, the rider detachable. Designed some 54mm models (medieval) of his own, and others (modern troops) for THE SENTRY BOX. Later designer of AIRFIX 20 and 54mm plastics and 7-inch plastic kits. Most outstanding recent performance a 54mm mounted 'Bruce' in plastic after Pilkington Jackson: sold as gold-plated, and expensive

OCHEL (Aloys) *Kiel* (1925 on) One of the most prolific distributors of modern flats. Two qualities: *Kilia* and *Oki*

PALOMEQUE (M.) *Madrid* (1922–36) Manufacturer of 54mm solids

PALX *Paris* Contemporary maker of 56mm models of 17–18th-century French civilians. We think they are synonymous with Alexandre, but cannot pontificate on this

PATMORE (Clive) *Ilford* Contemporary maker of plaster composition models on metal armatures. Specialised in officers of the Guards Regiments and Royal Horse Artillery. Also made officers of the 7th Queen's Own Hussars (1807), The Black Watch (1808) and the Highland Light Infantry (1778)

PFAB (Vincent) *Kennesaw, Ga.* Contemporary maker of 54mm solids. Creator of the Kennesaw Battlerama

QUIRRINAL *Paris* (*fl. c* 1950–60) Manufacturer of 54mm models in aluminium

RAY (Don and Honey) (*fl.* 1939–40) English manufacturers of a small and shortlived range of miscellaneous models, including Waterloo types

REAMSA *Barcelona* Contemporary manufacturers of 54mm and larger plastics. Riders detachable. Early models anachronistic, but new lease of life with designer G. Erik, formerly of Wimbledon, joining firm. Spanish-Napoleonic War and 'El Cid' series the two most recent and popular

REKA LTD. (C. W. Baker) *London* (*c* 1910–30) Manufacturer of hollow-casts in rivalry with Britains. Poor quality

RENVOIZE (James) *London* (*c* 1900–14) Manufacturer of 54mm hollow-casts. Rival of Britains. Poor quality

REYNOLDS (H.) *London* (*fl.* 1960) A shortlived firm making 54mm hollow-casts. A set of Vikings will be remembered

RICHARDS *London* (*c* 1930–50) Manufacturers of 54mm hollow-casts of little significance

RODE-ORME *Copenhagen* Manufacturers of 75mm aluminium models. After 1946 name changed to KROLYN

ROSKOPF-MINIATUMODELLE *Berlin* Contemporary manufacturers of 20mm solids and armaments; much used in war-game

RÖSSNER (Prof Georg Walter) *Schleswig-Holstein, Stockholm* Gifted contemporary maker of flats, harking back in style to early days, and unique in content

ROUSSELOT (L.) *Paris* Contemporary maker of fine quality, large models (mainly equestrian) of varied materials. One of the original partnership making flats for Mignot. Known universally as the authority on French Napoleonic uniforms, his paintings being in great demand

RUSSELL *London* (*c* 1914–18) Manufacturer of poor quality hollow-casts, only remembered as contemporary with Britains

SAINT LOUIS LEAD SOLDIER CO (C. Chichester Lloyd) *Detroit* (*c* 1925) Manufacturers of solids, the most curious productions ever made

SANCHEZ *Madrid* (–1930) Manufacturer of flats and 50mm solids

SANDOW *Berlin* Contemporary maker of flats

SANTESSONKA TENNGJUTERIET *Stockholm* (1843–1930) 35mm flats: 40mm semi-solids; 50mm solids

SAUNDERS (E. W.) *Taunton* Contemporary private maker of models in various sizes and materials, mostly as commissions, or for friends. 54mm solids, covering wide range, including Seven Years' War, Napoleonic period, American Civil War. Latterly 6–9-inch amalgam of plastic wood (from plaster moulds) heads of plaster cast in silicone rubber moulds, clothing of natural materials

SCHEIBERT (Hedwig) *Vienna* Contemporary maker of flats

SCHEID (John) *Easton, Pa.* Contemporary maker of 54mm solids

SCHWEITZER (Adam) *Diessen-Ammersee* (1797 on) Manufacturer of flats of various sizes. Unique series, the original designs of the late 18th–early 19th century still obtainable

SCRUBY (Jack) *Visalia, Calif.* Contemporary maker of 40 and 54mm solids. Smaller models much used by wargamers, on which pastime he has had a profound effect

SEGOM *Paris* Contemporary manufacturers of 54mm plastics. One of the first to issue their models in semi-kit form. Specialists in Napoleonic period. A characteristic is the archaic 'pigeon-chested' pose of the infantry

SELCOL PRODUCTS LTD. *London* Contemporary manufacturer of hollow-casts and plastics. Most outstanding achievement were their plastic kits designed by E. Meister. These, however, proved ahead of their time, and were ousted by smaller and cheaper competition

SELWYN-SMITH (Roy) *London* A contemporary maker who joined with Gottstein in SELWYN MINIATURES (1951–2) subsequently purchased by Britains. Designer for Zang (plastics) HERALD MINIATURES, later still incorporated in Britains, of whom he is a director

SIBORNE (Captain William) *London* Made two models of the Battle of Waterloo in 1838 and 1840–4, each containing a vast number of tiny solid models, those in the later model slightly larger, and with removable equipment

SKYBIRD (A. J. Holliday & Co) *London* 1939–51. Manufacturer of 30mm solids, mainly of khaki-clad Great War troops. Now rarely seen, but sometimes offered for sale at absurdly high prices

SOHLKE (F.) *Hanover-Regensburg-Augsburg* (*c* 1816) Flats

SOHLKE (G.) *Berlin* (1819–68) Manufacturer of semi-solids and solids

SPENKUCH (Georg) *Nuremberg* (19–20th century) Manufacturer of semi-solids and solids

STARLUX *Paris* Contemporary maker of 40 and 56mm plastics of a quality rivalling those of HERALD

STOCK (J. Duke) Contemporary American private maker of solids

SWEDISH AFRICAN ENGINEERS (F. Winkler and C. Wennberg, 'SAE') *Cape Town* (*c* 1954–68) Manufacturers of 30mm solids. Designed by Eriksson, but production very clumsy

TAYLOR & BARRETT *London* (*c* 1930–8) Manufacturers of 50mm hollow-casts. Poor quality

TENNGJUTERIET MARS (W. E. Lindberg) *Stockholm* (1913–*c* 1930) Manufacturer of flats and 40mm semi-solids

TENNGJUTERIET SCHREUDER *Stockholm* (1896–1920) Manufacturers of 40mm semi-solids. Later SCHREUDER AND OHLSON

THOMAS INDUSTRIES *Shawnee, USA* Contemporary manufacturer of 20mm models for use in the war-game. Also makes 54mm lead copies of wood-carvings by Cliff Arquette

TIMPO *London* (1943 on) Prolific manufacturer of hollow-casts and later plastics. Varying quality, slightly larger than standard size

TREFOREST MOULDINGS (F. Winkler) *Treforest* (1937) 32mm flats, 40mm solids, some designed by Henry Harris

TRU-CRAFT MODELS (Cecil Jackson) *Santa Monica, Calif.* Contemporary manufacturer of 54mm solids

TURNBULL *London* (?*c* 1914–18) Manufacturer of poor quality 54mm hollow-casts in rivalry to Britains

VALVERDE (Capitaine Carlos Martinez) *Barcelona* Contemporary maker of 54mm solids for museums

VANOT (B.) *Paris* Contemporary maker of fine 54mm solids. Protégé of Lelièpvre

VERTUNNI (G.) *Italy-Paris* (*c* 1900–?) Maker of splendid 54mm solid portrait models. Very rare

WARREN COMPANY *USA* (*c* 1914–40) 57mm solids

WEGMANN *Brunswick* (Before 1820–95) Manufacturer of flats. Successively Carl; Theodore. Purchased Denecke's moulds, substituting initials CW on base. Later purchased by B. Borning

WEHRLI (Rudolf) *Alt Arrau-Nuremberg* (1801–76) 30mm flats. Originally apprenticed to Gottschalk. Successively Rudolf (son); Friedrich continued business to 1887

WENDALL *Blandford* (*fl.* 1950–65) 54mm aluminium models for juvenile trade

WEST (Mrs Helen) *Baltimore* Contemporary private maker of 54mm fine quality solids

WEYGANG *Göttingen* (1810–1919) Manufacturer of flats. Successively Carl; Carl Friedrich Victor.

WILCOX (Peter) *London* Contemporary private maker of ancient and medieval types

WIRTHS (The) American private makers

WOLLNER *Vienna* (1866–1914) A firm of manufacturers specialising in 40mm and other size semi-solids. Still obtainable from Josef Kober in Vienna

WOOTEN (Peter) Contemporary Australian maker of 54mm solids

List of places where model soldiers may be seen

AUSTRIA
Deutsch-Wagram Heimatsmuseum (diorama)
Donaumuseum (Krauhs)
Herogenburg. Schloss Heiligenkreux (Krauhs)
Linz. Schlossmuseum (diorama; Krauhs)
Mistelbach. Schloss Loosdorf (Private collection of Ferdinand Graf Patti, thirty dioramas)
Salzburg. Haus der Natur (Krauhs). Rainer Museum (Krauhs) Schloss Mirabell (Krauhs)
Vienna. Kunsthistorischesmuseum (medieval; flats)
Petronell. Danube Museum (Krauhs)

BELGIUM
Bruges. Musée Grandhure (late eighteenth century moulds)
Brussels. Musée Royal de l'Armée (flats)

CANADA
Calgary. Glenbow Foundation (three dioramas from RUSI)
Minden Museum of Dioramas, Ontario
Montreal. Lake St Louis Historical Society (dioramas)
Quebec. Musée de Fort (dioramas); Musée du Citadel (dioramas)

DENMARK
Copenhagen. Teknisk Museum (moulds of flats dated 1760–1791: mould of Frederik VII by Høy)

FRANCE
Epinal Museum (paper sheets)
Janessy Museum (dioramas)
Mars-le-Tour Museum (dioramas)
Paris. Compiègne. (flats, dioramas, solids, carved wood)
Musée Carnavalet (paper sheets)
Musée de Cluny (medieval; sixteenth- and seventeenth-century solids)
Musée de l'Armée (paper sheets, flats, dioramas, solids)
Musée de la Marine (dioramas, Fouillé)
Periguex Museum (paper sheets)
Strasbourg Museum (paper sheets, flats, medieval)

GERMANY
Bischofswerda Museum (flats)
Celle. Bomann Museum (flats)
Eisenach. Thuringer Museum (flats)
Hoboe. (Private collection of dioramas by E. Schmidt)
Halle. Museum (flats)
Hanover Museum (flats, Waterloo diorama)
Leipzig Museum (flats, Leipzig diorama)
Munich. Bayerisches Museum (medieval, flats, solids, including Haffner)
Nuremberg. Germanisches National-museum (medieval, flats)
Plassenberg Castle, Kulmbach (large collection dioramas)
Potsdam Museum (flats)

GREAT BRITAIN
Battle Museum (diorama of Battle of Hastings)
Blenheim Palace (large collection of Lucottes; small collection of Staddens)
Chester Museum: King Charles Tower dioramas)
Derby Museum and Art Gallery (solids, flats)
Dover Castle (diorama of Waterloo)
Edinburgh. Museum of Childhood
Hastings Museum (diorama)
Irish Military College, The Curragh (solids)
Lewes. Anne of Cleve's House (diorama of Battle of Lewes; solids and hollow-casts)
London. Bethnal Green Museum (flats) Imperial War Museum (dioramas) London Museum (flats, hollow-casts, solids) National Army Museum (Coppin, Synge-Hutchinson, Surén dioramas) National Maritime Museum (Coppin, Synge-Hutchinson) Pollock's Toy Museum (hollow-casts, paper sheets); Tower of London (Siborne's second Waterloo model)
Norwich, Stranger's Hall (hollow-casts, solids)
Rottingdean. The Grange (National Toy Museum)
Tunbridge Wells Museum (Allgeyer, Lucotte)
Wilton House (Earl of Pembroke's collection)
Woburn Abbey (Major Rowe's collection)
York Museum (diorama of Marston Moor)
Many regimental museums

HOLLAND
Leyden Museum (Koeckeck collection of paper sheets in diorama form)
Zweeloo Drenthe (Spandauw collection of converted kits)

ITALY
Milan Museum (flats)
Naples Museum (paper sheets)
Padua. Toy Soldier Museum (Testi collection)
Turin. Pietro Millo Museum (carved wood and fabrics); Risorgimento Museum (carved wood and fabrics)
Venice. Musée Navale

NORWAY
Stavanger. Ledaal Museum (flats, solids)

SPAIN
Barcelona. Musée Industrias y Artes Populares de Pueblo Espanal (moulds by Ortelli, flats)
Madrid. Museo de Ejercito (400 carved wooden figures by Tellov); Naval Museum (Valverde)

Bibliography

Pontevedra Museum (Valverde)

SWITZERLAND

Coppet Castle. Museum of Swiss Regiment in Foreign Service (flats)
Grandson Castle (solids)
Lausanne. Cantonal and University Library (flats)
Lucerne Museum (flats)
Morges. Military Museum (flats)
Zurich. Landesmuseum (comprehensive collection of flats)

UNITED STATES OF AMERICA

Annapolis. Military and Naval Academy (dioramas)
Detroit. Children's Museum
Fort Still
Kennesaw Battlerama, Georgia (created by Vincent Pfab)
Lakewood. White Russian Museum (Hitrovo)
New York Museum (paper sheets, German solids, early Britains)
Philadelphia. US Marine Corps Memorial Museum (dioramas)
Providence. Mrs J. N. Brown Museum
Quantico. US Marine Corps Museum.
Washington, DC. Anderson House (solids)
Washington. Smithsonian Institution (Bussler; the Harles; the Wirths)
West Point. Museum (Métayer; plaster)

USSR

Leningrad. The Hermitage (flat wooden cutouts; part of Peter III collection)

Baldet (Marcel) Figurines et Soldats de Plomb. *Paris*, 1961
Bard (Bob) Making and Collecting Military Miniatures. *New York*, 1957
Blum (Peter) Military Miniatures. *New York*, 1964
Claretie (L.) Les Jouets: Histoire, Fabrication. *Paris*, 1894
Daiken (L.) Children's Toys through the Ages. *London*, 1953
The World of Toys. *London*, 1963
D'Allemagne (H.R.) Histoire des Jouets. *Paris*, 1903
Featherstone (Donald) Handbook for Model Soldier Collectors. *London*, 1969
Forrer (R.) Les Etains de la Collection Alfred Ritleng. *Strasbourg*, 1905
Fraser (Lady Antonia) A History of Toys. *London*, 1966
Freeman (R. and L.) Cavalcade of Toys. *New York*, 1952
Garratt (John G.) Model Soldiers: a Collector's Guide. Third Edition. *London*, 1971
Grober (C.) Children's Toys of Bygone Days. Translated P Hereford. *London*, 1932
Hampe (T.) Der Zinnsoldat. *Berlin*, 1924
Harris (Major Henry) Model Soldiers. *London*, 1962
Hert (Louis H.) Handbook of old American Toys. *New York*, 1947
Holme (C. G., Editor) Children's Toys of Yesterday. *London*, 1932
Jackson (Mrs Neville) Children's Toys of Other Days. *London*, 1908
McClintock (Inez and Marshall) Toys in America. *Washington*, 1961
Martin (Paul) Les Petits Soldats de Strasbourg. *Strasbourg*, 1950

Martin (Paul) Les Petits Soldats de Strasbourg. *Strasbourg*, 1950

Der Standhafte Zinnsoldat. *Berlin*, 1962
and Vaillant (M.) Le Monde Merveilleux des Soldats de Plomb. *Paris*, 1959
Model Soldiers, Armiesin Miniature. Introduction by Massimo Alberini. *Novaro*, 1972
Nicholson (Lieut-Col. J. B. R.) Model Soldiers (for Newman Newton Ltd). *London*, 1969
Nicollier (J.) Collecting Toy Soldiers. *Fribourg*, 1967
Percout (R.) Les Images d'Epinal. *Paris*, 1912
Richards (L. W.) Old British Model Soldiers, 1893–1918. *London*, 1969
Riff (A.) Les Etains Strasbourgeois du XVIe au XIXe siecle. *Strasbourg*, 1925
Risley (C. A.) and Imrie (W. F.) The Model Soldier Guide. *New York*, 1967
Scrine (J.) A Short History of Britains Ltd. *London*, 1955

Sources of Illustrations

Photographs and illustrations were supplied or are reproduced by kind permission of the following: Bird and Tassell 101, Blum Collection 42–3, 67, 130, 132, 188, 189; Custer Collection 203; 205; Dattilo Collection 69; David Collection 20, 21, 25 left, 155, 156, 157; Draeger Collection 71; Faulkner Collection 151; Fire Protection Review 12 above; Folio Fine Art 11 right; Garratt Collection 8–9, 16, 79, 80, *84*, 137 above left and right, 140–1, 214, 215 above and left; Germanisches Museum, Nuremberg 41; Grafton Collection 14 above; Hanington Collection 28; Harris Collection 45; Heeresgeschichtes Museum, Vienna 52 above; Historex 31 left and below, 32; Hitrovo Collection 209, 210; Judd Collection 24, 30, 218; Kröner-Grim Collection 179; Lentz Collection 131; Mansell Collection 227; Martin Collection 154; McDonnell Collection 197, 198, *216*; Montreal Military and Maritime Museum 55; Musée de Cluny 12 right, 13 above and left; Musée Historique de Strasbourg 14 below; 15 below; Musée de la Légion, Puyloubier 36; Musée de la Marine *72*; National Army Museum 85; National Maritime Museum 82; Nelli Collection 159; Norman Newton Ltd, 81 right, 102, 114, 116, 117, 227; Opie Collection 162; Pearce Collection 94, 229; Pestana Collection 27 below; Pfab Collection 38; Philipott Collection 76; Pollocks Toy Museum 27 above; Private Collection *59*; Puffer Collection *62*, *204*; Rees Collection 87, 88, 220, 221; Richards Collection 22, 163, 164; Robinson Sager 222, 223; Spandauw Collection 33 above left; Stearns 198; Taverner and Ekins Collection 106; Thoburn Collection *167*, 173, 174, 175, 176; Thompson 166, 168; Tunbridge Wells Museum 18, 19; US Marine Corps Museum 37; Wade Collection 34, 104, 194, 195; Wilson Collection 169; Winter Collection 172.

Photographs were taken by: I. D. Aston 172; Irv Bahrt 130; P. Birt 101; Peter Blum 96, 131, 188; Eric C. Cartwright 16, 80, 137, 212, 217; Hartford Courant 225; Humphrey Saunders Studio 229; Behram Kapadia 8–9, 140–1; S. K. Lazell 18; Alan Meek 181; Stig Nilsson 125; Edmund Osborn *204*; P. and M. 79, *84*, 100, 106, 137, 161, 162, 214, 215; Photo RTF 28 below; Photography (London) Studios 104, 195; Bruce M. Sharp 187; Philip O. Stearns 67, 189, *213*, *216*; A. R. Thiel 173, 176, 179; Harold G. Tilsey 105; Walker's Studios 232; Michael T. Wheeler 19.

Index

Abel and Fry, 165
accessories, models of military, 98, 122, 130, 149, 153, 165, 171, 179, 182, 189, 192, 199, 203, 220, 228, 229
Airfix models, 34–6 *passim*, 99, 144, 147, 207, 227, 228, 230
Alcocer, 214
Allen, T., 118
Allgeyer, 18, 19, 25, 36, 148, 153, 210
Almirall, 24, 184, 186
America, model making in, 24, 30, 35, 40, 46, 95–6, 127–41, 146, 172–6, 188–9, 196–9, 202–5, 207–11, 223–6, 232–3
American Indians, models of, 137, 155, 209
American Soldier Company, model makers, 24
American War of Independence, models of, 60, 90, 97, 116, 131, 134, 186, 188, 200, 203
Ammon, model makers, 18, 35
ancient peoples, models of, 11, 35, 88, 90, 91, 98, 104, 133, 134, 148, 149, 152, 155–8 *passim*, 186, 196, 199, 207, 209–11 *passim*, 214, 218, 220, 221, 224, 233, 234
Anderson, model maker, 24
Anderson House, Washington, 39, 60
Angenot, General, model maker, 46, 56–7
Antonini, F. and L., model makers, 159
'Argosy' models, 107
Armitage models, 195
Armont, (Petrocochino), model maker, 77, 153
Arnholm, model maker, 214
Arthur, model maker, 146
Ashton, model maker, 198–9
auction sales of models, 145
Aurora models, 207
Austria, model making in, 28, 51–3, 177–80
Austrian Collectors' Society, 177, 180
Authenticast series models, 25, 30, 124, 168, 180, 184, 197–9 *passim*, 218
Australia, model making in, 25, 147, 184–7
Aylmer, model maker, 35, 207, 226

Baldet, M., collector/author, 27, 28, 34, 37, 46, 55, 58, 60, 67, 73, 77, 172, 174, 176, 180, 189, 197, 200
Ball, Miss K., model maker, 45, 94–6, 158, 160, 188, 197
Ballada, model maker, 40, 46, 61, 64, 209
Banner-Model, model makers, 24
Bantock, A., collector, 148–9
Bantock, J. R. Granville, 151, 234
Baptiste, E., model maker, 46
Barclay, model maker, 24
Barker, H. J. junior, model maker, 174
Barnes, Dr L., model maker, 107–11
Bastian, K. C., collector, 149–51
Battaglia, E., model maker, 40
battle scenes, dioramas of, (see also Crécy, Waterloo) 36, 37, 40, 98, 149, 158, 177, 178, 184, 198, 199, 214, 221, 232
Becker, H., 133
bee—Imperial mark, 14, 15
Belgium, model making in, 24, 31
Belmont-Maitland, R., 112, 113
Benoy, J. F., model maker—see Grove and Benoy
Berdou, R., model maker, 40, 46, 55, 61–6, 77, 144, 172, 174, 176; collaboration with Imrie (qv), 66
Bergmann, model maker, 154
Berne, model maker, 23
Betjeman, J., 10
Biebel, model maker, 39
Bird, P. H. S., model maker, 46, 99, 101
Bittard, model maker, 40
Black Prince, models of, 87, 88, 97, 145, 158, 222, 231
Blenheim Palace, 15, 113
Blondel, model maker, 15
Blum, P., collector/author, 67, 68, 75, 96, 131, 188–9; collaboration with Gottstein, 214
Boer War, models of, 98, 156, 192, 195, 207
Bohler, model maker, 78
du Bois, model maker, 19
Boitard, M., model maker, 36
Boutet, R., 46
Britain, models, 21, 23, 26, 30, 45, 80, 94, 134, 142, 144, 145, 148, 151, 155, 157, 159, 160, 162–6, 168–72, 181, 182, 186, 190, 192, 197, 202, 207, 208, 210, 211, 219, 221–4, 226, 228, 231; Eastern peoples sets, 221; high auction prices of, 145; imitated in America, 24; Knights of Agincourt models, 23, 107, 158, 192, 212, 222, 231; Peninsular War British infantry, 80; Tournament set, 220, 221
British Model Soldier Society, 23, 40, 80, 94, 108, 112, 124, 142, 144, 148, 153, 165, 171, 180, 182, 184, 190, 210, 217, 225; *Bulletin* of, 144
Broker, model maker, 78
Broman, C. R., model maker, 137, 214; trading as H-R Products Inc 137
Brunoe, S., model maker, 53–5
Bucquoy, model maker, 64, 153
Bunte Rock, Der (Martin), 153
Bull, model maker, 20
Burkhardt, sheet publisher, 206–7
Bussler, K. G., model maker, 24, 35, 46, 197–9, 224
Bustelli, F. A., model maker, 54–5

Café Storme, model distributors and coffee merchants, 30, 31, 50, 184, 214
Canada, model making in, 25, 155, 222–3
Canadian National Maritime Museum, 85, 86
carabiniers, French, models of, 68
Carbago models, 107, 215
Carman, W. Y., model maker, 26, 107, 144, 195
Carnavale Museum, Paris, 14
Casanellas, model maker, 24
Cass, A., collector, 149
catalogues, production of, 16,

78, 92, 97, 98, 125, 130
cave drawings, 11
Cavendish Miniatures, model makers, 30, 118, 196
Cederstrom, artist, 55
Célébrations du Cheval (Angenot), 57
Central School of Arts and Crafts, London, 92
Charbens, model makers, 30, 165
Charge (Young), 230
Charles I, model of, 99, 222; II 222; VI 52; VI's coach 53; XII 126; XIV 126
Cherband, model maker, 23
Cherilea, model maker, 23, 30, 145, 160, 161, 231
chessmen, models of, 94, 118
Chiappa, E., model maker, 40, 122, 159, 160
Churchill, Sir Winston, 82, 96
Civil War, American, models of, 46, 97, 98, 104, 125, 129, 131, 133, 134, 171, 172, 199, 203, 209, 210, 228, 230, 231; English, 35, 68, 90, 98, 99, 186, 199–201, 220, 221
Clairet models, 162
Clans (M'Ians), 105
Clendennin, R., 144
Cliffe Arquette, model makers, 214
Cluny Museum, 13
Collecting Toy Soldiers (Nicollier), 61, 147
Comet, model makers, 24, 124, 180
Commission International d'Histoire Militaire, 153
Company of Military Collectors, and Historians, 76, 129, 197, 225
Conley, F., model maker, 24, 40
Connett, P., collector, 149
Connoisseur, the, 82
Conrad, J., model maker, 165
Cooke, N. H. and L., model makers, 40, 46, 127–9, 172, 214; Lance Historical Miniatures, 127–8
Coppins, the, model makers, 40, 45, 80–6
Cortum, model maker, 149; his Alexander the Great 151
Costume Militaire, Le (Martin), 153
Cotman, J. S., artist, 124
Courtenay, R., model maker, 35, 40, 45, 48, 57, 61, 86–8, 104, 105, 107, 142, 144–6, 158, 165, 172, 186, 202, 205, 208, 209, 211, 214, 218–21, 231
Courtenay, W., 195
Cox, L. H., collector, 104, 172, 212
Crawhall, J., artist, 124
Creese, M. J., collector, 151–3
Crécy, Battle of, model of, 37, 87, 96, 107, 230
Crescent, model makers, 23, 30, 161, 165
Crimean War, models of, 97, 117, 131, 214
Cromwell, Oliver, model of, 99
Crusaders, models of, 87
Cuperley, model maker, 15
Cushing, P., 104, 105
Custer, E. and W., model makers, 46, 77, 134, 172, 202–5, 210
Czechoslovakia, model making in, 24, 30

DYK models (Stadden), 113
Daiken, L., 10
Danube Museum, Petronell, 52
Dark Ages, models of, 104
David, model maker, 214
David, P., collector, 155–7; list of his collection, 155–7
Delhaert, sheet publisher, 207
Delion, F. C., designer, 201
Denecke, model maker, 19
Denmark, model making in, 24, 53–5
Detaille, E., 64
Deutsche Gesellschaft der Freunde und Sammler Kunsthistorischen Zinnfiguren, 153
Deutsche Zinnfigurenwerkstätte in Berlin, model makers, 78
Devil is an Ass, The (Jonson), 13
Dichtung und Wahrheit (Goethe) 14
Dickens, Charles, models of characters, 99
Dickinson, model maker, 214, 226
Diener, Dr E., 178
Dillet, J., collector, 63, 64
Dilley, R., collector, 182
Dinky models, 228
Dioramas, 35–7 *passim*, 39, 69, 70, 77, 78, 94–6 *passim*, 101, 146, 152, 158, 177, 178, 184, 190, 198, 200, 201, 207, 210, 219, 221–3 *passim*, 234; small figures for 35, 45, 73, 223, 224
Donath, R., model marketeers, 77, 149, 151
Doran, modeller, 86
Dorfler, model maker, 19
Duguay-Trouin, model of, 68, 189
Duchess of Malfi, The, 13
Durham Arts Centre, 171; Light Infantry Museum, 171
Durso, model maker, 190

Edmonds, Miss Y., model maker, 107–11
Edward I, models of, 221; III 88, 222; VII, Coronation of, 196
Egyptians, models of, 35, 88, 90, 151, 186, 200, 210, 214, 218, 221
Eisenhower, General, 53
Elins, Miss N., collector, 106, 107
Elizabeth I, models of, 99, 222; at Tilbury, 36, 37
Elizabeth II, models of, 123, 126, 147, 168, 209, 210; Coronation models, 45, 89, 180, 184
England, model making in, 20, 26, 30, 35, 40, 45, 80–122, 146, 157–8, 160–72, 180–4, 190–2, 199–201, 211–17, 219–22, 231–2
Erik, G., model maker, 31, 118, 214
Eriksson, H., model maker, 25, 35, 40, 46, 57, 63, 113, 117, 124–6, 144, 155, 165, 166, 168, 182, 184, 214, 218, 226–8, 230
Étains Strasbourgeois du XVIe au XIXe siècle (Riff), 10
Evans, L., dealer, 222
Fabre, model makers, 172
Fabrique Belge, models, 190
Farish, G., model makers, 89
Fattori, G., painter, 159
Faulkner, H. C., collector, 88, 107, 146, 157–8
Featherstone, D., war-gamer, 230
Figur, model makers, 23
figurines, 12, 73, 200; non-military, 200, 201, 215
First Empire, models of, 64, 70, 77, 111, 176, 211
First World War, models of, 28, 190, 224, 233
Fontaines, Josianne des, model maker, 40, 45, 61, 63, 66–8, 144, 146, 189, 200, 205; Venetian scene, 200–1
Fouillé, G., model maker, 46, 54, 69–71
Fragonard, painter, 55
France, model making in, 15, 16, 23, 26, 31, 36, 37, 40, 45, 46, 56–77, 146
Francesco, model maker, 24
Frank, engraver, 78, 153
Franz Josef, Emperor, models of, 27, 39, 126
Fraser, Lady A., 10
Frazer, C., collector, 53, 190, 205–7, 217
Frederick the Great, Hilpert's model of, 16, 39, 190, 215; troops of, 78, 90, 116, 149, 152, 153, 155, 158
Fry, model maker, 23, 195
Fylde, model maker, 195

Gainsborough, artist, 55
Gallandre, M., artist, 63, 64
Gammage, R., model maker, 35, 40, 45, 48, 89–93, 104, 144, 151, 158, 160, 162, 165, 168, 171, 172, 184, 186, 190, 197, 200, 209, 214, 218–22 *passim*, 225, 228, 230, 231; 'Cabalt' figures 91, 92; 'Connoisseur' models 91, 196; 'Rose' models 92
Garratt, J. G., author and collector, 86, 124, 154, 190, 207, 211–7
Garrett-Taylor, collector, 149

Gartner, L., collector, 177
Gerbeau, model maker, 15
Germany, model exports from, 18; model making in, 25, 26, 31, 35, 39, 77–81, 233–4
Gilder, P., model maker, 214, 228
Gillet, R., 74
Glenbow Foundation, Calgary, 36
Goethe, 14
Gottschalk, model maker, 18
Gottstein, O., model maker and engraver, 23, 25, 26, 36, 39, 95, 107, 149, 153, 209; Battle of Hastings 40, 99, 151; Gottstein-Blum 214
Grand Dictionnaire Larousse (illustrated Fouillé), 70
Grant, C. S., model maker, 201, 227–30
Granville Bantock, J. R. and A., *see* Bantock
Grassi, J., cast maker, 118
Green, model maker, 172
Green, Mrs G., 10
Greenwood, G. A., model maker, 35, 40, 45, 48, 94–6, 104, 144, 146, 158, 160, 188, 190, 197, 202, 205, 209, 225, 226, 228, 231; chessmen, 94
Greer, W. F., model designer, 77, 134, 171, 210
Griffith, M. D., author, 29
Griffiths, A., 112, 113
Grove and Benoy, model makers, 35, 195, 223, 226
Guilbert, model maker, 162
Guild of Military Antiquarians, 184; of Model Soldier Manufacturers, 111
Gustav Adolf, King of Sweden, 125, 126

Hafer, model maker, 25, 215
Haffner, model maker, 19, 20, 157
Hahn, H., model maker, 28, 215
Hahnemann, model maker, 39
Hamel, model maker, 77
Hames, L., modeller, 75
Hamleys' toyshop, London, 182, 217
Hampe, author, 10
Hanington, J., collector, 190–2
Hanks, model makers, 23, 163–5 *passim*, 195
Hannibal, models of, 126, 155, 196
Hardie, J. W., 34
Harle, model maker, 197
Harrington, collector, 146
Harris, H., author, 14, 69, 146, 180–4, 217, 226
Haselbach, model makers, 19, 78
Haus de Natur, Salzburg, 52
Hausser, O. and K. (Elastolin models), 28, 30, 31, 144–6 *passim*, 155, 186, 190, 218, 226, 231
Head, T., collector, 231
Heeresgeschichtliches Museum, Vienna, 52, 178
Heinrich, model maker, 20, 165
Heinrichsen, model maker, 19, 20, 25, 36, 39, 40, 78, 149, 153, 177, 208, 210, 214, 215, 223, 226
Henrietta Maria, model of, 99
Henry II of England, 107; V 106, 158; VII 99; VIII 99, 209, 222; IV of France 13, 107
Herald models, 77, 124, 146, 160, 161, 171, 182, 186, 190, 192, 196, 217, 231; 'Wars of the Roses' series, 222, 231
Heyde, G., model maker, 20, 23, 26, 30, 144, 145, 155, 157, 164, 165, 190, 194–7 *passim*, 199, 207, 211, 223, 231; imitated in America, 24
Higgins, L., model maker, 35, 40, 55, 99, 146, 214, 225
Hill, John and Co (Johillco), model makers, 23, 144, 145, 160, 164, 211, 231
Hilpert family, 16, 39; model of Frederick the Great, 16, 39, 190, 215
Hingle, C.B.O., model designer, 112
Hinsch, model maker, 151
Hinto, model maker, 35
Hinton, M., model maker, 40, 45, 96–8, 131, 144, 146, 172, 184, 186, 190, 196, 214, 220–2 *passim*, 226, 228, 230; Hinton Hunt figures 96; range of his military models 97
Historex models (R. Gillet Aeros SA), 33, 64, 74, 111, 145, 146, 214
Hitrovo, M. V., collector, 207–11, 214
Holmes, W., model maker, 201
Hoy, model maker, 215
Huber, Baron F. X., 27, 61, 63, 77
Hujos, sheet publisher, 207
Hummel (late Morrells—model shop), 94, 104, 105, 107, 171, 182, 217, 221, 231
Hunt, S., model designer, 96

Imrie, W. and H., model maker, 40, 46, 90, 129–32, 172, 174, 184, 186, 189, 197, 198, 209, 222, 224; collaboration with Risley, 129–32; Hellenic Miniatures, 129; Imrie Custom Miniatures, 129; supplier of riders to Berdou (qv), 64, 66
Industria Sopramobile Artistici, model makers, 24
Inter-Allied Museum, Arromanches, 96
Irish Army Military College, Kildare, 183
Italy, model making in, 16, 24, 40, 46, 122, 159–60

Jackson, General, model of, 131
Jackson, P., model maker, 45
Jackson, Samuel C., 'Jane', 25, 172, 214
Japan, model making in, 30
Jewson, collector, 212
Johnson, J., model painter, 201
Jones, J. E., model maker, 199, 209
Jonson, Ben, 13
José, Don, the first, of Portugal, 18
Judd, N. F., collector, 217–8

KS Miniatures, model makers, 24, 172
Kaufmann, M. L., model maker, 137, 214; Cockade Miniatures, 137
Kellet, artist, 153
Kennesaw Battle-Rama, Georgia, USA, 39
Kews, model maker, 165
knights, models of, 12, 86–8 *passim*, 105, 116, 145, 152, 158, 211, 214, 215, 219, 221, 222, 231; 'Ivanhoe', 145
Knotel, designer, 153, 174
Kramer, model maker, 40
Krauhs, model maker, 46, 51–3, 179
Krolyn (Rode Orm), model maker, 24
Kröner-Grimm, Dr E., 53, 177–80 *passim*, 217; editor of *Sammler-nachrichten*, 180
Kurdian, G., collector, 232–3

Lafayette, General, models of, 60, 68, 189
Lance Historical Miniatures, 127–8
Landsknechts, 53, 80, 101, 137, 214, 215
Land/townscapes, models of, 53
Latin-America, model making in, 25; models of races of, 104, 209, 210, 218
Lecouvreur, A., model of, 55
Lecke, model engraver, 78, 80, 149, 215
Lee, General, models of, 131, 199
LeGloahec, A., painter, 134, 136
Lelièpvre, E., model maker, 34, 39, 40, 46, 63, 64, 69, 73–5, 176, 189; collaboration with Métayer, 73, 77
Leroux, model maker, 64
Lineol, model maker, 155, 190, 205
Lockwood, C., 153
London, Tower of, 12
Lorenz, model maker, 18, 215
Louis XI of France, 107; XIII 13; XV (model of his coach), 74, 75; XVI 14
Loy, model maker, 149
Lucas, F. L., 13
Lucotte, model maker, 14, 15, 19, 144, 155, 190, 195, 197

McDonnell, A. G., author, 151
McDonnell, C. A., collector, 131, 196–9
McLoughlin Bros, model makers, 24, 155, 211
Madlener, model maker, 25, 77, 78
Maier, S., model engraver, 39, 77, 78, 149, 151
Malleable Mouldings, model makers, 30, 31, 124, 180, 182, 184, 195
Marat, model of, 67
Marc, model maker, 145
Marrion, model maker, 190, 214
Martin, Dr P., collector and author, 153–4, 206
Marx, model makers, 30, 162, 205
Mary, Queen of Scots, models of, 99, 222
Mathiot, designer, 34, 74, 75
Maximilian, funeral of, model, 53; knights of, models, 80
May, Commander, curator, 85
Meissonnier, artist-engraver, 64, 129
Meister, E., model maker, 33
Merlin, model maker, 13
Merten, model maker, 31, 217, 226
Metal Art Miniature Company (Moulded Miniatures), 24
Métayer, Mme, model maker, 40, 46, 61, 73, 76–7, 197, 200, 209, 218; *Petits Soldats de France*, 76
Middle Ages (medieval times), models of, 23, 25, 31, 40, 50, 53, 68, 87, 88, 97, 104, 105, 116, 133, 134, 152, 157, 158, 199, 200, 210, 212, 214, 215, 220–2, 224, 225, 228; personages of, models, 158
Mignot (CBG) model makers, 15, 23, 26, 39, 76–8 *passim*, 134, 142, 144–6 *passim*, 148, 153, 155, 164, 172, 190, 197, 202, 208, 209. 223, 224
Military Historical Society of Australia, 184
Military Miniatures, model makers, 24
Military Miniatures (Blum), 67, 68, 96, 189
MIM (Steinback), model makers, 24
Miniature Figure Collectors of America, 197, 225; of Pennsylvania, 209
Minifigure Company, model makers, 24
Mittman, model maker, 149
Model Soldier Guide (Risley and Imrie), 130
Model Soldiers (Harris), 14, 180, 226
Model Soldiers (Nicholson), 113
Model Soldiers: a Collector's Guide (Garratt), 86, 124, 154, 190, 207
models, religious, 11, 15, 51
Mohr, model maker, 149
Mokarex (coffee merchants and distributors of models), 30, 31, 182, 205, 214
Mond Collection, 144
Monde Merveilleux des Soldats de Plomb (Martin and Vaillant), 153
Montcalm, model of, 68, 189
Montgomery, model of, 90
More, Sir Thomas, model of, 106
Morrells—see Hummels
Morschauser, J., collector, 227, 228
Moulded Miniatures, model makers, 209
Mozart family, models of, 53
Müller, model maker, 39, 149, 151, 215
Murray, P., 10, 40, 46, 77, 172, 205, 209, 214, 224
Murray, W. H., collector, 133–6
Musée de la Marine, Paris, 69, 70
Musée de l'Armée, Paris, 36, 40
Musée Militaire, Montreal, 58, 60
Museo Navale, Venice, 53

Napoleon and his Marshals (McDonnell), 151
Napoleon I, 18, 20, 36, 66, 68–70, 99, 113, 126, 129, 151, 152, 176, 189, 190, 200, 205, 207; III 39, 200; model of, 28
Napoleonic models, military, 18, 46, 53, 70, 77, 78, 91, 97–9 *passim*, 101, 104, 108, 113, 125, 129, 131, 146, 148, 151, 153, 158, 173, 188, 199, 201, 209, 215, 218, 222–5 *passim*, 228, 230, 231, 233
National Army Museum, 85, 183
NATO troops, 137
Neckel, toy marketeers, 77, 149, 151, 152–3, 214
Nefertiti, model of, 35, 88, 215, 221
Nelli, P. and A., collectors, 159–60
Newton, N., Ltd, model makers, 99, 101, 113
Niblett, J., model designer, 34, 35, 40, 45, 99, 195, 214, 225, 231
Nicholas I of Russia, 39
Nicholson, J. R., model maker, 228
Nicollier, J., author, 61, 147
Niekirk, P. D., collector, 160
Norman Conquest, models of, 104
Norway, model making in, 24
Nymphenburg factory for toys, 55

Ochel, A., model distribution, 25, 77, 78, 80, 149, 151, 177, 179, 209, 214
Odiot, J. B. C., 14
Ohlsson and Mars, model makers, 124
Old British Lead Soldiers (Richards), 163
operas, models of, 104, 105
Opie, J., collector, 146, 160–2
Osbourne, L., 10, 35, 226
Otello, model maker, 46

Palomeque, model maker, 24
'Palx' models, 200
Patmore, model makers, 45
Pearce, W. F., model producer, 96
Pellerin, sheet publishers, 206–7, 211
Petits Soldats de France, models, 76; *de Strasburg* (Martin), 153, 154, 206
Pevsner, N., 10
Pfab, V. and Mrs, model makers, 39
Philip, Prince, model of, 120 (see also Royal family)
Phoenix plastic models, 160
Pietro Millo Museum, Italy, 40, 122
Ping, F., model maker, 40, 45, 48, 60, 61, 63, 86, 101, 104–7, 142, 144–6 *passim*, 158, 171, 172, 186, 196, 199–201 *passim*, 205, 209, 214, 217, 231; influence of Courtenay on, 105, 107; Tudor Court figures, 107
Pohl, model maker, 149
Poland, model making in, 24, 30
Polk's Hobby Store, New York, 134
Portugal, model making in, 18
Pranzetti, A., model maker, 40, 123, 159–60
Pre-Revolution regiments, models of, 70, 97
Puffer, E. L., collector, 63
pyrogravure iron, 74

Rainer Museum, Salzburg, 53
Ramsay, L. E. G. (editor *Connoisseur*), 82
Ray, H. and D., model maker, 144
Reamsa, model makers, 30, 145, 214
Reavley, C., 228
Rees, Bevan J. H., collector, 88, 219–22
Regiments, American, 50, 60, 90, 116, 120, 125, 129, 131, 133, 134, 137, 153, 155, 172, 174, 176, 188–9, 198–200 *passim*, 203, 218, 228, 230–2 *passim*; Austrian 27, 52, 128, 148, 149, 155, 177, 178, 186, 218; auxiliary services, 170, 171, 190, 192, 199, 211, 221, 224, 228, 230; British, 21, 23, 28, 33, 34, 36, 45, 68, 82, 85, 88, 90, 91, 94, 96–9 *passim*, 111, 113, 116, 117, 119, 120, 123, 125, 132, 134, 144, 145, 147, 149, 152, 153, 156–8 *passim*,

160, 165, 166, 168, 170, 171, 180, 184, 186, 189, 192, 195, 200, 203, 209–11 *passim*, 218–20*passim*, 222, 224, 225, 231; French, 20, 21, 28, 60, 63, 64, 68, 70, 74–8*passim*, 91, 97, 99, 113, 117, 128–30*passim*, 148, 151, 152, 155, 157, 158, 176, 180, 184, 186, 190, 196, 201, 203, 209, 210, 224, 228, 229, 231, 233; German, 20, 21, 28, 52, 91, 97, 116, 117, 126, 129, 131, 148, 149, 151–3*passim*, 157, 158, 168, 186, 190, 224, 228, 233; Highlanders, 28, 119, 156, 160, 205, 211, 224; Indian/Pakistani, 89, 90, 108, 120, 148, 156, 158, 160, 165, 169, 170, 180, 181, 186, 190, 194–6*passim*, 199, 228; Italian, 97, 122, 123, 156, 159, 160, 233; miscellaneous nations, 25, 53, 97, 117, 120, 124, 125, 129, 134, 136, 137, 145, 148, 149, 152, 155–7 *passim*, 166, 168, 180, 181, 192, 195, 210, 218, 224; Russian, 134, 136, 148, 152, 157, 168, 192, 208–10*passim*, 214, 233; Swedish, 125–6*passim*
Reka, model maker, 23, 163–5 *passim*, 195
Renvoize, model maker, 163, 165, 195
Retter, model maker, 151, 153; his Rommell, 90, 117, 151
Revell, model maker, 205
Reynolds, J., artist, 55
Richard I of England, 99, 158, 221; III 106, 107, 158
Richards, model maker, 165
Richards, L. W., collector, 146, 155, 157, 163–5, 192, 195
Richelieu, Duc de, model of, 99
Riedmatten, R. de, collector, 177
Riff, author, 10
Risley, model maker, 40, 46, 90, 129–32; collaboration with Imrie, 129–32, 205
Risorgimento, models of, 97; Museum, 40, 122
Riviere, R. B., sculptor, 107, 108
Robinson-Sager, A, collector, 222–3
Rochambeau, models of, 60
Roger, N., 13
Roskopf, gun modellers, 78
Rössner, G., model engraver, 26, 78, 214, 215
Rostrup-Bouesen, P., artist, 53
Roulle, S., engraver, 18
Rousselot, artist, 34, 55, 64, 77–8*passim*, 153
Royal family, models of, (see also Elizabeth II and Prince Philip), 170, 180, 209, 210, 222
Royal Gazette, the, 18
Royal United Service Institution, 36, 95, 144, 182, 232
Russell, model maker, 165
Russler, model maker, 172

St Louis Lead Soldier Company, model makers, 24
Sabretache, 58, 153
Saez-Alcocer, L., model maker, 24
Sala, G. A., author, 10
Sanchez, model maker, 24
Sandow, model engraver, 25
Santessonska Tenngjuteriet, model makers, 24, 124
Sardinia, model making in, 40, 123
Saunders, model maker, 171, 172, 201, 210, 230
Scheid, J., model maker, 46, 129, 172, 198, 199
Scheibert, model engraver, 25, 177
Schmitt, F. Th., painter, 153
Scholtz, W., model producer, 26, 77–80, 149, 151, 179, 214; Friederichianer, 78; Retreat from Moscow, 78, 151, 152, 223; Scholtz-Lecke, 215; Spitzweg shop of, 78
Schweitzer, model maker, 215
Scottish Model Soldier Group, 190, 207
Scruby, J., model maker, 24, 35, 40, 46, 172, 225, 228, 230
Second Empire, models of, 64
Second World War, model equipment of, 101, 132, 137, 228
Segom models, 31, 145, 146, 207, 218
Selcol, model maker, 33
Selwyn-Smith, R, model maker, 23, 30, 57, 118, 144, 196
Sentry Box, The, models, 40, 45, 107, 110, 111, 146, 231
Seven Years' War, models of, 53, 128, 186, 214
Sharpe, S., war-gamer, 230
Ships: a Picture History in Colour (illustrated Fouillé), 70
Siborne, Captain W., model maker, 20
Skybird models, 226, 228
Société des Collectionneurs, 40; *de Figurines Historiques*, 40, 56, 58, 69, 153, 200
Society for Army Historical Research, 184
Society of Industrial Artists and Designers, 89
Söhlke, model maker, 19, 78
Soldats et Figures de Plomb (Baldet), 37, 58, 67, 73, 180, 189, 200
soldiers, model, accoutrements, 15, 37, 46, 51, 52, 56, 64, 82, 90, 113, 120, 128; aluminium, 24, 27; 'animation' system, 58, 92, 95, 113; artists' *modus operandi*, 46, 54, 55–8*passim*, 60, 64, 66, 67, 70, 73, 74, 77, 78, 82, 85, 87, 88, 92, 95, 96, 99, 101, 106, 108–10 *passim*, 113, 119, 120, 129, 130, 134, 174; automatic, 226; background to, 11 ff; barbola, 220; bibliography of, 10; bronze, 12, 16; cannibalisation of, 44; cardboard, use of, 13, 14; cavalry, 15, 16, 24, 33, 63, 64, 70, 97, 108, 111, 148, 149, 152, 155, 156, 160, 164, 170, 174, 176, 183, 192, 195, 224, 228, 230; cavalry, removeable, 20, 24, 165; cessation of metal, 23; collections/collecting, 10, 23, 26, 28, 35, 39, 40, 44, 50, 66, 89, 91, 92, 94, 96, 99, 104, 106, 107, 111–13*passim*, 116, 117, 127, 142 ff, 226, 231 ff; conversation pieces, 50, 52; costume of, 46, 48, 56, 63, 82, 113, 120, 184, 210, 231; criteria of status, 39; enamels, use of, 48, 165, 170; engraving on, 25, 39, 53, 78, 80, 98, 223; equestrian, 15, 19, 23, 24, 53, 56, 57, 63–5*passim*, 68, 73, 74, 80, 86–8*passim*, 91, 99, 109, 111, 113, 120, 123, 126, 131, 145, 146, 155, 157, 158, 174, 176, 182, 212, 214, 215, 218, 221, 225, 231; exports from Germany, 18, 19, 124; flats, 11, 12, 15, 18–20*passim*, 25, 28, 37, 39, 40, 64, 76, 77, 95, 99, 107, 124, 144–6 *passim*, 148–54, 177, 179, 190, 207, 208, 210, 215, 223; flats, painting of, 48, 76, 78; foot soldiers/infantry, 15, 19, 21, 27, 68, 70, 77, 97, 110, 111, 126, 129, 134, 144, 148, 149, 155, 156, 158, 164, 192, 195, 215, 221, 222, 228, 230, 231; gold, 92; heraldic aspects of, 46, 87, 107, 157, 221; historical accuracy of, 21, 39, 46, 63, 70, 74, 85, 95, 99, 104, 120, 129, 132, 184, 201, 205; hollow-cast, 21, 23, 40, 144–6*passim*, 207, 223; humour in, 137, 180, 217; importation of, 24; improvisation in making, 56, 57; interchangeable figures, 30, 33, 37, 74, 92; kits, 33, 34, 109, 111; lead, 13–15 *passim*, 24, 40, 70, 74, 82, 92, 94, 95, 107, 108, 118, 127, 144, 145, 159, 160, 161, 182, 210; lead, prohibition of, 144, 145; leather used in, 27, 40, 48, 51, 56, 57, 74, 122; mass-produced, 39, 44, 94; mountings for, 205; oils used in painting, 48, 50, 60, 64, 65, 77, 120, 126, 165, 170; painting of, 34, 46, 48, 50, 55, 60, 63–5*passim*, 73, 76, 77, 101, 110, 111, 118, 119, 126, 153, 203, 228; paper/paper sheets, 26, 27, 73, 142, 144, 206, 207, 211; paper used in making, 57; papier-mâché, 11, 27, 40,

122, 144; plaster, 27, 28, 31, 73, 82, 107, 108; plaster moulds, 70, 74, 120, 134, 149, 169, 208; plastic, 30, 31, 34, 35, 45, 74, 118, 142, 144, 145, 160, 161, 196, 199, 205, 207, 210, 218, 227, 230; plastic wood, 220; plasticine, use of, 46, 54, 73, 99, 220; plugged-in heads etc., 15, 24, 31, 92; regulations concerning manufacture, 144, 145; repainting of, 44, 171, 205, 207, 231; royal collections, 13, 14; silver, 13, 92; semi-flat, 19, 20; semi-solid, 19, 20, 24, 51, 124; semi-solids for war-games, 35; solder, use of, 15, 58, 64, 88, 96, 201, 220; solid, 11, 13, 15, 19, 20, 24, 40, 76, 94, 124, 144, 159, 207, 215, 223; standard sizes for, 19, 21, 33, 74, 80, 94, 97, 106, 112; tin, 16, 19, 28, 29, 40, 73, 234; types of 10, 11, 39, 142; wooden, 39, 40, 57, 73, 112, 113, 126, 142, 144

Sollner, model maker, 149
Spain, model making in, 18, 24, 30, 35, 46
Spandauw, E., 34, 99
Spenkuch, model maker, 19
Stadden, C. C., model maker, 30, 35, 36, 40, 45, 48, 57, 77, 104, 112–18, 126, 131, 142, 144, 146, 149, 158, 160, 172, 174, 184, 186, 188, 189, 190, 196–203*passim*, 205, 209, 214, 218–20*passim*, 222–6*passim*, 228, 230, 231; 'Shoulder-Knot' models, 118
Stadmuseum, Austria, 53
Standhafte Zinnsoldat, Der, (Martin), 153
Starlux models, 31, 35, 124, 145, 146, 162, 226, 231
Statutory Regulations, 1967, 144, 145
Stearns, P. O., collector, 67, 68, 146, 201
Steinback (MIM), 24
Steiner, model maker, 40
Stevenson, R. L., author, 35, 226
Stock, model maker, 46, 205
Stokes, D., 36, 45, 95, 96
Studio, The, 86
Surén, E., model maker, 35, 40, 55, 98–9, 200, 201, 214, 223, 226, 230
Sweden, model making in, 16, 24, 26, 40, 124–6
Swedish African Engineers (SAE), 124, 225, 226, 230
Swedish Army Museum, 55
Sweet, C., Jnr, collector, 113, 214, 223–6, 228
Switzerland, model making in, 16
Synge - Hutchinson, model maker, 40, 45, 80–6

T and B, toymakers, (Taylor and Barrett), 163, 195
Tassell, L., model maker, 46, 99, 101; 'Lasset' models, 101; Restoration gallant, 99
Taverner, Miss J., collector, 106, 107
Tenngjuteriet Schreuder, model makers, 124
Teuber, Weckersdorff, W., collector, 177
Thirty Years' War, 53, 104, 214
Thoburn, L., collector, 63, 64, 172–6
Thomas, model maker, 35, 227, 228
Thompson, F. G., collector, 165–8
Thornborough, F. B. and P., collectors, 184–7
Timpo, model makers, 23, 30, 145, 161, 182, 212, 222; 'King Arthur' series, 212, 231; 'Quentin Durward' series, 231
Tobinnus, model maker, 149
Toft, A., artist, 82
Toy Armies of the World, The, (Griffith), 29
Tradition, 113
Tradition (model shop), 217, 231
Trafalgar period, models of, 85
Treforest Mouldings, models, 184
trellis tongs, 226
Triang Toys, models, 118
Trucraft models, 172
Turnbull, model maker, 165

Ulundi, model of, 36
Umberto I, King of Italy, model of, 159
United States—see America
USSR, model making in, 30

Vaillant, M., author, 153
Valverde, model maker, 46
Vanot, B., model maker, 46, 176
Vertunni, model maker, 40, 197, 208, 209
Vienna, siege of, models of, 36, 177, 178; Hofburg, 178
Vie Quotidienne dans les Armées de Napoléon (Baldet), 58
Vollrath, model maker, 149

Wade, General, model of, 105, 196
Wade, Shamus O. D., collector, 192–6, 223
War-games, models for, 19, 35, 39, 53, 92, 96, 117, 145, 146, 148, 149, 201, 225–30; societies for, 35
Warren Company, model makers, 24, 197
Wasa Museum, Stockholm, 55
Washington, G., models of, 28, 60, 68, 131, 189, 198, 215, 218
Waterloo, Battle of models/dioramas of, 18, 20, 36, 37, 90, 111, 152, 160, 190, 192, 219, 224, 231
Waterloo Convention, 98
Watteau, artist, 55
Wavell, General, model of, 90
Webster, J., playwright, 13
Wegmann, model maker, 19
Weiss, W., collector, 233–4
Wellington, Duke of, models of, 20, 99, 189, 195
Wells, H. G., author, 226
Wendall models, 195
Wennburg, C., 124, 180
Werhli, model maker, 18
Werner, Hofrat Dr, collector, 177
West, Helen, modeller, 210
Weygang, model makers, 19
West Point Museum, USA, 129
Wilcox, P., collector, 146
Wild West, model of, 23, 28, 125
Wilke, K. A., painter, 179
Willetts, model makers, 40, 45, 118–22, 146, 231; 'Matchlock Military' models, 107, 118
Wilson, F. W., collector, 169–71
Winkelmüller, model maker, 149; his Napoleon at the Pyramids, 151
Winkler, H., model maker, 30, 180; Fred, 182
Winter, D., 127
Winter, D. and Y., collectors, 171–2
Wolfe, General, model of, 152
Wollner, model maker, 51, 179
Wolrab, J., model maker, 13
Wootten, P., model maker, 25, 186, 214
Wright, J. L. (Lincoln Logs), 24, 195
Wynne-Jones, Nancy, model designer, 108, 109

Young, Brigadier P., collector, 35, 68, 104, 146, 199–201, 230

Zang, M., model maker, 30
Zinnfiguren, 15, 16, 77, 78, 151
Zinnsoldat, Der (Hampe), 10
Zinnsoldaten, 53, 153
Zulus, models of, 23, 137, 221